Cooperative Mexican-U.S. Antinarcotics Efforts

A Report of the CSIS Simon Chair in Political Economy

AUTHORS
Sidney Weintraub
Duncan Wood

November 2010

ITAM | INSTITUTO TECNOLÓGICO AUTÓNOMO DE MÉXICO
CSIS | CENTER FOR STRATEGIC & INTERNATIONAL STUDIES

About CSIS

In an era of ever-changing global opportunities and challenges, the Center for Strategic and International Studies (CSIS) provides strategic insights and practical policy solutions to decisionmakers. CSIS conducts research and analysis and develops policy initiatives that look into the future and anticipate change.

Founded by David M. Abshire and Admiral Arleigh Burke at the height of the Cold War, CSIS was dedicated to the simple but urgent goal of finding ways for America to survive as a nation and prosper as a people. Since 1962, CSIS has grown to become one of the world's preeminent public policy institutions.

Today, CSIS is a bipartisan, nonprofit organization headquartered in Washington, D.C. More than 220 full-time staff and a large network of affiliated scholars focus their expertise on defense and security; on the world's regions and the unique challenges inherent to them; and on the issues that know no boundary in an increasingly connected world.

Former U.S. senator Sam Nunn became chairman of the CSIS Board of Trustees in 1999, and John J. Hamre has led CSIS as its president and chief executive officer since 2000.

CSIS does not take specific policy positions; accordingly, all views expressed in this publication should be understood to be solely those of the author(s).

Library of Congress Cataloging-in-Publication Data

Weintraub, Sidney, 1922-
Cooperative Mexican-U.S. antinarcotics efforts / Sidney Weintraub and Duncan Wood.
p. cm.
ISBN 978-0-89206-607-0 (pbk. : alk. paper) 1. Drug traffic—Mexico. 2. Drug traffic—United States. 3. Drug control—Mexico. 4. Drug control—United States. 5. United States—Foreign relations—Mexico. 6. Mexico—Foreign relations—United States. 7. Narco-terrorism—Mexico. 8. Organized crime—Mexico. I. Wood, Duncan R. (Duncan Robert), 1968- II. Title.

HV5840.M4W45 2010
363.450972—dc22 2010044343

Center for Strategic and International Studies
1800 K Street, N.W., Washington, D.C. 20006
Tel: (202) 775-3119
Fax: (202) 775-3199
Web: www.csis.org

CONTENTS

ACKNOWLEDGMENTS

The preparation and writing of this report took place in spring and summer 2010. Alaina Dyne, the William E. Simon Chair's research assistant, handled much of the logistics and guided the research for the various chapters in the report. Following Ms. Dyne, Michael Graybeal joined the office of the Simon Chair in May 2010 as research associate and assisted in compiling and editing the chapters. Both were very helpful in the preparation of this report.

Simon Chair interns also wrote several chapters for the report. Chapter 7, on Mexican public opinion on antinarcotics efforts, was written by interns David Angel, Asmeret Asghedom, and Michael Graybeal, who was then an intern. The discussion of murder rates in Mexico in chapter 5 was prepared by David Angel. All three provided much research assistance for the numerous topics discussed in this report.

Funding for the report was provided by the Open Society Institute (OSI) with the support of Kasia Malinowska-Sempruch, director of the Global Drug Policy Program at OSI. We also received support from Tamas Varga, program officer for the Global Drug Policy Program, and David Holiday, program officer for the Latin America Program at OSI. Their recognition of the need to address current antinarcotics efforts between Mexico and the United States proved instrumental in producing the report.

We also wish to thank the various authors whose background papers provided valuable insights and helped shape our thinking on antinarcotics efforts. Six background papers were prepared to help with the report: Armand Peschard-Sverdrup on the Mérida Initiative; George Grayson on cartel structure; Raul Benitez on organized crime and security in Central America; Samuel Logan on drug-trafficking routes and methods; Johanna Mendelson Forman on arms trafficking; and Aaron Houston on the possibility of decriminalization and legalization in the United States. Three additional papers that helped shape this report are included here as appendixes: Jonathan Caulkins and Eric Sevigny on imprisonment rates in the United States; Jonathan Winer on money laundering of narcotics profits; and Nathan Jones on the various arms used by the cartels.

At CSIS, the Publications Office provided much help with shaping the report into its final form.

1 INTRODUCTION

Background

Because of high U.S. narcotics consumption and Mexico's role as the main transit country for cocaine from Colombia, the dominant narcotics activity in the Western Hemisphere takes place between the United States and Mexico. Competition among the large Mexican drug-trafficking organizations (DTOs) to maximize their share of sales in the United States has led to terrible violence in Mexico, and that country's "war" against the drug-trafficking organizations has amplified that violence. Mexico was a small player in the movement of cocaine to the United States before the 1980s, when the main route was from Colombia through the Caribbean to Florida. After that route was largely abandoned because of heavy U.S. sea and land interdiction, Colombian cocaine began to enter the United States through Central America and Mexico.

This report will focus on four drugs: cocaine, heroin, methamphetamine, and marijuana. Mexico produces the last three of these drugs, which are shipped directly to the United States. If reliance on Mexico as the final transit country for cocaine sales to the United States were to become too costly for the drug-trafficking organizations, the route could change again. And while the violence in Mexico might then diminish, cocaine would still come into the United States because of the demand for the drug.

For many years, the United States and Mexico were at odds over which country bore the greater responsibility for the drug trafficking. The United States, which argued that Mexico was not doing enough to interdict drugs before they crossed the border, actually closed the border several times for days on end to "send a message" to the Mexicans to do better. The Americans were themselves unable to interdict the drugs once they moved into the United States. The Mexicans, in turn, insisted that the United States was not doing enough to reduce consumption. In fact, even as the United States was spending vast amounts on imprisoning drug dealers and users, many believed the country was wasting resources on enforcing the wrong policies.

As the two countries moved closer toward each other in political and economic relations under the North American Free Trade Agreement after it went into effect in early 1994, their cooperation in other areas also increased. In March 2007, the two presidents, George W. Bush and Felipe Calderón, agreed in Mérida, Yucatán, to have a cooperative program under which the United States would support Mexico's antinarcotics efforts. The Mérida Initiative, although modest, is now the main joint antinarcotics program between the two countries—and it will be discussed in this report.

For many years the U.S. government was unwilling to admit explicitly that U.S. narcotics consumption bore some responsibility for the violence in Mexico. During a visit to Mexico in March 2009, however, Hillary Clinton, the U.S. secretary of state, finally stated the obvious: that U.S. narcotics demand was fueling drug violence in Mexico. This report thus comes at a time of antinarcotics cooperation between the two countries. This cooperation does not mean that the problems related to drug trafficking and consumption are on their way to solution, only that issues not discussed earlier can now be put on the table. The purpose of this report is to provide a full discussion of such issues.

Current Issues

The major issues are how to best deal with the large consumption of narcotics in the United States and the violence in those Mexican states where the drug-trafficking organizations, frequently referred to as drug cartels, operate.[1] To get at these issues, one must first examine how each country deals with its narcotics problems.

The United States

Drug sales and use are criminal offenses in the United States, and policy until recently was to imprison these criminal offenders. According to one informed estimate, that by Caulkins and Sevigny (see appendix C), slightly more than 335,000 drug offenders were in federal and state prisons in 1994, as well as another 150,000 in local jails. That total conforms to an *Economist* article of March 7, 2009, that reports that the United States arrests 1.5 million people a year for drug offenses and imprisons up to 500,000 of them. The *Economist* article also notes that arrests for drug offenses explain why one in five black Americans spends some time in jails. Incarceration has been a particularly pronounced component of U.S. drug policy in comparison with imprisonment policy in other countries. Imprisoning so many people is costly, even without taking into account the effect on the lives of those incarcerated. A Zogby International poll carried out in September 2008 found that large majorities of U.S. voters believed that the U.S. "war on drugs" was a failure.[2] This view held true for all regions of the country and when broken down by race, age, and education.

Mexico

Antinarcotics policy in Mexico, at least since the advent of Felipe Calderón as president on December 1, 2006, has been to declare all-out war on the drug cartels. The government has had many successes, including confiscating drugs, capturing cartel kingpins and extraditing many of them to the United States for prosecution, and using well-planned raids and killing many cartel leaders. Violence by the cartels has escalated, however. More than 22,000 people have been killed and many more wounded, kidnapped, extorted, or threatened in Mexico since December 2006.[3] The rate of killings was 1–2.2 per 100,000 people from 2001 to 2007; 4.8 per 100,000 in 2008; an estimated 6.1 per 100,000 in 2009; and rising again in 2010.[4] Most of the killings have taken place in Mexican states near the border with the United States where the drug-trafficking organizations are most active, particularly in Chihuahua and Sinaloa but also in Guerrero, Durango, Michoacán, and others.

---

1. Strictly speaking, the DTOs are not cartels because they compete with each other.

2. Zogby International, "Zogby Interactive Likely Voters 9/23/08 thru 9/25/08 MDE +/- 1.5 percentage points," September 25, 2008.

3. U.S. House of Representatives, Bureau of Western Hemisphere Affairs, "Testimony of Roberta Jacobson, Deputy Assistant Secretary of State," before the Western Hemisphere Subcommittee and the Counterterrorism Subcommittee, May 27, 2010.

4. Trans-Border Institute, University of San Diego, January 2009.

The most violence-wracked city in Mexico—perhaps in the world—is Ciudad Juárez, Chihuahua, the city opposite El Paso, Texas.

The estimated profits of the drug-trafficking organizations from narcotics sales to the United States range from $10 billion to $40 billion a year, a large range indicating that the actual amounts are unknown. Not all of this money is necessarily brought back to Mexico, but enough is to bribe government officials, police, and army personnel assigned to confront the cartels. The federal police force has grown to an estimated 26,000, and the federal government has provided funds to local police forces. These efforts followed many police reforms, which included sacking many officers and replacing them with others believed to be more reliable. In addition to police, President Calderón has used up to 45,000 military personnel to quell the violence. Some 5,000 troops were dispatched to Ciudad Juárez in early 2009, for example. None of these measures, however, has worked as effectively as the government had hoped, and the military were later withdrawn and the federal police built up.

The drug cartels have not confined themselves to selling narcotics. They engage in kidnapping for ransom, extortion, human smuggling, and other crimes to augment their incomes. They have spread their activities into the United States and at least 19 Latin American countries and, according to the U.S. National Drug Intelligence Center, have reached as far as Australia. Central to their operations is the laundering of their profits, and the United States and Mexico cooperate, as do other Latin American countries, in countering such activities. (See appendix B, in which Jonathan Winer seeks to trace the money laundering activities of the cartels.)

President Calderón has expressed concern about what has been called the "iron river" of small arms and ammunition that crosses the border from the United States into Mexico. These include various weapons, such as AR-15s, AK-47s, MP5 submachine guns, 50-mm machine guns, ground-to-air missiles, bazookas, Belgian Five-SeveN pistols, .50 caliber Barrett sniper rifles, and fragmentation grenades. In November 2008, in a cache in Reynosa, Tamaulipas, bullet-proof vests were found that belonged to the Zetas, initially a protective army for other cartels—most notably the Beltran Leyva organization—and now one of the most bloodthirsty cartels in its own right. The Mexican government believes that more than 2,000 weapons flow daily from the United States through many crossing points, carried by *hormigas* (ants) individually across the border or by more sophisticated "straw purchasing."[5] The tracing of guns captured in Mexico indicates that straw buying is most prevalent in Arizona, California, and Texas. More than 90 percent of the guns captured in Mexico have been traced back to the United States, although it is uncertain whether that is the correct percentage for all guns entering Mexico from foreign suppliers. Although obtaining guns from nearby locations in the United States is convenient, the market for buying weapons is global.

The Organization of American States adopted the Convention against the Illicit Manufacture of and Trafficking in Firearms, Ammunition, Explosives and Related Items (CIFTA), which was opened for signature in November 1977. Thirty-three member states signed the convention, and 22 have ratified it—not including the United States. On April 16, 2009, U.S. President Barack Obama called on the Senate to ratify it.

While murders have increased in the states where drug-trafficking organizations are operating and are being confronted by the Mexican police and military, murder rates for Mexico as a whole

5. In this process, individual legal buyers of weapons buy guns in the United States and then sell them to organizations linked to the DTOs, which then smuggle them into Mexico.

have been declining. According to United Nations data, murder rates in Mexico fell from 14.9 per 100,000 inhabitants in 1998 to fewer than 11 in 2006. This rate is lower than in much of the rest of Latin America but higher than the 5.6 per 100,000 in the United States.

The issues discussed in this section stem from current policies within the two countries and in their interactions. As was made clear in the Zogby poll cited above, most Americans believe current policies are unhelpful. Many Mexicans are also skeptical about their government's policies, especially because of the deadly results.[6] Potential new policies will be discussed in the next section.

Policy Options

One option for Mexico is to increase antinarcotics activity in the hope of making the cocaine transit operation so costly that the narcotics-trafficking organizations will change the drug routes. This approach would be expensive for the government and would almost surely lead to more drug-related deaths. It would most likely fail, and Mexico's war on drugs would lose further popular support. Changing the routing for cocaine would not affect the other three drugs discussed in this report because they are produced in Mexico.

Mexico, in essence, has few meaningful independent options that would affect the United States. The influence works primarily in the opposite direction, the U.S. influence on Mexico. Mexico could end its war on drugs, and this decision would probably reduce the drug-related killings but probably not end the turf wars between the cartels for better access to the U.S. market. Mexico could either decriminalize or legalize drug use, but the main drug traffic is to the United States, which would not be greatly affected by either of these actions. Drug addiction in Mexico is modest, especially when compared with the United States. Jorge Castañeda, based on what he calls consistent surveys by specialists over the years, reports that the number of drug users in Mexico went from 307,000 to 465,000 between 2002 and 2008—an increase of 26,000 addicts per year in a country of 110 million people. The overall addiction rate, he reports, is 0.4 percent of the population. He writes that even in Ciudad Juárez, the city most afflicted with drug-related killings, the addiction rate was just 4 percent in 2005—just one year before the Calderón administration declared its war on drug cartels.[7]

"Decriminalization" in drug parlance relaxes punishment for users, not sellers or producers. Use of drugs remains an illegal activity but does not involve criminal prosecution. Decriminalization may, in fact, raise drug prices above what prevails under "prohibition" (current U.S. policy) because the seller is aware that incarceration of the user will not occur. Decriminalization, however, does not appear to have had much effect on drug use in countries that have tried it.

"Legalization," by contrast, would lead to a system that creates a regulated cultivation and distribution system and licensing requirements for both sellers and buyers. Excise taxes could be imposed on drugs under legalization, but if the taxes were too high, a black market to undersell the official prices might be the result. Excise taxes cannot be imposed on illegal products.

---

6. Carlos Fuentes, Mexico's famous novelist, has stated that direct confrontation with narcotics traffickers is a losing proposition and that the problem should not be handled as one of criminality but rather of health. *Reforma*, February 12, 2010, 6.

7. Jorge Castañeda, "What's Spanish for Quagmire?" *Foreign Policy* (January/February 2010): 78.

It is unlikely that either the U.S. president or the Congress would accept legalization for cocaine, heroin, or methamphetamine. Decriminalization may be a possibility for these drugs, particularly to remove the imprisonment that has been so prevalent in the United States. It may be possible to legalize marijuana, however, which is already in common medical use to ease pain. Many Americans support legalization of marijuana. The policy of prohibition has become largely inoperative because it is relatively simple to obtain marijuana and the U.S. government is already reducing or forgoing prosecution for its use—although arrests still occur and remain part of an arrestee's record. If marijuana were to be legalized, the government may wish to control the tetrahydrocannibinol and the cannabidiol content because of their psychological effects. The government cannot mandate the composition, however, if marijuana production and use remain illegal.

There is also much support in the United States for providing more education on the effects of narcotics use, much as is now provided for tobacco, and for helping addicts break the habit. Such support would be especially strong with either decriminalization or legalization.

The Latin American Commission on Drugs and Democracy recently issued a report titled "Drugs and Democracy: Toward a Paradigm Shift." The position of the three former Latin American presidents who cochaired the commission—César Gaviria of Colombia, Ernesto Zedillo of Mexico, and Fernando Henrique Cardoso of Brazil—received much media attention. According to the report, "It is imperative to rectify the 'war on drugs' strategy pursued in the region over the past 30 years." The report explicitly refers to current policies as a failure and calls for breaking the taboo on discussions leading to safer and more efficient and humane drug policies.

In the United Kingdom, the drug policy foundation Transform called on the UK government to lead the world by carrying out an impact assessment of domestic drug prohibition, because it has consistently delivered the opposite of its stated goals, with the poor and marginalized hit hardest.

Structure of the Report

The report that follows will discuss the themes listed in the table of contents designed to cover the relevant narcotics issues within and between Mexico and the United States and to make policy proposals based on the available options. The foregoing sections of the introduction are intended to provide a précis of the more complete discussions that follow.

The two principal authors of this report, Sidney Weintraub (Center for Strategic and International Studies) and Duncan Wood (Instituto Tecnológico Autónomo de México) have relied much on material provided by experts from the two countries. Three papers from among these experts appear as appendixes to the report: Jonathan Caulkins and Eric Sevigny on imprisonment in the United States; Jonathan Winer on money movement and laundering; and Nathan Jones on the use of guns purchased in the United States by drug-trafficking organizations. In addition, six papers were commissioned to provide essential information to the two principal authors for incorporation in the report. These are Armand Peschard-Sverdrup, CSIS, and independent consultant, on the Mérida Initiative; George Grayson, College of William and Mary, on the drug cartel structure and operations; Raúl Benitez, Universidad Nacional Aútonoma de México, on drug cartel activity in Central America; Samuel Logan, independent consultant, on drug-trafficking methods and routes; Johanna Mendelson Forman, CSIS, on arms trafficking; and Aaron Houston, Executive Director of the Students for Sensible Drug Policy, on decriminalization and legalization of marijuana in the United States.

2 NARCOTICS CONSUMPTION

The variety of drugs used in the United States is substantial. The most widely used reference on illicit drug consumption in the United States is prepared by the U.S. Department of Health and Human Services. The data that follow come from the "Results from the 2008 National Survey on Drug Use and Health: National Findings."[1] Most of the detailed information in this chapter deals with the illicit use of four drugs: marijuana, cocaine, heroin, and methamphetamines.

U.S. Drug Use Data

In 2008, an estimated 20.1 million persons aged 12 or older living in the United States had used an illicit drug (all illicit drugs, not just the four primary ones) in the month before the survey. That number represents 8.0 percent of the 12-and-older population, a percentage that has been relatively stable since 2002.

Marijuana is the most commonly used illicit drug of persons aged 12 and older living in the United States. In 2008, the number of past-month users was 15.2 million, which constituted 75.7 percent of all illicit drug users. Marijuana was the only drug used by 57.3 percent of illicit drug users. The overall rate of past-month marijuana users was 6.1 percent of persons living in the United States aged 12 or older, a rate that has changed little since 2002. Illicit drugs other than marijuana were used by 8.6 million persons, or 42 percent of illicit drug users aged 12 and older in 2008. The 12-and-older age group used marijuana on 300 or more days in 2008. That is, 3.9 million persons in this group used marijuana on a daily or almost daily basis over a 12-month period.

Past-month users of *cocaine* in 2008 were estimated at 1.9 million or 0.7 percent of persons aged 12 and older. These figures were similar to those in 2007 as well as in 2002. The number of past-month *crack* users aged 12 and older was 359,000 or 0.1 percent in 2008, a number lower for this age group than in all years going back to 2002 except for 2004.

The number of past-month *methamphetamine* users aged 12 or older was 314,000 in 2008, less than half the number of methamphetamine use by this age group in 2006 (731,000) and a substantial reduction of users in 2007 (529,000). Past month usage of *heroin* by persons 12 and older was estimated at 0.2 percent in 2008.

1. Substance Abuse and Mental Health Services Administration, Office of Applied Studies. Information from this source is provided on illicit drug use of marijuana, cocaine, heroin, hallucinogens, and inhalants, as well as nonmedical use of prescription-type pain relievers, tranquilizers, stimulants, and sedatives. The phrase *all drugs* when used in this discussion refers to all of the above. The source also provides comparative information on alcohol and illicit drug use.

Figure 2.1. Past-Month Illicit Use of Marijuana, Cocaine, Methamphetamines, and Heroin among Persons Aged 12 or Older in the United States, 2008

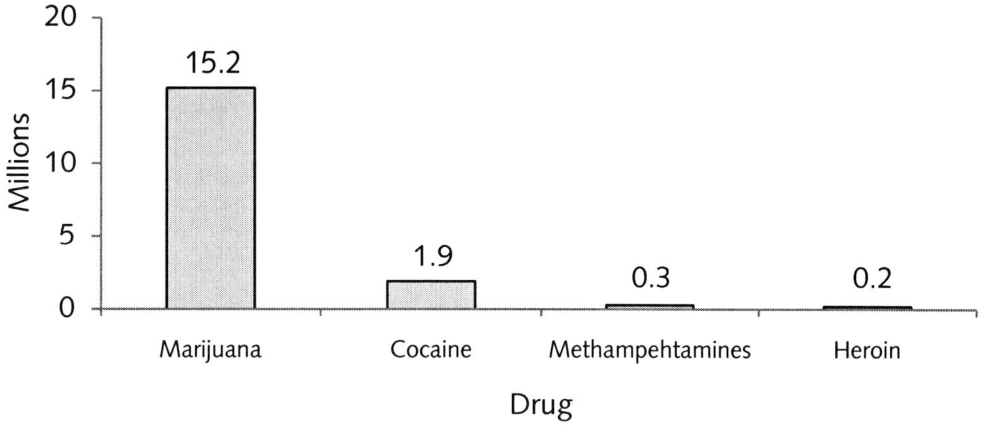

Source: U.S, Department of Health and Human Services, "Results from the 2008 National Survey on Drug Use and Health: National Findings."

By gender, the rate of 12-and-over past-month drug use was higher for males (9.9 percent) than for females (6.3 percent) in 2008. The rate for females increased from 5.8 percent in 2007 to 6.3 percent in 2008, however, while the rate for males went down slightly between those two years. In the specific case of marijuana, 12-and-older past-month use went from 3.8 percent in 2007 to 4.4 percent in 2008 for females and declined from 8.0 percent in 2007 to 7.9 percent in 2008 for males. Among pregnant women aged 15–44 years, the average past-month use was 5.1 percent based on data averaged for 2007 and 2008, a modest increase in pregnant-women use in 2003–2004 and 2005–2006.

Among adults aged 18 or older, the rate of current drug use (all drugs, not just the four featured in the discussion in this report) was lower in 2008 for college graduates (5.7 percent) than for those who did not graduate from high school (8.1 percent), high school graduates (8.6 percent), and those with some college (9.4 percent). Adults who had graduated from college, however, were more likely to have tried illicit drugs in their lifetime (51.8 percent) compared with adults who had not completed high school (37.7 percent).

The rate of illicit drug use (all drugs) for Asians 12 and older was 3.6 percent in 2008. Use in 2008 was higher for persons of other races: 14.7 percent for persons reporting two or more races; 10.1 percent for blacks; 8.2 percent for whites; and 6.2 percent for Hispanics.

Among adults aged 18 or older, the rate of illicit drug use in 2008 was 19.6 percent for unemployed persons, 8.0 percent for those employed full time, and 10.2 percent for persons employed part time.

In 2008, the rate of illicit drug use (all drugs) was more than nine times higher among youths aged 12–17 who smoked cigarettes in the past month (49.0 percent) than among youths in this age group who had not smoked cigarettes in the past month (5.3 percent). Among youths aged 12–17 who were heavy drinkers (consumed five or more drinks on the same occasion on each of 5 or more days in the past 30 days), 68.5 percent were current illicit drug users in 2008, whereas the rate of illicit drug users among nondrinkers in 2008 was 4.3 percent. In 2008, 10.0 million persons aged 12 or older were reported driving under the influence of illicit drugs during the past year; this number corresponds to 4.0 percent of the 12-or-older population. The rate of driving under the influence of illicit drugs in 2008 was highest among young adults aged 18– 25 (12.3 percent). According to the study, in 2008 every day 2,000 people 12 or older used cocaine for the first time.

In 2008, an estimated 2.9 million persons aged 12 or older used an illicit drug for the first time within the past 12 months, which averages almost 8,000 initiates per day. A majority (56.6 percent) reported that their first drug use was marijuana.

Some Financial Estimates

Although no hard data on the revenue generated by drug-marketing organizations from their sales of illicit drugs in the United States are available, the U.S. Congressional Research Service estimated those revenues at $13.6–48.4 billion in 2007.[2] An estimated range this wide reflects uncertainty. In appendix C, Caulkins and Sevigny discuss the vast differences in prices to growers, prices to buyers in source countries, and retail prices U.S. consumers pay for illicit drugs. The quantity of illicit drugs cannot be kept uniform in user countries, and there is some price elasticity of demand; consequently, the earnings from these sales will vary. Another way of getting at the financial outcomes is to examine the amount of money laundered domestically or outside the United States. The National Drug Intelligence Center, in a 2007 study, reports that at least $17.2 billion was smuggled into Mexico in bulk cash shipments, as well as additional amounts through other techniques.[3]

Data on Mexican Drug Use

Data from a national survey in 2008 indicated that 4.2 percent of the population aged 12–65 used *marijuana* that year: 7.2 percent for the 12–65 male population and 1.4 percent of the female population.[4] *Cocaine* use in 2008 was 2.4 percent for the 12–65 population: 4.1 percent for males and 0.7 percent for females. The cocaine figures include crack use, which applied to 0.6 percent of the 12–65 population: 1.0 percent for males and 0.6 percent females. Use of *amphetamine* stimulants was 0.5 percent for the 12–65 age population: 0.8 percent for males and 0.2 percent for females. *Heroin* use for this age group in 2008 was 0.1 percent: 0.3 percent for males and less than 0.1 percent for females.

Jorge Castañeda, in an article in which he concludes that the Mexican drug war is "costly [and] unwinnable," asserts that the war was launched using "distorted" statistics.[5] This assertion is based on the addiction surveys taken since 1988, which show that the overall addiction rate in Mexico

---

2. Colleen W. Cook, October 16, 2007, "Mexico's Drug Cartels," Congressional Research Service report for Congress.

3. National Drug Intelligence Center, Department of Justice, "National Drug Threat Assessment, 2010," Product No. 2010-Q317-001, February 2010.

4. Consejo Nacional contra las Adicciones (CONADIC), Instituto Nacional de Psiqiatria Ramon de la Fuente, Instituto Nacional de Salud Pública, and Fundación Rio Arronte, I.A.P., "Encuesta Nacional de Adicciones 2008."

5. Jorge Castañeda, "What's Spanish for Quagmire? Five Myths That Caused the Failed War Next Door," *Foreign Policy* (January/February 2010): 78–81.

(all drugs, not just the four noted here) of 0.4 percent is lower than that in the United States and Western Europe. The data he cites are that total addiction went from 307,000 in 2002 to 465,000 in 2008—an increase of 26,000 a year in a country with 110 million inhabitants. Mexico, he says, jumped into its war on drugs without debate or reflection.

Transportation of Drugs

Most of the locations where drugs illegally enter the United States are the same border crossings where money and guns illegally enter Mexico. Cocaine normally makes its way from Colombia, through Guatemala, and then into Mexico, from where it passes into the United States.

The nine most important border crossing routes between Mexico and the United States, going west to east, are the following: (1) Tijuana–San Diego, where illicit drugs are brought into the United States by both land and sea; (2) Mexicali-Calexico, which is an important route for the Tijuana cartel but also for the Sinaloa cartel; (3) Agua Prieta–Douglas, which does not connect to any major highway but is a prime route for illegal aliens; drugs are often tossed over the fence at a prearranged time and then immediately picked up on the U.S. side; (4) Nogales-Nogales, an area through which many unauthorized immigrants also pass; (5) Ciudad Juárez–El Paso, which is now one of the most dangerous border crossings in the world because of the high murder rates on the Mexican side; (6) Piedras Negras–Eagle Pass, along the Rio Grande; (7) Nuevo Laredo–Laredo, allowing movement further into the United States on I-35; (8) Reynosa-McAllen, in the Rio Grande Valley; and (9) Matamoros-Brownsville, which is at a strategic location along the Gulf of Mexico coast and major Mexican and U.S. highways.

Drugs are moved on all kinds of vehicles (some stolen)—bicycles, all-terrain vehicles, aircraft, personal automobiles, buses, rail cars, and tractor trailers—and there are many mechanics preparing the vehicles to store drugs. "Ant trafficking" involves large numbers of people carrying small amounts north. Narcotunnels have been found at different entry points. The smugglers must move large amounts of drugs across the border, and they have been doing it for years. Consequently, they can be creative, and authorities have found drugs hidden in tables, chairs, other furniture, toys, and food products, among other places.

3 THE STRUCTURE OF THE MEXICAN CARTELS

Since the 1980s, Mexican drug-trafficking organizations (DTOs) have undergone large-scale changes in size, reach, and practices. From being largely concerned with the transshipment of cocaine from Colombia and the growing and shipment of marijuana into the United States, Mexican DTOs have increased dramatically in wealth and power. This growth has occurred largely because control of major drug markets in the United States has passed from Colombian DTOs to their Mexican counterparts.

Mexican DTOs collectively offer a wide range of narcotics, including cocaine, marijuana, methamphetamines, and heroin. This diverse "product line" has helped them establish a thriving business across the United States, offering narcotics for poor, middle-class, and richer consumers. To satisfy and grow this demand, Mexican DTOs now engage in the production, trafficking, and distribution of different narcotics.

Mexican DTOs differ extensively from one another in size, power, internal organization, and geographical reach (see table 3.1). What's more, these attributes seem to vary considerably over time, depending on levels of violence and competition for markets among the cartels and on the actions of public security forces. What can be said about all DTOs is that they appear to be highly mobile, fast-reacting organizations. When pressure is applied to a DTO by government authorities, the reaction can take the form of retaliatory attacks, of a shift in activities from one region or state to another, or a movement across national borders. It has often been noted that DTOs are similar to balloons: when pressure is applied at one point, the DTO will expand its presence somewhere else.

If we are to understand the structure of drug trafficking, we must analyze the industry along a range of different dimensions. In this report, we propose looking at the structure of drug trafficking in three main ways:

- The international structure of drug trafficking
- The distribution of power and influence among DTOs
- The internal structure of DTOs

The balance of power and the overall structure of the drug trade have undergone dramatic changes since the 1980s. Perhaps the most obvious change has been the shift from predominantly Colombian DTOs to their Mexican counterparts. This change occurred for a number of reasons: partly because of the success of U.S. government attempts to close down drug-trafficking routes through the Caribbean to Florida and partly because of successes against the DTOs in Colombia. The most important factor in the rise of Mexican DTOs, however, was their decision to accept payment from the Colombian DTOs in kind rather than in cash, allowing them to build up their own cocaine distribution networks in the United States. Over time, this factor has greatly increased their power vis-à-vis the Colombian organizations, as well as the resources available to them.

Table 3.1. The Major Mexican Drug-Trafficking Organizations

Organization	Base	Profile
Beltran-Leyva	Morelos, Guerrero	Led by Arturo Beltran-Leyva and his brothers, the cartel began life as an affiliate of the Sinaloa cartel but split from it in 2008. It is now allied with the Zetas. The cartel has been severely weakened recently by the killing or capture of three of the four Beltran-Leyva brothers; only Hector remains in control.
La Familia Michoacana (LFM)	Michoacán	The newest actor in the Mexican DTO universe, LFM is notorious for its use of symbolic violence (decapitations, messages cut into the flesh of its victims' bodies) and for its semi-religious or moralistic rhetoric.
Gulf	Nuevo León, Tamaulípas	Although severely weakened by the arrest or killing of senior members of the cartel in recent years, the Gulf DTO continues to play a central role in drug trafficking in northeast Mexico. Allied with the Juárez cartel, it is engaged in conflicts with both the Tijuana cartel and the Zetas.
Juárez	Chihuahua	The Juárez cartel derived its power and influence from its geographic location at one of the most important crossing points for drugs passing from Mexico to the United States. Although the cartel has been weakened in recent years, its alliance with the Gulf DTO has helped strengthen both cartels.
Sinaloa	The Golden Triangle—Sinaloa, Durango, Chihuahua	One of the most important cartels, the Sinaloa DTO is at the center of "the federation," an alliance with a number of smaller cartels. Through this structure, the Sinaloa cartel has a presence in 17 Mexican states and has distribution networks throughout the United States.
Tijuana	Baja California Norte	Just like the Juarez DTO, the Tijuana cartel, also known as the Arrellano Félix cartel, has gained power by controlling the lucrative corridor from Tijuana to Mexicali, both moving drugs and charging other cartels for their shipments through its territory.
Zetas	Eastern Mexico	The former military wing of the Gulf cartel, the Zetas now operate as a fully fledged DTO independently in a number of states and regions of Mexico and have engaged in turf wars with the Gulf cartel and the LFM

Source: George Grayson, "Status of Cartels," CSIS background paper (January 2010), 6–12.

As Mexican DTOs have grown in power, they have not only established a presence in the United States and throughout Mexico but have also built up networks throughout Central America, into Colombia, and even as far afield as Africa and Europe. In South America, all the major Mexican DTOs, with the possible exception of LFM, have made significant inroads throughout the continent. As such, Mexican DTOs need to be viewed as truly transnational, and increasingly transregional, actors.

As can be seen from tables 3.1 and 3.2, in recent years Mexican DTOs have built up a network of connections and a presence throughout Latin America. Of particular importance is, of course, their presence in major cocaine-producing countries such as Peru and Colombia, but looking forward, we should also note that they have formed alliances with gangs and organized crime groups in the countries of Central America. These connections are becoming increasingly prevalent and deep-rooted as the Mexican government's attacks on DTOs in Mexico have progressed since 2008. When thinking about U.S. policy toward the drug trade in the future, and in particular the shape of post-Mérida initiatives, we must consider this Central American connection.

According to the Drug Enforcement Administration, the extent of Mexican DTO activity in the United States is steadily increasing and has now reached major cities in the entire continental United States, as well as some major cities in Canada. In the United States, Mexican DTOs appear to rely on decentralized distribution networks that lack rigid organization. Although arrests of drug dealers may have a short-term impact on local supply, the effect on the DTO itself is minimal. The same can be said of drug distribution in Mexico itself, an increasingly important but still relatively small market for Mexican DTOs. *Narcomenudeo,* or drug dealing on the streets of Mexican cities, has become another income stream for the DTOs and a further challenge for the authorities, with its consequent impact on public health and security.

The second major change affecting the Mexican DTOs has been the shifting balance of power among them. From a largely unipolar system that brought significant stability, the landscape of Mexican drug trafficking has become fractured, highly competitive, and unstable. This change has come about largely because of government actions against the cartels and because of the ongoing war among them that has led to a splintering and then partial consolidation of DTOs. With the notable exception of Operation Condor in the post-World War II period, Mexican drug trafficking enjoyed an existence largely unmolested by government actions, which led to the establishment of a dominant DTO in the Pacific corridor led by Miguel Angel Félix Gallardo. On his arrest in April 1989, Félix Gallardo divided up his territories among his captains, establishing a precarious peace among the different factions that gradually dissolved into open conflict. Since then, the geographic division of Mexico among the cartels has been in almost constant flux, waxing and waning with power shifts among individual DTOs caused by government arrests and competition among the organizations. Whether DTOs will continue to fracture, or whether there will be a consolidation of power to restore some stability to their universe, remains to be seen.

Recognizing the fluid network of alliances and partnerships among Mexican DTOs is also vital. Partly in response to increasing attention from the Mexican government, partly because of the economics of the drugs trade, and partly because of the emergence of rival alliances, DTOs may fracture or show signs of merging. In recent years, the major developments in this regard have been the emergence of "the federation," formed by the Sinaloa, Juárez, and Valencia cartels, and an alliance between the Gulf and Tijuana cartels. Although each of these DTOs remains independent, they have formed alliances based on the division of business and markets and on collaborative

Table 3.2. The Presence of Mexican Drug-Trafficking Organizations in Latin America

Cartel	Number of Latin American Countries with Mexican DTO Presence	Latin American Countries with Mexican DTO Presence
Cártel de Sinaloa	15	Argentina, Belize, Chile, Colombia, Costa Rica, Cuba, Dominican Republic, Ecuador, El Salvador, Guatemala, Nicaragua, Panama, Peru, Uruguay, Venezuela
Los Golfos-Zetas	10	Argentina , Belize, Brazil, Colombia, El Salvador, Guatemala, Honduras, Nicaragua, Uruguay, Venezuela
Cártel de Tijuana	5	Colombia, Costa Rica, El Salvador, Guatemala, Nicaragua
Los Beltran-Leyva	2	Colombia, Guatemala
Cártel de Juárez	1	Argentina

Source: *El Universal*, various issues.

operations. This partial consolidation of the Mexican DTOs has been matched by the emergence of the former military wing of the Gulf cartel—the Zetas—as an independent organization and the rise of La Familia Michoacana (LFM) in the west of Mexico.

The third structural dimension of drug trafficking refers to the internal organization of the DTOs. Given the dynamic nature of these criminal networks, internal structures are subject to frequent change, but it is useful to adopt Adler's "double-funnel" model of drug trafficking.[1] In this model, the production and distribution functions of the cartel are seen as diffuse and labor intensive, whereas the trafficking of drugs across the border, particularly a difficult one such as the U.S.-Mexican border, is undertaken by a small group of specialized personnel. As a result, the structure of DTOs can be described as "thick" at the point of origin and the point of sale but relatively "thin" at the center, creating a double-funnel appearance. The "center" of the DTO involves business management, security, and political connections, among other functions.

This internal structure also helps show where profits from the business are generally concentrated. A small number of participants at the center, those who organize the business of smuggling drugs across the border, control the organization and reap the rewards. Should either a drug producer or a drug distributor be apprehended by law enforcement authorities, the impact on the DTO will be minimal. Capturing leading figures at the center and disrupting the business of trafficking across borders, however, are likely to be more effective.

Because of the concentration of profits, power, and management expertise at the center of the DTO, government actions directed against the center not only will be more disruptive but also

1. Patricia Adler, *Wheeling and Dealing: The Ethnography of an Upper Level Drug Dealing Community* (New York: Columbia University Press, 1989).

will draw a stronger reaction from the cartel. Such action will lead to a "thickening" of the center as the security functions of the DTO are expanded to protect key personnel from arrest and to protect against threats from other cartels. The same can be said of the impact of post-9/11 border measures by the U.S. government. As transporting drugs into the United States has become more risky and more costly, DTOs have become more sophisticated in their internal structures and in the methods they must use to get drugs across the border.

Alternatively, should government authorities succeed in arresting or eliminating high-ranking DTO personnel, a struggle within the cartel for succession may result. Government authorities have repeatedly given this explanation to account for peaks in violence and have cited it as evidence of progress. We will return to this theme in a later section.

It is important to point out that in times of intense competition among the cartels, and increasing attacks on the cartels by government forces, change occurs frequently in their internal structure. A 2008 case study of the Gulf cartel by Nathan Jones[2] showed how the cartel, a formerly hierarchically organized DTO, responded to the arrest of high-ranking figures in its hierarchy. In the wake of the 2003 arrest of Osiel Cárdenas Guillen, the head of the cartel, the Gulf DTO saw a "flattening" of its command structure, with a number of different individuals, known as "gatekeepers," running different areas of business. This development raised questions about the ability of the DTO to respond to rising competition from its former military wing, the Zetas, particularly after the 2007 extradition of Cárdenas Guillen to a U.S. jail, from which he has found it much more difficult to coordinate the cartel's operations. The arrest of 175 members of the Gulf cartel in 2008 by U.S. authorities further weakened the DTO, leading to a belief that it would not be able to continue dominating drug corridors in the Mexican northeast. The rise of the Zetas as an independent organization, and its spread to other states throughout Mexico, seemed to confirm this assessment. The Gulf cartel has recently shown its resilience, however, pushing back against its former military ally in Tamaulipas. Although the Gulf cartel appears to be able to continue to prosper by employing a decentralized chain of command, it may be the exception rather than the rule.

2. Nathan Jones, "Using Counterinsurgency Strategy to Reassert the Westphalian State against Criminal Networks: The Case of the Gulf Cartel in Mexico" (paper presented at the Annual Convention of the International Studies Association, New York, March 2009).

4 GUNS AND DRUGS

In his address to the joint session of the U.S. Congress on May 20, 2010, President Felipe Calderón respectfully called on U.S. lawmakers to reexamine gun laws in the United States and to make efforts to halt the stream of weapons south to Mexico: "There is one issue where Mexico needs your cooperation, and that is stopping the flow of assault weapons and other deadly arms across the border." Although the likelihood of U.S. legislators changing the country's gun laws is slim, Calderón's appeal was directed toward increasing interdiction efforts for weapons moving across the border. This theme has been a permanent feature of the Calderón government's discourse on the drug war for the past four years and has succeeded in gaining recognition from both President Obama and Secretary of State Clinton, who have publicly accepted that the United States must do more to stem the "iron river" of guns flowing into the hands of drug cartels.

During his tenure as Mexico's attorney general, Eduardo Medina-Mora had drawn attention to illegal gun movements into Mexico as part of the government's broader strategy to secure recognition of coresponsibility from the United States. Medina-Mora consistently emphasized the fact that, in many situations, Mexican government forces found themselves "outgunned" by the cartels, whose foot soldiers had access to more impressive weaponry than their counterparts in the police or army. Of course, guns and other weapons are only part of the problem: Mexican DTOs have increasingly been using sophisticated military technology such as night-vision goggles and scopes, body armor, and armored vehicles. The growing firepower of the cartels, however, is the major driver of the rising violence and casualties.

During his talks, Medina-Mora became well known for using an impressive "show and tell" approach to convincing audiences of the need for stricter gun controls in the United States, displaying large-caliber sniper rifles that had been traced back to gun stores in the United States and explaining in graphic language the impact of such weapons on Mexican soldiers and law enforcement officials.

It is certainly true that the scale of weaponry used by the cartels has now become an important factor in the Calderón administration's attempts to suppress both drug-trafficking activity and narco-violence. Rising competition and conflict among the cartels and the government's war on the cartels have also served to drive demand for guns; as Nathan Jones notes, "The current increased demand for weapons in Mexico has been sparked by the militarization of the Mexican drug cartels."[1]

Tracing the Guns

Thanks to the use of eTrace software, guns seized from the cartels in raids and operations by Mexican government agents have been tracked back to their point of sale. Although some in the

1. See appendix A, p. 59.

United States have disputed the figures of the Mexican authorities,[2] it seems that an overwhelming majority of the weapons used by the cartels in Mexico originate in gun stores in the United States, predominantly located near the southern border. In a study by Nathan Jones commissioned for this report, two factors seem to explain which U.S. states serve as the source of the cartels' guns: proximity and leniency or strictness of gun laws. According to a report by the GAO,[3] 70 percent of all the guns seized by the Mexican government between 2004 and 2008 came from three states: Arizona, California, and Texas. The Mexican government has identified the large number of gun stores or pawnshops that sell guns along the border (particularly in the Southwest where the U.S. government estimates there are 6,700) as a serious problem that aggravates the flow. Although a small percentage of the total, a significant number of guns have also been traced back to stores in Florida and Washington State, showing that proximity is not the only factor. These two states have lenient firearms controls, and when leniency and proximity are combined, as in the cases of Arizona and Texas (from which 39 percent and 10 percent of the total number of guns seized come), a pattern begins to emerge. Gun shows are also an important source of weapons, particularly because in some states (including Arizona and Texas) buyers may purchase guns without having to submit to a background check. The federal government has yet to address properly this "gun show loophole" in U.S. firearms regulation.

Not all weapons, however, can be traced back to the United States. As the "arms race" among the cartels has heated up, organized criminals have begun to use heavier artillery. Although grenades, antitank rockets, .50 caliber machine guns, and grenade launchers are not officially available in U.S. gun markets, the Mexican government has increasingly found them in raids and arrests, and these weapons have been used against government forces. These weapons seem more likely to have come from Central America, entering Mexico through the porous southern border, although they could also have been stolen from U.S. or Mexican military armories.

Moving the Guns

Guns find their way to Mexico through "straw-purchasing" procedures, whereby individual legal buyers of weapons buy guns in the United States and then sell them to organizations linked to the DTOs, which then smuggle them into Mexico. The individual purchasers in the United States will normally have clean criminal records, be licensed to carry weapons, and will make a substantial profit from their role as intermediaries. The straw-purchasing rings that take the weapons to Mexico are able to cross over the border easily because of the relative laxity of border checks on the Mexican side.

Where Are Guns Recovered in Mexico?

Although drug cartels use guns throughout the country, according to Mexico's Center for National Planning and Information to Combat Crime, eight states predominate in weapons seizures: Baja California Norte, Chihuahua, Distrito Federal (DF), Guanajuato, Jalisco, Michoacán, Oaxaca, and Tamaulipas. With the exception of the DF and Guanajuato, these states are notorious for their

2. Fox News has claimed that the Mexican numbers are exaggerated.

3. J.T. Ford, "Firearms Trafficking: U.S. Efforts to Combat Arms Trafficking to Mexico Face Planning and Coordination Challenges" (Washington, D.C.: GAO, 2009).

drug violence and for known activity of the major Mexican DTOs. Studies using eTrace software have also shown the same eight states as being important locations for weapons seizures.

What Can Be Done?

Three main policy options exist for addressing the flow of weapons feeding the drug violence and growing insecurity in Mexico:

- Strengthening U.S. domestic gun legislation
- Expanding bilateral interdiction of weapons flows
- Ratifying the Inter-American Convention against the Illicit Manufacturing and Trafficking of Firearms (CIFTA) by the United States

Although changes to U.S. domestic gun laws are unlikely to come about as a direct result of drug violence in Mexico, the remaining two options have some potential. On both the northern and the southern borders of Mexico, increased cooperation between U.S. and Mexican government agencies through the Mérida Initiative could have an impact on the ability of the cartels to get hold of weapons. Project Gunrunner, an operation implemented by the U.S. Bureau of Alcohol, Tobacco, and Firearms in 2006, was the source of the eTrace software now being used by Mexican authorities (and which has been recently translated into Spanish to facilitate its use). Further efforts to interdict arms shipments across the U.S.-Mexican and Mexican-Guatemalan borders involving the coordinated actions of U.S., Mexican, and Central American security and intelligence services would be an important use of Mérida resources. In particular, the strengthening of Mexican border controls would likely have an impact on the flow and the cost of transporting weapons into Mexico. The ratification of CIFTA, although controversial and facing powerful opposition in the United States, "would reinforce the Obama administration's commitment to engagement on issues such as organized crime, seeking a multilateral approach to a problem and reminding our citizens of the interdependence of both the U.S. and Mexico when it comes to security," according to Johanna Mendelson Forman of CSIS.[4] Furthermore, Mendelson Forman argues, "A ratified treaty would send a clear signal to U.S. gun merchants, large and small, that our government is serious about illegal arms deals."[5]

---

4. Johanna Mendelson Forman, "Draft Paper on Small Arms," CSIS background paper (January 2010), 1–2.

5. Ibid., 5.

5 VIOLENCE AMONG MEXICAN DRUG-TRAFFICKING ORGANIZATIONS

Mexican society has been paying the price for the war against the drug cartels being waged by the Calderón administration since 2008 in a way, and to an extent, never before seen. Although the Mexican government argues that almost all the violence takes place between rival DTOs in turf wars or in targeted hits, Mexico's population has suffered both directly and indirectly from the violence and growing insecurity in the country.

Since 2007, more than 23,000 people have lost their lives in drug-related violence in Mexico, according to accounts kept by the Transborder Institute at the University of San Diego. The year 2010 is shaping up to be the bloodiest year on record in the drug conflict: from January to the end of May, 3,365 people died in the violence, double the number killed in the same period in 2009. Government sources in both Mexico and the United States frequently claim that the rise in violence is a direct result of the success of the authorities against the cartels and of the cartels' growing desperation, but this explanation is of little consolation to the Mexican people whose lives are directly or indirectly touched by insecurity. In opinion polls in 2010, Mexicans are showing a growing concern over insecurity and have identified it as one of the major problems facing them and the country.[1] Although their predominant concern since 2007 has been the economic crisis (in 2005 and 2006 insecurity was identified as the number-one challenge), opinion polls have consistently identified violence in the country as the second-most important problem, and as economic recovery continues, we can expect insecurity to challenge the economy for first place.

The numbers of lives lost in the struggle among and against the cartels is particularly horrific when viewed beside the number of U.S. casualties in the Iraq war, where 4,287 U.S. service personnel were lost between 2003 and the end of 2009. What's more, the death toll in Mexico has gotten progressively worse, giving most Mexicans the impression that the government is losing control of the situation. In 2007, 2,477 people were killed in the violence, but this number more than doubled to 6,290 during 2008. That number was again exceeded in 2009 when 7,724 casualties were reported, and up to June of 2010, more than 5,000 people have been killed in the violence.[2] With no slowdown in the rate of killings likely in the foreseeable future, Mexicans are increasingly questioning the Calderón administration's strategy of open confrontation with the cartels.

It may be useful to organize the violence into different categories. First, some violence stems directly from the competition among cartels and the retaliatory violence that generally follows. Second, some violence comes as a direct result of government actions against the cartels, when gun fights erupt between police or army forces on the one hand and DTO foot soldiers on the other. Third, symbolic or graphic violence has increased in recent years, whereby the cartels com-

1. Consulta Mitofsky, "Economia, Gobierno y Politica," *Monitor Mitofsky* (June 2010), http://72.52.156.225/Docs/FusionCharts/EPG.pdf.

2. Estimates taken from *El Universal*, various issues, http://www.eluniversal.com.mx/coberturas/esp207.html.

mit specific gruesome actions against their competitors or against government personnel, in a way that is designed to send a message. Fourth, the violence that takes place in Mexican territory and is well reported across the border in the United States. Last, some of the violence affects innocent bystanders who have increasingly become victims, with mistaken identity often being the cause of the loss of innocent life in conflict-affected areas of the country.

Violence among cartels has occurred mostly in those areas where they come into direct competition for markets or supply corridors (*plazas*). As a result, violence has been concentrated mostly in the north of Mexico, close to the U.S. border, particularly in the area around Ciudad Juárez and the Tijuana-Mexicali corridor, important areas for transporting drugs across the border. That said, competition for routes and markets extends across Mexico, and clashes have escalated into more general conflicts among DTOs. Major cities such as Monterrey, Guadalajara, and Morelia have all witnessed such violence, although at the time of writing, drug violence had barely touched Mexico City.[3]

The violence is usually committed by individual assassins or groups of foot soldiers, known as *sicarios*. Despite the arrest or killing of thousands of these *sicarios* in intercartel violence or government attacks, there appears to be a never-ending supply of young men who are willing to kill and commit other grisly deeds in the service of the Mexican DTOs. This availability is directly tied to the dire state of local economies in many regions of Mexico, so that the fast money promised by the cartels presents an opportunity that many cannot refuse. Low-ranking foot soldiers may be paid as little as $45 a week for their work, highlighting the desperate situation of many young Mexicans in areas with little or no well-paid employment.[4]

Although the arrest or killing of senior officials in the DTOs are on orders of the cartel leaders, since 2006 the *sicarios* have moved progressively higher up the cartel hierarchy or have acquired autonomy or independence from the cartel leaders. This change has most famously been observed in the case of the Zetas. Created by the Gulf cartel in the 1990s to act as a military wing, the Zetas were originally recruited from the Grupo Aeromóvil de Fuerzas Especiales (Special Forces Airmobile Group, GAFE) or Mexican Special Forces, and thus have a reputation for being professional soldiers of the highest capabilities. They are extremely well equipped and trained and have also recruited new members from Guatemala's Special Forces (the *kaibiles*), famed for their brutality and obsessive commitment to battle. Recruitment has also brought in former and current members of the police and intelligence services, making the Zetas a formidable organization. In recent years, the Zetas, who have become a force in their own right and have expanded both their activities and their geographic scope, now challenge the Gulf cartel for dominance in the northeast.

Violence that has come as a direct result of government antinarcotics operations has of course become a lot more prevalent since the Calderón administration stepped up the federal government campaign in 2006. Major shootouts have occurred across Mexico, such as in the city of Cuernavaca near Mexico City, where a two-hour gun battle between Mexican navy forces (including 200 troops, two tanks, and a helicopter) and members of the Beltran Leyva cartel resulted in the

3. The major exception was, of course, the assassination of Edgar Bayardo, a former senior federal police official who had been co-opted by drug cartels and then turned state witness; his testimony led to the indictment of the federal police chief and other top cops. His murder in December of 2009 was a major shock to the Mexico City establishment, particularly considering that the hit took place in a Starbucks in broad daylight.

4. Matthew Price, "Mexico's Struggle to Win 'War' on Drugs," BBC News, http://news.bbc.co.uk/2/hi/world/us_and_canada/10275565.stm.

killing of Arturo Beltran Leyva, along with four of his *sicarios*.[5] Although such major confrontations are not common, smaller gunfights between government forces and the DTOs have become part and parcel of Mexico's daily news.

Graphic or symbolic violence is playing a growing role in the drug conflict in Mexico, especially with the emergence of two new warring actors, the Zetas and La Familia Michoacana (LFM). The Zetas have long used brutality and symbolic acts as a way of striking fear into their opponents, both in the government and in other cartels. In Nuevo Laredo, burning alive of police officers inside barrels of diesel oil in 2008 was particularly gruesome, but the group has consistently used such methods to exact revenge and to send messages to its rivals. Partly due to its former links with the Zetas (several members of LFM used to be involved with the Zetas), the LFM has also become notorious for its use of symbolic violence, which first gained public attention in 2006 after a horrifying incident in a Michoacan nightclub when five human heads were rolled onto the dance floor.[6] Since then, the LFM has built its reputation for graphic violence through torture, mutilations, and castrations.

In the growing conflict between the Zetas and the LFM, graphic violence has therefore played an important role, but an ideological or ethical dimension has also emerged, complicating the economic or personal motives for conflict more typically seen. The LFM has increasingly used moralistic rhetoric as a justification for its actions in its attempt to demonize rival drug cartels and in particular the Zetas. The LFM is best known for saying, "The Family doesn't kill for money; it doesn't kill women; it doesn't kill innocent people; only those who deserve to die, die. Everyone should know… this is divine justice," a motto included in a note left behind after the 2006 nightclub incident.

Symbolic violence involves not only the grisly nature of the killing but also the timing and impact. The June 2010 murder of Rodolfo Torre Cantu, the gubernatorial candidate of the Partido Revolucionario Institucional (PRI), was designed to send a message to the government, both state and federal, that nobody is safe and that the government has failed to maintain control of the country even during elections as important as those of the summer of 2010.

Many fear that the violence from border towns such as Ciudad Juárez or Nuevo Laredo will spill over into the United States. While such spillover has thus far been limited, it remains a constant concern for both U.S. and Mexican authorities. Authorities on the U.S. side of the border have repeatedly warned about the growing threat from Mexican DTOs within their jurisdiction, and one Texas official, Department of Public Safety director Steve McCraw, has stated publicly that it is already occurring:

> The state of Texas defines "spillover violence" as Mexican cartel-related violence that occurs in Texas including aggravated assault, extortion, kidnapping, torture, rape and murder….The victims of these crimes include illegal immigrants being smuggled into the United States, Mexican or U.S. citizens working with the cartels or their innocent family members, and those who are not associated in any way with the cartels or transnational gangs.[7]

Other officials are less willing to categorize such incidents as spillover violence because they

---

5. "Muere Arturo Beltrán Leyva en *Cuernavaca*," *El Universal*, December 16, 2009, http://www.eluniversal.com.mx/notas/646490.html.

6. George Grayson, "Status of Mexico's Drug Cartels," CSIS background paper (January 2010), 17.

7. Jeremy Roebuck, "DPS Director: 'Spillover' Is Here," *Brownsville Herald*, March 31, 2010, http://www.brownsvilleherald.com/articles/spillover-110342-drug-ago.html.

fear causing panic among local residents, but it is clear that Mexican DTOs are becoming increasingly bold in their incursions into U.S. territory.

Finally, we must make note of the impact of violence on innocent bystanders in areas of drug conflict areas. As the war among and against the DTOs heats up, a growing number of ordinary citizens with no connection to the cartels have been affected. The shooting of two students on the Tec de Monterrey University campus in a gun battle between police and *sicarios* in March 2010 and the massacre of a group of 15 teenagers at a party in Ciudad Juárez in late January served to highlight the growing cost to the Mexican public of the war against the cartels. To make matters worse, officials first reported that all the victims were associated with the cartels, necessitating an embarrassing retraction later. But regular Mexican citizens are suffering in other, less direct ways from the violence:

- First, the general climate of fear and insecurity
- Second, the impact on local economies, particularly in the north, as businesses lose income or are forced to close
- Third, a rise in other forms of violent crime not directly associated with the cartels, as the "culture of impunity" encourages more people to engage in crimes such as kidnapping and extortion

The Trend in Murder Rates in Mexico

States and Regions

Murder rates in Mexico show differences in violence throughout the country. Homicide was trending down overall from 1990 until 2007, when homicides decreased from approximately 14,520 to about 8,868. Data for the year 2008, however, showed a dramatic increase in murders, about a 37 percent increase from the year before (table 5.1). With the exception of the states of Nuevo León, Veracruz, and Yucatán, all other states suffered from rising homicide rates that year. The increase in homicides, though, was not spread equally. Chihuahua, Baja California Norte, Durango, and Sinaloa showed the highest increments in homicides in 2008 of 402, 179, 141, and 107 percent changes, respectively. Campeche, Hidalgo, and Oaxaca experienced homicide increases of about 10 percent in 2008.

Figure 5.1 shows average annual homicides by region from 1990 through 2008. The northern border states experienced the largest increases in murders. In fact, the northern region is the only one that shows an overall increasing trend in homicides since 1990.

Table 5.1. Number of Murders in Mexico by Region, 1990–2008

	1990	1991	1992	1993	1994	1995	1996	1997	1998	1999	2000	2001	2002	2003	2004	2005	2006	2007	2008
Aguascalientes	43	56	35	33	23	35	29	23	44	23	17	23	29	25	21	26	26	42	59
Baja California	277	286	313	293	353	399	383	340	582	643	444	404	428	454	478	441	465	369	1,031
Baja California Sur	12	18	18	21	28	32	24	35	20	34	29	22	32	25	29	34	26	35	38
Campeche	85	67	87	78	75	98	79	77	86	77	66	53	54	44	36	48	33	50	54
Chiapas	277	472	437	502	645	708	653	606	825	609	429	173	475	444	224	305	539	101	263
Chihuahua	315	467	480	469	577	760	669	663	643	567	612	650	653	537	476	570	648	518	2,601
Coahuila	180	231	226	218	216	178	168	152	144	148	123	155	139	119	117	152	107	111	181
Colima	78	99	121	72	87	64	43	53	62	60	58	60	45	43	53	51	44	43	57
Distrito Federal	1,259	1,059	1,201	1,156	1,155	1,360	1,292	1,216	1,226	1,046	930	985	942	982	948	880	818	847	930
Durango	285	334	618	349	343	310	241	239	244	207	161	164	174	210	158	173	170	174	420
Guanajuato	372	419	362	398	337	306	287	294	307	254	232	222	209	221	177	216	206	219	295
Guerrero	784	1,019	1,589	1,307	1,209	1,262	1,032	1,079	1,137	962	804	644	624	602	594	591	789	766	1,005
Hidalgo	205	153	130	132	165	163	127	142	166	125	95	130	59	73	88	73	47	74	75
Jalisco	834	782	797	785	703	785	744	625	558	545	474	490	481	475	409	441	478	445	542
México	3,465	3,503	3,407	3,412	3,210	2,756	2,769	2,476	2,386	2,150	2,024	1,941	1,962	1,927	1,735	2,016	1,748	1,239	1,579
Michoacán	1,164	1,165	1,404	1,362	1,286	1,151	1,148	859	661	660	617	647	546	564	550	681	992	563	658
Morelos	383	342	379	496	462	354	351	305	314	310	241	213	177	171	159	138	141	128	215
Nayarit	245	233	249	253	272	197	126	157	130	124	110	114	153	110	138	133	106	108	155
Nuevo León	73	91	131	122	153	134	109	131	140	121	118	98	108	149	116	150	168	279	241
Oaxaca	1,214	1,286	1,274	1,337	1,177	1,183	1,130	977	962	789	709	640	609	620	626	547	520	564	616
Puebla	518	419	537	591	491	594	477	506	512	461	404	432	396	372	364	316	354	273	354
Querétaro	84	77	77	79	102	86	102	106	82	92	105	108	69	83	75	79	61	55	74
Quintana Roo	58	51	54	80	155	74	64	90	81	86	75	104	71	136	137	77	67	121	144
San Luis Potosí	241	212	273	242	245	227	209	202	315	284	276	229	157	147	135	138	158	143	199
Sinaloa	451	550	595	555	600	627	670	612	572	541	463	503	479	428	394	436	463	398	824
Sonora	166	190	243	213	250	315	331	277	302	283	202	257	223	233	253	260	251	323	436
Tabasco	133	119	137	156	241	238	183	161	146	148	93	101	97	116	111	100	144	146	153
Tamaulipas	266	340	413	376	358	323	280	282	325	290	266	186	188	229	216	348	359	193	266
Tlaxcala	48	33	45	47	42	74	62	67	67	76	56	53	52	39	51	49	44	37	53
Veracruz	780	843	753	695	703	618	551	634	500	444	422	383	351	409	330	344	360	380	340
Yucatán	62	66	47	59	47	49	44	46	45	34	44	36	51	52	36	37	41	49	49
Zacatecas	163	161	173	168	134	165	131	130	132	94	89	104	110	100	96	76	81	75	100
Total	14,520	15,143	16,605	16,056	15,844	15,625	14,508	13,562	13,716	12,287	10,788	10,324	10,143	10,139	9,330	9,926	10,454	8,868	14,007

Source: Instituto Nacional de Estadística y Geografia, May 2010.

Figure 5.1. Murder Rates in Mexico by Region, 1990–2008

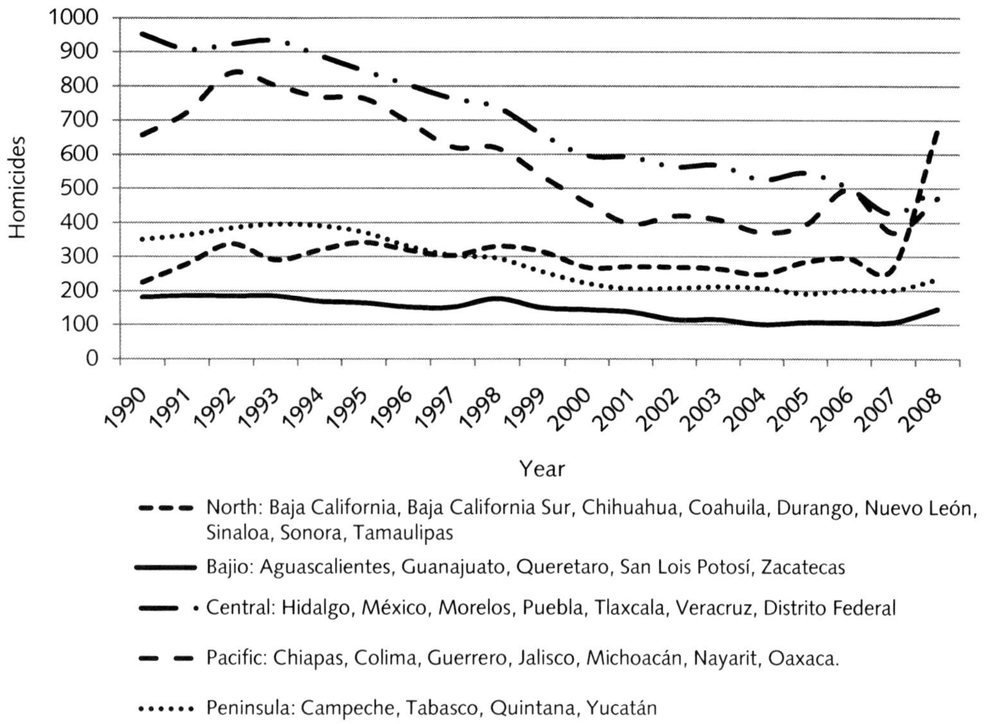

Source: Instituto Nacional de Estadística y Geografía, May 2010.

6 MEXICAN PUBLIC OPINION ON ANTINARCOTICS EFFORTS

The Mexican Government's Antinarcotics Efforts before Calderón

This section will briefly explore the main reforms that defined antinarcotics efforts leading up to the Calderón administration: eradication of crops to stop production (1970s–1980s), institutional and legal reforms to expand and strengthen law enforcement capacity (1990s), and today's approach of direct confrontation with drug cartels. Because the deployment of troops to counter drug trafficking has sparked much debate, the chapter will provide information on Mexican public opinion on the role of the military. Last, the chapter will examine media coverage of the drug violence and government efforts to allow for a better understanding of the extent to which drug cartels and violence are limiting the reporting on issues related to Mexico's drug conflict.

Eradication to Halt Production

Large-scale Mexican antinarcotics efforts took off in the 1970s as U.S. pressure forced the Mexican government to adopt a more aggressive antinarcotics strategy. Much of the antinarcotics efforts quickly became focused on crop eradication as a way to show commitment to the cause while minimizing direct confrontation with drug traffickers. This strategy was highlighted by Operation Condor, a multimillion dollar eradication campaign that featured spraying chemical defoliants on marijuana fields. Initial results were positive, as marijuana and opium production declined in the late 1970s and early 1980s.

The initial successes of the eradication campaign proved illusory for two main reasons. First, drug traffickers quickly adapted, dispersing production to new areas of Mexico and improving efforts at avoiding detection. Second, as U.S. efforts in southern Florida proved successful in stemming the flow of narcotics through the Caribbean, Mexico became the major transit point for delivering cocaine to the United States. As the Mexican cartels came to replace Caribbean traffickers, the power of the Mexican cartels increased. Corruption in Mexico grew as the cartels found increasing profits from cocaine shipments, undermining previous gains made in antinarcotics efforts.

Institutional Reforms

The Salinas and Zedillo administrations of the late 1980s and 1990s brought new energy to reforming Mexico's institutions while increasing the funding of antinarcotics efforts. In 1993, for example, the Salinas administration created the National Institute for the Combat of Drugs to better coordinate antinarcotics policies. That same year saw new legislation to combat money laundering and increase the lengths of sentences for drug-trafficking convictions. In 1999, the Zedillo administration created the Federal Preventive Police (Policía Federal Preventiva, or PFP). The PFP was created as an attempt to streamline various specialized federal police forces into one federal agency with greater centralized control.

Police reforms continued during the Vicente Fox administration (2000–2006). In 2001, the Agencia Federal de Investigación (AFI) was created to replace the federal judicial police, which had suffered numerous accusations of corruption. The AFI was intended to strengthen the investigative capacity of law enforcement by becoming a more technically adept police force, giving its officers the skills to assist the work of federal prosecutors. In addition to police reforms, the Fox presidency moved toward integrating military personnel, either retired or "on leave" from active duty, into civilian law enforcement institutions to carry out leadership functions. While Fox did send a small number of troops to the border, it was not until the Calderón presidency that a more confrontational approach was used against the drug-trafficking organizations (DTOs).

Confrontation with Drug Cartels

The Mexican army has played a significant role in the antinarcotics efforts from the beginning of President Felipe Calderón's government. After his first week in power, Calderón sent more than 6,000 federal troops and police officers to the state of Michoacán. Three weeks later, he sent 3,000 more troops to Tijuana.[1] During his first three years in office, Calderón sent approximately 49,000 soldiers across Mexico in the fight against drug cartels.[2] The policy shift to a larger-scale confrontation, however, has had violent consequences as many bystanders have died in the midst of the conflict. While declaring Mexico's drug problem a national security problem has helped justify and solidify the deployment of military troops to confront drug cartels directly, the many alleged reports of human rights violations committed by the military have tainted their reputation. Support for the use of troops, as the following section will show, appears to be waning as the violence shows no signs of subsiding.

Mexican Public Opinion on the Use of the Military

The expanding role of the army has generated different opinions across Mexico. To explore this heated debate and the views of the public, we must examine some pivotal factors mentioned earlier. Previous administrations in Mexico generally took a passive stance against drug cartels. Various approaches have been taken by successive Mexican governments to counter drug trafficking from 1970 to the present: crop eradication, institutional and police reforms, and military confrontation. Despite the reforms throughout the past decades, the Mexican government has not been able to decrease the power of the DTOs.

In fact, Calderón's military deployment is the most recent major effort to counter narco-violence, which had escalated by the end of Vicente Fox's administration. Likewise, by the time Calderón took office, many within the academic and political sphere assumed that using the army

---

1. Manuel Roig-Franzia, "Calderón's Offensive against Drug Cartels," *Washington Post,* July 8, 2007, http://www.washingtonpost.com/wp-dyn/content/article/2007/07/07/AR2007070701280.html.

2. Mica Rosenberg, "Drug War Abuses by Mexican Army Rise Sharply," Reuters, December 10, 2009, http://www.alertnet.org/thenews/newsdesk/N10203151.htm.

at the front lines of the counternarcotics campaign was the only option for regaining some control of the country. In particular, that assumption rose in parallel to the recognition that the state and municipal police forces could not satisfy such a role, given that high levels of corruption, poor institutional performance, and widespread public distrust of police are common.[3] In contrast, critics of the militarization of public safety and antinarcotics efforts have argued that the army could end up corrupted as well, especially taking into account their low salaries and high desertion rates.

General Public Opinion

Figure 6.1 shows the range of public opinion on security in Mexico.[4] Overall, after three years of extensive military deployment, a majority of the public still favored the use of the military and its antinarcotics efforts. When people were asked if they thought the army could become corrupt in dealing with drug cartels, however, 54 percent of those questioned answered yes, 29 percent answered no, and 17 percent had no comment or did not know.[5] One reason for the lack of agreement in public opinion could be that violence in Mexico, particularly drug-related violence, is not spread equally throughout the country. For example, areas bordering the United States have shown greater levels of violence: Ciudad Juárez, for example, is considered one of the most dangerous cities in the world. Likewise, regions where cartels fight over territory—mainly to expand their share of the illegal drug trade—experience higher violence and murder rates.

Some political observers, academics, and human rights organizations have been more critical about the deployment of army troops. A contending opinion argues that the strong military presence increases violence because more intense confrontations with drug cartels take place. Likewise, some have argued that the Mexican army may not be qualified or trained to interact appropriately with civilians, leading to abuses and the weakening of civilian democratic institutions.[6] Meanwhile, several human rights organizations have asserted that complaints against the army have increased as the role of the military has expanded. For example, the National Human Rights Commission reported that 182 complaints were received in 2006, compared with 1,230 in 2008 and approximately 2,000 in 2009.[7] In a 2009 survey, however, 56 percent of Mexican respondents reported that they considered it more important for the government to try to maintain law and order than to protect personal freedoms (see annex to this chapter). Only 18 percent placed greater importance on protecting personal freedoms, and 24 percent argued that both were important priorities.[8] Thus, while the Mexican army has not been able to curb violence, people generally approved of its expanding role in antinarcotics efforts.

---

3. Moses Moloeznik, "The Militarization of Public Security and the Role of the Military in Mexico," in *Police and Public Security in Mexico*, ed. Robert A. Donnelly and David A. Shirk (San Diego: University Readers, 2009), 65–92.

4. CASEDE-SIMO, "Encuesta Seguridad Nacional Julio-Agosto 2009," 13, http://www.seguridadcondemocracia.org/biblioteca/segnalagosto09.pdf.

5. Ibid., 14.

6. Laura Carlsen, "Militarizing Mexico: The New War on Drugs," *Foreign Policy in Focus*, July, 11, 2007, http://www.fpif.org/articles/militarizing_mexico_the_new_war_on_drugs.

7. Tracy Wilkinson, "Rights Group Faults Mexico over Alleged Army Abuse," *Los Angeles Times*, December 9, 2009, http://articles.latimes.com/2009/dec/09/world/la-fg-mexico-abuse9-2009dec09.

8. The Pew Research Center for the People and the Press, "Mexico: Drugs, Military, May 26 to June 2, 2009." Polling the Nations Online Database.

Figure 6.1. Mexican Public Opinion on Use of the Military for Antinarcotics Efforts, 2009

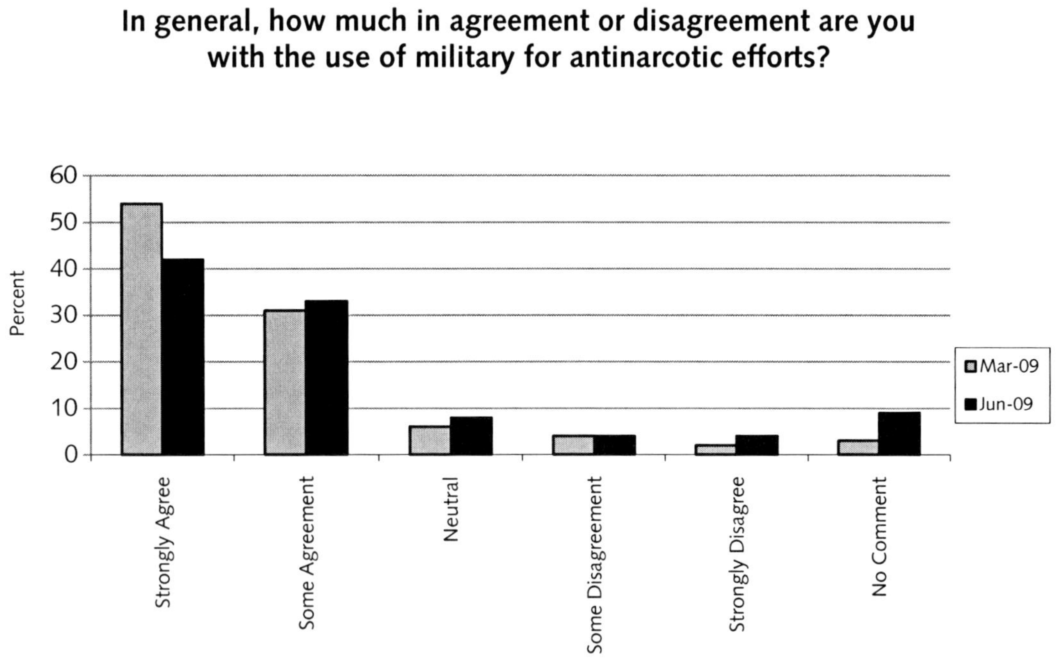

Source: CASEDE-SIMO, "Encuesta Seguridad Nacional Julio-Agosto 2009."

The Military Viewpoint

In a speech in May 2009, the minister of national defense, Guillermo Galván Galván, asserted that the expanding role of the armed forces in the antinarcotics efforts was a mandate given by Mexican civil society through its governments. Such a duty, Galván Galván argued, requires the intervention of the army to maintain and guarantee internal order and public security. The military viewpoint is inherently tied to government documents such as the National Security Act and the Programa Sectorial de Defensa Nacional 2007–2012, the strategic document of the Secretaría de la Defensa Nacional (SEDENA) that postulates the military's missions and priorities. The goals of antinarcotics efforts determined for the armed forces are to regain strength and the security of the state through frontal attack—168 "high impact operations" from 2007 through 2012— designed to eradicate drug trafficking and other expressions of organized crime.[9] Another legal framework that shaped the army's internal mission and its viewpoint is a Supreme Court ruling of 1996. This ruling allowed all three branches of the military "to participate in civilian activities to protect public safety."[10] Thus, the military viewpoint not only embraced the increasing role of the army in the antinarcotics efforts but also considers it essential for the advancement of Mexican society and a valuable support for the preservation of homeland interests.[11]

9. SEDENA, "Programa Sectorial de Defensa Nacional, 2007–2012," Secretaría de la Defensa Nacional, 2007, 12, http://www.sedena.gob.mx/pdf/psdn.pdf.

10. Moloeznik, "The Militarization of Public Security," 79.

11. Ibid., 7.

Media Coverage of Mexico's Antinarcotics Efforts

The rising violence of the conflict between the Mexican state and the cartels in the border regions of northern Mexico and the increasing lack of security for reporters are limiting the ability of the Mexican media to cover antinarcotics activities. Because of the violence levied against reporters who focus on the drug wars, Mexico has replaced Colombia as the most dangerous nation for journalists in Latin America. Since 2000, 55 reporters have been murdered, most likely because of the content of their reporting.[12] In addition, 9 reporters have been missing since 2003 with little progress made in determining what happened to them.[13] Many of the crimes against journalists have not resulted in a conviction, which has left a general sense of impunity in the border region. Absent any likelihood of conviction, such crimes continued unabated in 2010, with 5 journalists murdered by mid-March and 8 reporters kidnapped in the city of Reynosa between mid-February and early March.

With the Mexican government unable to protect journalists, many have decided to censor themselves. Threatened with violence by the drug gangs, or sometimes bribed, journalists have increasingly shied away from reporting on DTO activity or battles occurring between the cartels and the government.[14] A journalistic "void" has thus emerged, and much of the civilian population has found it difficult to know what is going on in their own towns with respect to the drug war. This lack of information has emboldened some citizens to take such reporting into their own hands. Instead of local newspapers reporting on cartel activity, other sources are now providing this information, with Facebook and Twitter offering first-hand accounts of what is transpiring in the border region.[15] As increasing numbers of reporters are assigned to different topics or relocated to safer reporting areas, the ability of the Mexican media to document the government's antinarcotics efforts appears to be diminishing.

Thus, as Calderón has made a shift in dealing with the drug cartels, the ability of the Mexican media to cover this profound change has been severely hampered by increasing violence against them. The lack of media protection has undermined the ability of reporters to recount the effectiveness of the government's antinarcotics efforts and to shed light on alleged human rights abuses by the military and hence has crippled the ability of the media to conduct the investigative journalism that is expected in democratic states. As media sources in Mexico and the United States have continued to note the intensifying violence perpetrated against journalists in Mexico in the midst of the drug war, the inability of the Mexican government to protect the freedom of the press has seriously diminished the right of Mexican citizens to be informed about the effectiveness of the government's antinarcotics efforts. Until the security of journalists is improved, the ability of the Mexican press to engage in investigative journalism will be severely compromised.

---

12. Reporters without Borders, "Mexico behind the Scenes of Impunity: Security Offensive and Bureaucratic Red Tape," September 2009, http://www.rsf.org.

13. Ibid.

14. Marc Lacey, "Fearing Drug Cartels, Reporters in Mexico Retreat," *New York Times*, March 13, 2010. The article points out that many news outlets on the U.S. side of the border have banned reporters from traveling to Mexican border regions, because of the threat of violence against them.

15. Not only have citizens found Facebook and Twitter useful in reporting on events in their towns, but the cartels have been using these media sources to their advantage as well. Cartels have used these tools as a form of communication, using code words to alert other members to police checkpoints and military raids. This development has led to the drafting of a bill by several members of the Partido de la Revolución Democrática (PRD) calling for stricter regulation of these sites. See Alexis Okeowo, "To Battle Cartels, Mexico Weighs Twitter Crackdown," *Time*, April 14, 2010.

Public Support for Calderón's Efforts in Light of Increasing Violence

President Felipe Calderón enjoyed high approval ratings when his administration took office in December 2006. In fact, public approval showed very strong momentum during the presidential campaign. In May 2005, Calderón had only a 14 percent approval rating. His two main opponents, Andrés Manuel López Obrador of the Partido de la Revolución Democrática (PRD) and Roberto Madrazo of the PRI, had approval ratings of 39 and 25 percent, respectively. By December 2006, however, Calderón had gained about 49 percent of the public's support, followed by López Obrador with only 19 percent.[16]

Figure 6.2. Public Approval of President Calderón, December 2006–March 2010

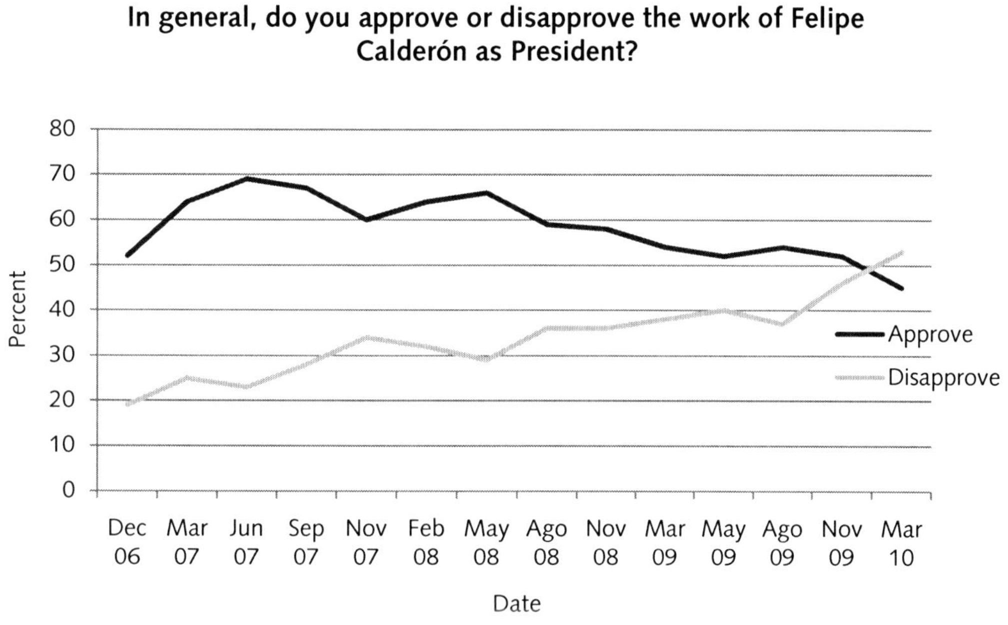

Source: GEA-ISA, Primera Encuesta Nacional, March 2010.

Figure 6.2 shows survey results of public support for Calderón's efforts as president.[17] Calderón received his highest support in the first six months of his presidency. During this period, the administration launched an immediate military offensive against the DTOs. In 2007, the number of murders in the north, Pacific, and central regions of the country substantially decreased. Public approval ratings, however, show a downward trend after May 2008, and by the end of 2009, disapproval ratings surpassed public approval of Calderón's efforts as president.

16. GEA-ISA, "Escenarios Políticos, 2004–2006: Gobernabilidad y Sucesión," Encuestas Nacionales, Mexico, http://www.isa.org.mx/contenido/GIMX0612p.pdf. This survey was conducted with a sample of 1,200. The results published have a ±3.3 percent margin of error at 95 percent confidence.

17. GEA-ISA, "Escenarios Políticos, 2010–2012: Gobernabilidad y Sucesión," Encuestas Nacionales, Mexico, 13, http://www.isa.org.mx/contenido/GIMX1003p.pdf.

This decrease in public support since 2008 mirrors an increase in violence throughout the country in that year. In fact, 2008 showed the highest percentage increase in violence in the past two decades, with a 37 percent increase in murders from the previous year. While Calderón currently has an approval rate of 45 percent, it is clear that public support has decreased in the light of the growing violence during his presidency.

Annex: Research Polls on the Use of the Military in Antinarcotics Efforts in Mexico, 2009 (percent of those polled)

In your opinion, at this time is it more important that the government try to maintain law and order or try to protect people's personal freedoms?

Law and order	56
Personal freedoms	18
Both	24
Don't know/refused to answer	2

What kind of influence is [the military] having on the way things are going in Mexico?

Very good	31
Somewhat good	46
Somewhat bad	14
Very bad	4
Don't know/refused to answer	4

Do you support or oppose: providing money and weapons to the Mexican police and military personnel?

Support	63
Oppose	28
Don't know/refused to answer	8

Source: The Pew Research Center for the People and the Press, "Mexico: Drugs, Military, May 26 to June 2, 2009." Polling the Nations Online Database.

Note: Polling was conducted by face-to-face interviews; the sample size was 1,000. Percentages are rounded and do not necessarily add up to 100.

7 CORRUPTION

A key element in the power the drug-trafficking organizations (DTOs) are able to exert is that the drugs are illicit where sold; it is this factor that allows the marketers to charge relatively high prices in the United States and other user countries. When combined with the substantial narcotics consumption in the United States, these high prices generate billions of dollars for corrupting the police, for corrupting the military when used in the Mexican antinarcotics effort, and for corrupting officials at all levels of government from the top to the bottom of hierarchies. The DTOs bribe both Mexican and U.S. officials.

Corruption of Senior Officials

Examples abound on how deeply this bribery reaches into Mexican organizations. In 1997, Jesús Gutiérrez Rebollo, then Mexico's antinarcotics drug czar, was convicted of cooperating with a drug cartel and passing on intelligence to them, including that coming from the United States. Noé Ramírez, a former head of Mexico's elite antidrug agency, was detained in November 2008 on charges of taking a bribe of $450,000 for leaking information to a drug cartel; he was Mexico's envoy to the United Nations Office on Drugs and Crime in Vienna when detained.

In May 2010, Mexico extradited Mario Ernesto Villanueva Madrid, a former mayor of the city of Cancún and subsequently governor (elected in 1993) of the state of Quintana Roo (where Cancún is located). He was charged with providing police protection to the Juárez cartel as it smuggled large shipments of cocaine into the United States. He was allegedly paid $400,000–500,000 for each shipment, coming to millions of dollars in total. He was also charged with laundering nearly $19 million through accounts with Lehman Brothers. As mayor and then as governor, he was well positioned as a valuable asset to the cartel.[1] According to an article in the *Washington Post*, Villanueva Madrid was the highest-ranking former official extradited to the United States. Before 2000, Mexico was reluctant, on sovereignty grounds, to extradite its own nationals. But the country extradited 107 alleged narcotics criminals to the United States in 2009, and extraditions continue at this pace or higher in 2010.[2] These extraditions are an example of the antinarcotics cooperation that now exists between the two countries.

1. Federal Bureau of Investigation, "Former Governor of Mexican State Extradited for Conspiring to Import Hundreds of Tons of Cocaine and Laundering Millions in Bribe Payments Through Lehman Brothers," press release, May 10, 2010.
2. Ceci Connally, "Mexico's Extradition Strategy Yields Mixed Results," *Washington Post*, May 22, 2010.

Police Corruption and Use of the Military in the Antinarcotics Effort

Mexican police forces are divided jurisdictionally into municipal, state, and federal police departments. The functional division is between preventive and investigative departments. Drug trafficking is a federal crime and therefore is under the jurisdiction of the federal police. The homicides that have been a tragic accompaniment of drug trafficking in Mexico are state crimes and therefore are investigated mostly by state police.[3] The literature on the corruption of the various police forces in Mexico is extensive.

Mexican society has little confidence in its police. It has long been normal practice to bribe transit police officers to avoid formal traffic charges.[4] Robbery is often not reported to police for fear that such action may lead to further extortion. The very word *police* arouses instinctive distrust in the minds of most Mexicans. Going beyond the police, Mexicans have little confidence in their judicial system. They do not expect equal treatment under the law. Under these circumstances, police reform is hard to carry out. These realities surely contribute to the willingness of police, particularly at state and municipal levels, to accept bribes from drug cartels. Drug marketers are normally able to provide more money to police officers than they receive in compensation in their official positions; in any event, any bribe paid augments a police officer's total compensation. In addition, some reports indicate that drug marketers bribing police and other Mexican officials offer them the choice of "*plata o plomo*"—money or a bullet.[5]

Each of the last three administrations has reorganized Mexico's police forces. The administrations of Ernesto Zedillo (1994–2000), Vicente Fox (2000–2006), and Felipe Calderón (2006–) focused their efforts on expanding and upgrading federal police capacity. Federal police officers numbered 11,000 in 2000 and grew to approximately 37,000 in 2009 in two separate bodies, the Policía Federal Ministerial, designed to focus on investigations, and the Policía Federal, intended to gather intelligence, combat organized crime, and operate under cover.[6] Few of the federal crimes reported are actually investigated, and even fewer ever reach a judge.

Mexico has an estimated 350,000 police officers, about 90 percent of whom are state and municipal. In addition to low pay, the average level of education is low—elementary school (up to ninth grade or less). There have been repeated purges of state and local police forces, along with instituting examinations and lie detector tests for replacement personnel. These actions have not really altered the generally unsatisfactory performance of state and local police, nor is it likely that they could because the underlying circumstances have not changed. Although successive Mexican presidents have placed increasing emphasis on federal police forces, most police officers work at state and local levels.

---

3. Daniel Sabet, "Police Reform in Mexico: Advancement and Persistent Obstacles" (Working Paper Series on U.S.-Mexico Security Collaboration, Mexico Institute, Woodrow Wilson International Center for Scholars, Washington, D.C., 2010). We have drawn heavily on this paper for organizational aspects of Mexican police forces and also for examples of police corruption, abuses, and ineffectiveness.

4. Sabet cites Transparencia Mexicana, *Informe ejecutivo: Indice nacional de corrupcinó y buen gobernio*, Mexico City, 2007, to the effect that bribes to transit police officers top their list of the most common acts of corruption in Mexico.

5. William Finnegan, "Silver or Lead," *New Yorker*, May 31, 2010, 39–51, has a subhead: "The drug cartel La Familia gives local officials a choice: Take a bribe or a bullet."

6. Sabet, "Police Reform in Mexico," 9.

Some military personnel have long been assigned to antinarcotics efforts, but President Calderón vastly increased the numbers to about 45,000 because of the lack of confidence in state and municipal police forces as well as the solid reputation of the military.[7] In the end, this decision has not turned out well. The military leaders would have preferred not to work on police issues or in collaboration with the police in Mexico's antinarcotics efforts. Military personnel may not have been as receptive to bribes from drug cartels, but neither were they immune. Ill-equipped with the street intelligence to do a good job on their assigned tasks, the armed forces could not easily acquire the necessary skills. The National Human Rights Commission received some 3,500 complaints concerning military abuses over the past three years.[8] Unfortunately, the sterling reputation of the military has been sullied by its involvement in the antinarcotics effort, and its role has now been largely eliminated in favor of federal antinarcotics specialists.

Shortcomings on the U.S. Side

Most of the sales of illicit drugs that generate the large revenues of the drug-marketing organizations take place in the United States, and most of the weapons used by the DTOs come from the United States. These issues are discussed elsewhere in this report.

While President Calderón has noted corruption on the U.S. side and not just in Mexico, he has cited no specifics.[9] One such case, however, involved Luis F. Alarid, a customs inspector on the U.S. side of the border with Mexico who was sentenced to seven years in federal prison in February 2009 for accepting bribes for waving in trucks from Mexico carrying marijuana and illegal immigrants. The Alarid case seems to have been one of a number of cases in which Mexican drug cartels sought to infiltrate official U.S. antinarcotics organizations. [10] The number of cases of U.S. officials accepting bribes similar to those common in Mexico is not known; however, the comparison made by President Calderón in his interview with Agence France Press has little validity.

---

7. "Dealing with Drugs," *Economist*, March 27, 2009, special briefing section, 30.

8. Data from presentation at the Woodrow Wilson Center on May 25, 2010, by Ana Paula Hernández, specialist in drug policy and human rights in Mexico.

9. This was done in an interview with Agence France-Press in early 2009.

10. Randal C. Archibald, "Hired by Customs, but Working for Mexican Cartels," *New York Times*, December 18, 2009. This article cites other cases of other Americans with Mexican backgrounds who were instructed to apply for jobs at Customs and Border Protection of the Department of Homeland Security precisely to enhance objectives of the drug cartels.

8 EFFECTS OF DRUG TRAFFICKING ON CENTRAL AMERICAN AND CARIBBEAN COUNTRIES

Colombian shipments of cocaine paste to the United States became important in the 1970s. The early cocaine shipments were predominantly from Colombia across the Caribbean to Florida, but this route became costly when the United States stepped up its interdiction efforts. Later in the 1970s, the movement of the paste was primarily from Colombia through Central America into Mexico, and from there to the United States.[1]

Effects on Central America

Considerable criminal activity takes place in Central America, especially in the northern triangle of Guatemala, Honduras, and El Salvador. Their combined murder rates are double those of Mexico.[2] The most serious case is Guatemala, where political elites dispute control over the state.[3] Armed conflict in Guatemala lasted 36 years, and the peace agreements in 1996 were merely the starting point for new violence that continues to this day. Large-scale unauthorized human movement occurs from Guatemala into southern Mexico from where most migrants continue into the United States. Cocaine shipments from Guatemala into the United States were estimated to be 250 tons in 2009. The two main Mexican drug-trafficking organizations (DTOs) in Central America are the Sinaloa cartel and the Zetas. The two do battle with each other, as well as with local groups, for control of shipments into Mexico, largely destined for further shipment into the United States. The Mexican DTOs have penetrated key Guatemalan government national and local agencies, the police, and even the courts.[4] Similar situations exist in El Salvador and Honduras.

Beyond the insertion of Mexican DTOs, an estimated 70,000 gang members or *maras*, as they are known in Central America, are concentrated in the three northern triangle countries.[5] With roots in different countries in Central America, Mexico, and even the United States, the gangs engage in extortion, kidnappings, and even murders. The *maras* have also become drug dealers.

---

1. Steven S. Dudley, "Drug Trafficking Organizations in Central America: *Transportistas*, Mexican Cartels and *Maras*" (Working Paper Series on U.S.-Mexico Security Collaboration, Woodrow Wilson International Center for Scholars, Washington, D.C., and the University of San Diego, San Diego, Calif., 2010). Mexican commentators sometimes think aloud that if the Mexico route could be made costly for the drug-trading organizations, perhaps another country or region might be chosen for shipments into the United States.
2. Ibid.
3. Raúl Benitez Manaut, "Organized Crime and National Security in Central America and Mexico," CSIS background paper (March 2010).
4. Dudley, "Drug Trafficking Organizations in Central America."
5. Ibid.

Effects in the Caribbean

In a speech in September 2009, U.S. President Barack Obama cited four Caribbean countries as major drug-producing or transit countries: the Bahamas, the Dominican Republic, Haiti, and Jamaica.[6] Evidence suggests that the official antinarcotics effort in Mexico, despite its lack of overall success in reducing the power of the DTOs, is helping drive the expansion of narcotics transit routes through the Caribbean into the United States.[7] Drug-related murders have been increasing in a number of Caribbean countries, particularly in Jamaica, the Dominican Republic, and Puerto Rico.[8] In a speech in Barbados in April 2010, U.S. Secretary of Defense Robert Gates expressed his concern that traffickers are likely to use Caribbean routes to bring drugs to the United States; he was told by Caribbean leaders that drug trafficking in the region is already increasing.[9]

Current Situation in Colombia

The United States and Colombia agreed to Plan Colombia in 1999 to deal with guerrilla activities in the country and the government's inability to enforce the rule of law. One analyst noted that for the U.S. public Plan Colombia was seen as a way to stop cocaine paste from being shipped from Colombia to the United States.[10] Much aerial spraying of coca and poppy fields was undertaken, reaching a peak of 172,000 acres in 2006. This approach was later changed to manual eradication because it was a more durable method of destroying the crops. In addition, the public was strongly averse to spraying because it was thought to have harmful health and environmental effects. Colombia today is still the world's largest producer of coca and cocaine. Narcotics money continues to generate corruption and play a large role in the country's high levels of crime. Coca and cocaine production, however, has become less a national security threat than it was before Plan Colombia was instituted, although production remains a law-enforcement problem. Colombia still produces the cocaine paste that finds its way to markets, but the important financial players are now the Mexican DTOs who dominate the trade in the United States.

U.S. Government Antinarcotics Structure

The most important U.S. action for combating narcotics coming from Mexico and Central America is the Mérida Initiative, announced in 2007 to begin in fiscal year 2008 and run through FY2010. The details of this initiative will be discussed in chapter 10.

In 2010, Congress separated funding for Central America, which totaled $83 million, from the Mérida Initiative and created a new Central American Regional Security Initiative (CARSI).

---

6. U.S. Department of State, "Presidential Determination for Major Illicit Drug-Producing Countries," September 15, 2009.

7. BBC News, "U.S. to Fight Caribbean Drug Routes," April 17, 2010.

8. Ezra Fieser, "Caribbean Re-emerges as a Drug Corridor," *Global Post*, June 1, 2010. The major violence was in Jamaica where the U.S. government asked for the extradition of Christopher "Dudus" Coke on drug-trafficking charges. When the Jamaican police came to arrest Coke in the Tivoli Gardens neighborhood of Kingston on the weekend of May 22, 2010, armed gangs confronted the police, and 74 people were killed and 500 were arrested. Coke was later successfully extradited to the United States.

9. BBC News, "U.S. to Fight Caribbean Drug Routes."

10. Peter DeShazo, Johanna Mendelson Forman, and Phillip McLean, *Countering Threats to Security and Stability in a Failing State: Lessons from Colombia* (Washington, D.C.: CSIS, September 2009), 51–59.

The administration requested $100 million for CARSI in its FY2011 budget submission. President Obama announced the creation of the Caribbean Basin Security Initiative (CBSI) at the Summit of the Americas in April 2009 to help the region address such challenges as transnational crime, illicit drug trafficking, and maritime and aviation security. The framework for and details of the cooperative programs of the CBSI are planned for discussion with Caribbean nations in 2010. Congress provided "not less than" $37 million for FY2010, of which "not less than" $21million was for social justice and education programs. The FY2011 administration request for CBSI is for $79 million.

These are modest programs.[11] It is not clear, however, how much of the U.S. antidrug program the CBSI will represent because the United States has provided such assistance in the past through bilateral programs. The U.S. Agency for International Development has a Caribbean Regional Program, and the State Department's Western Hemisphere Program includes the Caribbean. Operation Bahamas Turks and Caicos is an international interdiction program established in 1982. The Dominican Republic has a joint antinarcotics program with the U.S. Coast Guard. The administration requested $45 million in initial funding in FY2010 for a security dialogue with the 14 countries of the Caribbean Community.

The Department of Defense has its own counterdrug programs in Latin America and the Caribbean. In the past, it has focused on Colombia but may now be coordinated with Mérida programs in Mexico, Central America, and the Caribbean.

Final Comment

The Mérida Initiative was first conceived as a U.S.-Mexican counternarcotics effort. It became clear when the administration discussed approval and funding for Mérida that the shipping routes for cocaine from Colombia also included countries in Central America and the Caribbean. Mérida was therefore expanded to include Central America; and the recognition that Colombian cocaine paste was shipped at times to the United States via the Caribbean meant that antinarcotics programs were required there as well. The structure of U.S. antinarcotics cooperation is still being developed, as is evident from the discussion taking place on the size and structure of the CBSI.

11. Clare Ribando Seelke, Liana Sun Wyler, and June S. Beittel, "Latin America and the Caribbean: Illicit Drug Trafficking and U.S. Counterdrug Programs," Congressional Research Service Report for Congress, April 30, 2010.

9 THE MÉRIDA INITIATIVE

President Felipe Calderón was declared president of Mexico on December 1, 2006. When he actually assumed office on December 10, he announced—without preliminary public debate—that he would conduct a "war" (his word) on drugs by directly confronting the Mexican drug-trafficking organizations (DTOs). President Calderón also called on the Mexican army to play a large role against the drug traffickers.

These were fateful decisions. Since December 2006, more than 22,000 drug-related deaths have occurred, with countless more wounded. The DTOs are powerful organizations that dominate the marketing of narcotics both inside and outside Mexico and are involved in related criminal activities, such as kidnapping, extortion, and arms trafficking. They are quite ruthless, as murders of public officials and decapitations have demonstrated. While police corruption was well known earlier to all Mexicans who drove cars and trucks, the war on drugs has made clear the extensive corruption of just about all state and municipal police, as well as many federal police officers. The ability of the DTOs to bribe officials at just about all levels in federal, state, and municipal hierarchies has reduced the prestige of public service. The army, which had a positive reputation before assuming a major role in the antinarcotics effort, is now known just as much for its violations of human rights and has been largely removed from the war on drugs. The impunity with which drug-related crimes can be carried out is evident to Mexicans, given that almost no one arrested for narcotics-related crimes has been convicted.

Before the Mérida Initiative went into effect in October 2007, Mexico was on its own in confronting the DTOs. The Mexican ambassador to the United States, Arturo Sarukhan, openly complained that the United States was not doing its share in what was intrinsically a binational antinarcotics effort; the word he used to describe the U.S. contribution was *zilch*. He also said that stepped-up U.S. efforts were needed to stop the flow of weapons from the United States to Mexico.[1] The two presidents discussed the issue of U.S. collaboration in the antinarcotics program in March 2007, when George W. Bush was in Mérida, the capital of the state of Yucatán, on the final stop of a trip to Latin America. A few months later, the Calderón administration proposed that the effort to combat organized crime, including narcotics trafficking, should have three parts: actions of the Mexican government, actions of the U.S. government, and collective actions, such as the kinds of equipment the United States would supply to Mexico. The actual appropriations bill for the Mérida Initiative was signed into law on June 30, 2008.[2]

---

1. Sidney Weintraub, "The High Cost of Criminalizing Drug Use," *Issues in International Political Economy*, No. 94, CSIS, October 2007.

2. Armand B. Peschard-Sverdrup, "The Mérida Initiative: Its Origin, Appropriations, Implementation, and Beyond," CSIS background paper (February 2010). This paper was drawn on for the discussion of first-year appropriations. Peschard-Sverdrup's paper will be included in that portion of the CSIS Web site related to this report. Peschard-Sverdrup is an independent consultant who specializes on Mexico-U.S. issues and is a senior associate of CSIS.

The Mérida Initiative as launched by the two presidents was for U.S. assistance of $1.4 billion over three years for equipment and training to cooperate in dealing with the problem of illicit drugs. The initiative called for inspection equipment (such as helicopters) to interdict drugs, equipment and training for the armed forces, the improvement of communications systems, and technical advice for strengthening the rule of law.[3] A proposal of $1.4 billion over three years is modest, certainly as compared with the extent of the Mexican contribution, and much lower than had been provided for Colombia. The amount was low considering that Mexico is a neighbor and that what happens there inevitably affects the United States. Nevertheless, the Mérida Initiative was intended to be the beginning of antinarcotics cooperation between the two countries. The initiative and its funding went through a number of variations to take into account the needs of Central American countries, as described in chapter 8.

The Appropriations Process

It took a year and nine separate versions before the first appropriation bill was enacted by the U.S. Congress. It contained supplemental appropriations for FY2008 and bridge fund supplemental appropriations for FY2009. These appropriations amounted to $400 million, of which 66 percent came from the International Narcotics Control and Law Enforcement (INCLE) account, 30 percent from the Foreign Military Financing (FMF) account, and 4 percent from the Economic Support Fund (ESF). The State Department is responsible for the INCLE and ESF accounts and the Department of Defense for the FMF account. More than one-third of the funds went to the Office of the Mexican Attorney General and the Secretariat of Public Security. After that, the Mexican military (army and navy) was the largest recipient (amounting to 31 percent) of year-one government agencies. Some 15 percent of the INCLE and FMF for FY2008 could not be obligated until the Department of State reported to the committees on appropriations that Mexico had taken a variety of actions, particularly that Mexican agencies were not violating human rights in their antinarcotics programs.

Evolution of the Mérida Initiative

The initiative got off to a slow start. At the end of September 2009, a total of $1.3 billion had been appropriated for Mexico, about two-thirds or $830 million had been obligated, and about 2 percent or $26.3 million had been spent. As of the same date, $165 million had been appropriated for Central America, $72.8 million obligated, and $2 million spent.[4] Mérida aid obligated to Mexico totaled more than $1 billion after 2008, but of this actual aid delivered as of May 11, 2010 was only $159 million.[5]

In the first phase of the initiative, the majority of U.S. funding went for equipment, particularly for aircraft. The dominant focus in 2010 was on institution building. The current approach is taking shape around "four pillars": disrupting and dismantling criminal organi-

3. Office of National Drug Control Policy, "National Southwest Border Counternarcotics Strategy," June 2009, 41–42.

4. U.S. General Accountability Office, "Status of Funds for the Mérida Initiative," report prepared at the request of Representative Eliot L. Engel, December 3, 2009.

5. "More Aid to Mexico," Just the Facts blog, May 18, 2010, http://justf.org/.

zations, institutionalizing the rule of law, building a twenty-first century border, and building strong and resilient communities.[6]

Assessment of the Mérida Initiative

John Bailey has written that there have been two important U.S. government pronouncements on U.S.-Mexican security strategy—Mérida and the Southwest Border Strategy.[7] In addition, he notes that other significant innovations in bilateral security cooperation in states and localities and along the border. He then goes on to say that significant gaps exist in interagency coordination within and between the two countries, particularly when it comes to intelligence sharing.

Mérida is surely an advance in that the security and intelligence agencies of the two governments have been ordered to cooperate whenever feasible. Secretary of State Hillary Clinton, in connection with an official visit to Mexico in March 2009, stated that U.S. failures to curb both drug use and shipment of guns to Mexico have fueled the drug trade and stimulated the drug-related violence in Mexico. Even casual observers of the Mexican-U.S. narcotics scene knew that to be so, but no senior U.S. official had ever before admitted this reality publicly.[8]

The shortcomings of Mérida were that the amounts provided by the United States were modest, especially in relation to the seriousness of the problem Mexico faced; and this imbalance was further complicated by the venality of Mexican police and other officials who accepted bribes from the cartels. Mexico has been increasing the role of the federal police, as opposed to state and local police forces, for more than 15 years, but the latter are inevitably far more numerous. The response by the DTOs to the efforts of the Mexican government to combat narcotrafficking has been far greater than President Calderón undoubtedly anticipated when he declared war on the drug cartels. President Calderón also learned that the cartels were often able to outgun the police and even the army in many head-to-head battles. The Mexican authorities have had successes in seizing drugs and capturing and even killing cartel leaders, but these seem to be tactical victories in a ferocious, and perhaps unwinnable, war.

Was Calderon's decision to confront the DTOs in this war wise or unwise? There is no simple answer to this question. The war yet may succeed if the drug traffickers find it necessary to find another route for transporting narcotics (cocaine is the only one of the four drugs highlighted in this report that Mexico does not produce) to the United States. Calderon's war has been costly, however, and it is therefore unclear how long it will endure.

---

6. Eric L. Olson and Christopher E. Wilson, "Beyond Mérida: The Evolving Approach to Security Cooperation" (Working Paper Series on U.S.-Mexico Security Cooperation, Woodrow Wilson International Center for Scholars, Mexico Institute, Washington, D.C., and the University of San Diego, San Diego, Calif., 2010).

7. John Bailey, "Combating Organized Crime and Drug Trafficking in Mexico: What Are Mexican and U.S. Strategies? Are They Working?" (Working Paper Series on U.S.-Mexico Security Cooperation, Woodrow Wilson International Center for Scholars, Mexico Institute, Washington, D.C., and the University of San Diego, San Diego, Calif., 2010), 17, 18.

8. Mary Beth Sheridan, "Clinton: U.S. Drug Policies Failed, Fueled Mexico's Drug War," *Washington Post*, March 26, 2009.

10 ALTERNATIVES TO CURRENT ANTINARCOTICS POLICIES

The prevailing conclusion of Mexicans and Americans who have studied antinarcotics policies is that they have failed in the United States, in Mexico, and in what is now the cooperative program between them (i.e., the Mérida Initiative).[1] Indeed, many observers go further and argue that the policies have inflicted harm in the two countries.[2] Proceeding from these assessments, the logical follow-on is to examine policy alternatives that may have a better chance of succeeding—or at least of doing less harm.

Alternative Policy Proposals

A natural place to start this examination is to ask whether the Mérida Initiative discussed in chapter 9 can be altered or made more expansive. Mérida is already being changed in that earlier emphasis on equipment, such as helicopters, is giving way to strengthening the Mexican institutions engaged in the antinarcotics program. The Calderón government initially relied on the military, particularly the army, to confront the drug-trafficking organizations (DTOs), the number of troops peaking at 45,000. Although its involvement antedated Mérida, the military continued in this role for several years after Mérida. Using the military in this fashion did not succeed, and the front-line antinarcotics organization is now the federal police. Mexico is changing its judicial structure, and U.S. help is being provided to Mexico in this effort. The amount of U.S. assistance made available to Mexico under Mérida could be increased, but it is not clear that more U.S. money would translate into meaningful improvements in building the relevant Mexican institutions. Mérida will surely change in content and structure as the two countries gain more experience in working together in the antinarcotics campaign, but this approach is essentially an evolution of an existing program rather than a changed policy. Most observers who comment on Mérida tend to think about it, consciously or unconsciously, as a step in the antinarcotics effort. Hence, much thought needs to be given to what comes after Mérida.[3] In general, what most observers believe must come next—indeed, what must accompany Mérida—is socioeconomic improvement, including lowering poverty.

---

1. Ethan A. Nadelman, "Reducing the Harms of Drug Prohibition in the Americas," Drug Policy Alliance, 2005, http://www.drugpolicy.org/docUploads/ReducingHarmofProhibitionEN1005.pdf.

2. U.S. House of Representatives, Committee on Foreign Affairs, Subcommittee on the Western Hemisphere, statement of John M. Walsh, senior associate for the Andes and drug policy, Washington Office on Latin America, "Assessing U.S. Drug Policy in the Americas: Time to Revisit Goals and Strategies," October 15, 2009. A pertinent quotation from his statement follows: "In the past, evident failures of our traditional drug control strategies prompted escalation of essentially the same approaches."

3. U.S. House of Representatives, Committee on Foreign Affairs, Subcommittee on the Western Hemisphere, and Committee on Homeland Security, Subcommittee on Border, Maritime, and Global Counterterrorism, statement of Shannon O'Neil, "Moving beyond Mérida in U.S.-Mexico Security Cooperation," May 27, 2010. The hearings themselves were on "U.S.-Mexico Security Cooperation: Next Steps for the Mérida Initiative."

Antinarcotics policy in both the United States and Mexico before Mérida focused on punishment for buying and selling narcotics, particularly in the United States. A 2006 paper by Caulkins and Reuter noted that U.S. drug prisoners would soon surpass the half-million mark, more than Western Europe locks up for all criminal offenses.[4] That paper argued that cutting imprisonment in half—or by one-third or two-thirds—would still leave the United States with a comfortable prisoner lead over any other Western nation. U.S. imprisonment for consumption of narcotics has decreased; although it remains higher than other nations that have similar zero-tolerance drug policies such as Japan and Sweden. Total (not just drug-related) Mexican prison inmates in 2009 numbered 225,000 or 202 per 100,000 population.[5] Conviction rates of those charged for drug-trafficking offenses in Mexico are negligible.

Imprisonment for the use of small amounts of narcotics could be reduced in several ways. One practiced in many countries is "decriminalization." The appendix by Caulkins and Sevigny states that decriminalization means substantially reducing or even eliminating criminal penalties for drug users, while continuing to prohibit production and distribution. The supply, they note, would still be provided by criminal enterprises. Caulkins and Sevigny believe that demand for illicit drugs is apt to be greater under decriminalization than under prohibition because the former eliminates important risks for buyers. Portugal decriminalized all drugs, including cocaine and heroin, in 2001, while drug trafficking continues to be a criminal offence. According to one source discussing this policy, Portuguese decriminalization has been a "resounding success" and has had no adverse effect on drug use.[6]

Legalization of what are now illicit drugs would be quite a different action. The main argument in favor of legalization in the United States is that it would remove the high profits that accrue to the DTOs because it would no longer be illegal to sell or buy narcotics. (U.S. prohibition of a legal drug existed with alcohol, and the subsequent violence and struggle for control of this illicit product led to its relegalization.)[7] Removal of the billions of dollars of profits would make it impossible for the DTOs to bribe police, military, civilian officials, and others to the extent that it now does. Under legalization, the United States would have to set up a structure for the marketing of drugs, as was necessary when alcohol prohibition ended. The government could use excise taxes to determine the sales prices of various drugs, but only up to a limit that would not encourage drug dealers to make a profit by selling for a price below what the excise tax would add. It is not clear what the long-run effect of legalization would be on consumption of narcotics, but short-term use would probably spike, and the authorities would have to provide some relief for drug addicts over that time period.

Because governments would no longer have to maintain the same institutional structure to deal with criminal activity—such as prisons and drug police—the resources saved could be used to increase drug treatment and education, as is now done for both tobacco and alcohol. Despite all these advantages, however, neither the public at large nor their elected representatives are prepared to legalize all drugs. At most, the United States might accept decriminalization, which could be

4. Jonathan P. Caulkins and Peter Reuter, "Reorienting U.S. Drug Policy," *Issues in Science and Technology* (Fall 2006).

5. Kings College London, International Centre for Prison Statistics.

6. Glenn Greenwald, "Drug Decriminalization in Portugal: Lessons for Creating Fair and Successful Drug Policies" (white paper, CATO Institute, Washington, D.C., 2009).

7. The Eighteenth Amendment to the U.S. Constitution on alcohol prohibition went into effect in 1920 and was repealed by the Twenty-first Amendment in 1933.

accomplished de facto without legislation. As noted above, however, the effect that decriminalization would have on U.S. consumption is uncertain.

Mexico could also adopt new antinarcotics policies. Indeed, President Calderón has a strong incentive for such action because he is losing support for Mexico's current policy.[8] Andrés Rozental, a former deputy foreign minister of Mexico, together with senior business executive Stanley Weiss, has argued that attacking the supply side of the drug war is unwinnable as long as the United States is unable to reduce the demand for illicit drugs.[9] Rozental and Weiss conclude that the United States must begin to think about "the gradual legalization of some drugs." The drugs they believe the United States can legalize are marijuana and methamphetamines.

Although Mexico could itself legalize drug sales and consumption at home, it has not done so because of uncertainty about the effects and about taking the corollary measures that would be needed. Mexico could decriminalize drug use and thereby reduce the number of people imprisoned for that purpose. Legalization of drug use would have to take place in the United States, however, if the objective is to reduce the funds available to the Mexican DTOs.

Arguments for Maintaining Current Mexican Policies

Mexican DTOs are criminal organizations that are run as businesses. They earn money primarily from selling narcotics but also engage in other criminal activities such as extortion, kidnapping for ransom, and smuggling.[10] Many analysts have therefore argued that if the United States legalized drug use and cut off the revenue of DTOs from that activity, the DTOs would most likely increase what are now their ancillary revenue earners—and the levels of violence in Mexico might not diminish.

Much of the earnings of the DTOs from narcotics sales in the United States are laundered in Mexico. In the appendix on money laundering, Jonathan M. Winer estimates that this activity amounts to $10–39 billion a year. The laundering can take many forms, such as investment in legitimate businesses, smuggling the funds into Mexico, and going through banks by layering the funds, among others. To the extent that the laundering takes place by investing in legitimate businesses, Mexico receives important benefits. George Friedman, in a Stratfor article, argues that, on the whole, "Mexico is a tremendous beneficiary of the drug trade."[11] The argument made to support this position is that billions of dollars flow into Mexico, which are then laundered, frequently in ways beneficial to Mexican investment; and, in addition, what else is Mexico to do as long as the United States is unable to reduce demand for drugs and is unprepared to legalize the harmful drug with the highest economic value, namely, cocaine? The argument that Mexico is a beneficiary of drug trafficking mentions the problem of the drug-related violence only in passing, giving the article a tongue-in-cheek quality.

---

8. William Booth and Steve Fainaru, "New Strategy Urged in Mexico: Calderón's U.S.-Backed War against Drug Cartels Losing Political Support," *Washington Post*, July 28, 2009.

9. Andrés Rozental and Stanley A. Weiss, "Only the U.S. Can Win War on Drugs," *Dallas Morning News*, February 25, 2009. Weiss is the founding chairman of Business Executives for National Security.

10. Scott Stewart, "The Struggle for Balance," *Stratfor Global Security & Intelligence Report*, April 8, 2010, http://www.stratfor.com/weekly/20100407_mexico_struggle_balance.

11. George Friedman, "Mexico and the Failed State Revisited," *Stratfor Geopolitical Intelligence Report*, April 6, 2010, http://www.stratfor.com/weekly/20100405_mexico_and_failed_state_revisited.

Implications of Legalizing Marijuana

Proposals to legalize marijuana are now common.[12] The underlying reasoning is that because drugs are not equally harmful, differentiating their legal treatment is therefore logical. Marijuana is the most widely used of the four drugs featured in this report, overwhelmingly so in the United States.[13] A brief background paper on marijuana was commissioned from Aaron Houston and was drawn upon in writing this report; Houston's paper will be posted on the CSIS Web site.

The Global Cannabis Commission concluded in its 2009 report that clear health problems are associated with cannabis use, such as the risk of psychotic symptoms, but that these risks are modest compared with those of other drugs. The commission also found that the risks incurred through prohibition were greater than those presented by cannabis itself.[14] If production and use of marijuana were legal, national health authorities would have flexibility in regulating it and could determine the strength of potentially harmful ingredients, such as tetrahydrocannibanol, or THC. This flexibility does not exist under prohibition. If the drug were legal, federal and state authorities could impose excise taxes to help cover the costs of treatment and of education. The legal use of marijuana for medical purposes is already common, especially in California. Marijuana is also readily available in the United States, despite its designation as an illicit drug. In sum, the legalization of marijuana is a real possibility. The political opposition to legalizing the three other illicit drugs featured in this report—cocaine, opium, and methamphetamine—still remains strong.

Other Policy Suggestions

Peter Reuter has asserted that the advice the U.S. government gives other countries in dealing with cocaine, opium, and methamphetamine does more harm than good. He writes that the only policy he can recommend with confidence is that the U.S. government keep a lower profile in dealing with international drug policy.[15]

Many organizations and individuals are advising the Mexican government to cease its war with the drug cartels, because the government is losing and the deaths from this policy keep mounting. Former Mexican foreign minister Jorge Castañeda has also taken that position. When it was in power, the PRI did not directly confront the DTOs, and the party may revert to this policy if it returns to power. A position heard often in Mexico is that while the United States does the consuming and provides the money that gives Mexican DTOs much of their power, the killings are largely confined to Mexico—not the outcome of a sensible policy for Mexico.

---

12. Four former Latin American presidents have proposed this (Fernando Henrique Cardoso of Brazil, César Gavaria of Colombia, Ernesto Zedillo of Mexico, and Vicente Fox of Mexico). This recommendation was preceded by the report of the Latin American Commission on Drugs and Democracy that included Presidents Cardoso, Gaviria, and Zedillo in its membership; the report criticized the prohibitionist policies toward marijuana. The Drug Policy Alliance has been in the forefront of this campaign for many years.

13. See chapter 2.

14. R. Room, B. Fischer, W. Hall, S. Lenton, and P. Reuter, *Cannabis Policy: Moving Beyond Stalemate: The Global Cannabis Commission Report* (Oxford: Beckley Foundation, 2008).

15. Peter Reuter, "Do No Harm: Sensible Goals for International Drug Policy," *American Interest* 4, no. 4 (March/April 2009).

11 CONSUMPTION EFFECTS OF LEGALIZATION
MARIJUANA, ALCOHOL, CIGARETTES

This chapter will discuss three related issues: (1) How much, if at all, would consumption of marijuana increase if it is legalized? (2) What were the consumption effects of ending alcohol prohibition? and (3) How effective has education been in reducing cigarette consumption?

Marijuana Use after Legalization

On July 19, 2009, the *New York Times* printed responses to the following question: If marijuana is legal, will addiction rise? The answers tended to dance around the issue. One respondent focused on the de facto legalization in the Netherlands, which allows coffee shops to sell marijuana; this concession had little overall effect on consumption, although there were age variations.[1] Another academic said that there was no definite answer because legalization permitted imposing a tax on marijuana to reduce its use.[2] (Drug marketers also charge the equivalent of a tax because of the illicit nature of marijuana.) Another said that although legalization would permit authorities to set the potency of the marijuana, the number of very heavy users would rise.[3] Still another said that legalization in the United States would be a more commercial activity than was the de facto legalization in the Netherlands.[4] Finally, one respondent argued that given the fact that the United States is already the world's largest per capita marijuana consumer despite the penalties, it is hard to imagine a large and lasting surge in consumption.[5]

The question itself is inadequate because its answer depends on the conditions attached to the legalization of marijuana. The Dutch case cited in some if the answers is unsatisfactory because it is a de facto legalization in a country with mores quite different from those in the United States. No country has yet taken the step of openly legalizing marijuana production and use.

The contention that legalization of marijuana should not be considered because of the presumed rise in consumption is extreme: we do not know if marijuana use would rise from the already high consumption, by how much, and for how long. Another argument against legalization is that marijuana is more potent today than it was earlier; and while this contention is true, it is flawed because only legalization would permit the authorities to regulate the potency. The debate on legalization should instead focus on the harmful effects of current policies and whether legalization with appropriate conditions would be preferable.

---

1. Roger Roffman, professor of social work at the University of Washington.
2. Wayne Hall, professor of public health policy at the University of Queensland, Australia.
3. Mark A.R. Kleiman, professor of public policy at the University of California at Los Angeles.
4. Peter Reuter, professor at the School of Public Policy and the Department of Criminology at the University of Maryland.
5. Norm Stamper, police chief in Seattle, Washington, from 1994 to 2000.

Alcohol Consumption after the End of Prohibition

The criminality and violence that erupted after alcohol use became illegal ultimately brought about the end of prohibition in the United States. Alcohol consumption has surely risen since 1933, when Prohibition ended, but we have no way of knowing what it would be if its prohibition had continued. If alcohol use were still illegal, the situation would probably be similar to that of marijuana: there would undoubtedly be petitions for medical use of alcohol and spirits, and alcohol would be easily available, just as marijuana is. Two researchers found that alcohol consumption dropped by 30 percent immediately after alcohol prohibition went into effect in 1920 and then rose slowly to 70 percent of the pre-prohibition level by 1929.[6] The implication is that alcohol consumption would have continued to rise with or without prohibition.

Education and Cigarette Consumption

The most deadly of all narcotics use is cigarette smoking. Some 450,000 people die each year in the United States from smoking cigarettes: statistics show that smoking kills more Americans than alcohol, car accidents, suicide, AIDS, homicide, and illegal drugs combined.[7] After the harmful effects of cigarette smoking were known, some action clearly had to be taken. The technique chosen was education—making sure that all Americans understood the potential consequences of smoking. This approach has worked, although not completely. Some 57 percent of men smoked cigarettes in the mid-1950s, a percentage that has now dropped to about 22 percent; for women, the figures came down over this same period from 28 percent to 17 percent. Overall, 20.6 percent of all adults in the United States were smokers in 2008. About 20 percent of high school students now smoke cigarettes.

Final Comments

U.S. policies on the production, sale, and consumption of different drugs vary, as they do in just about all countries. The variations depend in part on their different national histories. Cigarette smoking was common, even considered chic, for a long time. It would have been hard to declare cigarettes illegal even after research demonstrated the dangerous consequences of the smoking habit.

Use of alcohol also has a long history in the United States and throughout the world. It took a sui generis set of circumstances that led to alcohol prohibition in the United States. Prohibition led to the kinds of violence that have accompanied the prohibition of other illicit drugs, as marketers competed with each other over control of the market. Prohibition in the United States actually made it chic to drink alcohol in illegal speakeasies. After alcohol use was re-legalized, education was used to demonstrate the harmful consequences of excessive drinking—with some of the same positive effects education has had on reducing addiction to cigarette smoking.

Marijuana, the most commonly used of the four illicit drugs featured in this report, seems destined to go the way of alcohol, that is, legalization at some point, with conditions. When the legal

6. James Roumasset and Min Min Thaw, "The Economics of Prohibition: Prices, Consumption and Enforcement Expenditures during Alcohol Prohibition," *Hawaii Reporter,* September 2003.

7. Data are from www.cancer.org.

status of marijuana changes, education will almost surely be used to teach users about its harmful effects.

How the United States will handle the three other illicit drugs featured in this report is much harder to predict. The public has shown little support for their legalization, although many would agree that current U.S. policies for handling them are not working. The earlier policy of extensive imprisonment for users of these drugs is already changing. It is highly likely U.S. authorities will provide more education, with more sophistication approaches, in efforts to reduce their consumption.

Mexico's current policy of direct combat with its drug-trafficking organizations (DTOs) has been going on for more than three years. This confrontation has led to annual increases in killings that are likely to exceed 15,000 in 2010. President Felipe Calderón, who initiated this policy when he assumed office, stated in a recent public message that it is his government's constitutional obligation to combat crime and do what it can to limit drug consumption in Mexico.[8] He likely felt compelled to issue this declaration because he realized that his policy of confrontation with the DTOs is losing public support. It is hard to predict how long this policy will last.

8. Presidential communication of June 13, 2010.

12 THE SOCIOECONOMIC SITUATION IN MEXICO

The two most pressing problems in Mexico are the narcotics trade along with its concomitant violence and the high level of poverty in the country. The two are related: poor people use drugs; many work for drug-trafficking organizations (DTOs); and the antinarcotics program reduces budgetary funds that might otherwise be used to alleviate poverty.[1]

Poverty in Mexico

About 35 million people live in relative poverty in Mexico, about 40 percent of its population of 110 million. Although those in relative poverty can eke out a bare existence, they live on the edge. An additional 15 million live in extreme or absolute poverty and lack clean water, nutrition, shelter, and health care and must rely on government help for these necessities. The government does provide help to Mexico's poor, mainly through a program called *Oportunidades,* which focuses on nutrition, health care, and education.

Mexico's complex labor market—which consists of two broad classes of workers, those registered with national authorities and others who work informally—complicates the poverty situation. The registered workers pay taxes and receive many government-mandated benefits; the informal workers, who make up about half the labor force, pay no income taxes and receive fewer benefits. Mexican companies often use part-time as well as informal workers to reduce the cost of providing benefits such as job security and large payments when workers are let go. Mexico's tax collection is low, normally about 12 percent of gross domestic product, largely because of the large contingent of informal workers.[2]

Mexico's income inequality is the highest of the 31 member countries of the Organization for Economic Cooperation and Development, despite the fact that inequality has fallen by more than that in any other OECD country during the past 10 years.

Drugs and Jobs

A recent article in the *New Yorker* on the drug trade in Mexico referred to many young people as "*ni-ni,*" meaning that they go neither to school nor to work. Many of these young people have

1. This second point was highlighted by Samuel González Ruiz of the Universidad Nacional Autónomo de México at a forum at Georgetown University in Washington, D.C., entitled "Law, Justice, and Public Security: Challenges for Mexico and its Neighbors," held on March 26, 2010.

2. The federal government in the United States collects about 18 percent of GDP in taxes. Most Latin American and Caribbean countries collect more taxes than does Mexico, but generally less as a percentage of GDP than the United States. Brazil collects about 35 percent of GDP in taxes. Part-time workers are not counted as unemployed in Mexico. The unemployment figures in Mexico and the United States are not comparable because the two are calculated differently.

become the "cannon fodder" for the traffic in illegal narcotics.[3] For Latin America as a whole, the *ni-ni* cohort amounts to about 20 percent of those aged 15–25, and the figure for Mexico is similar. Creating decent jobs for these young people would facilitate their exit from the drug trade, and keeping them in school would equip them for the future—and both would contribute to easing the problem of poverty and to removing them from the drug trade.[4]

Creating enough suitable jobs that would be true alternatives to working for the DTOs is a complex task. Job creation is a function of growth in gross domestic product, and, except for about five years after 2002, Mexican GDP growth has averaged only about 1.5 to 2.0 percent a year since the early 1980s.[5] Mexico needs sustained growth of around 6 percent a year to create enough jobs for those left behind by the low economic growth of the past 30 years and to accommodate the new entrants into the labor force. Mexico has many shortcomings that have to be corrected, such as changing the structure of the labor market, collecting more taxes, eliminating monopolies, improving the justice system, reducing corruption, and enlarging the number of young people who remain in school. In addition, labor productivity is lower in Mexico than in the United States. The failure to make these corrections has held back Mexico's growth potential. Legislation is now under discussion on a new labor law, an antimonopoly law, and educational reform, but whether they will be enacted or be adequate to the task is not known. Nor is it clear if recently enacted changes in the legal system will improve the administration of justice.

Mexico's social shortcomings also contribute to the country's inadequate economic growth and to the severity of drug violence. Reducing poverty and making income distribution more equal are imperatives for raising GDP growth and are also essential for success in Mexico's antinarcotics efforts.

Final Comments

Mexico's socioeconomic situation requires improvement in its own right. Poor Mexicans are nationalistic, but their poverty, both relative and absolute, does not make for strong allegiance to any particular administration. Mexico's poor are relatively less concerned about the "war on drugs" declared by President Calderón than they are about correcting their own situation. The poor are aware of their inequality before the law compared with higher-income Mexicans. They see the corruption that surrounds everyday life in Mexico, especially in their dealings with the municipal police. They are cynical about a government that says it will reduce corruption when it is the government officials who are the most evident form of corruption they witness. Although the absolute poor would like to emulate their compatriots who flee for work and higher income in the United States, most lack the resources to hire a *coyote* to shepherd them across the border. Most unauthorized Mexican workers in the United States have jobs at home but are seeking income improvement.

Young Mexicans who lack the skills to find decent jobs at home, or who have not had the opportunity or energy to attend school long enough, are natural recruits for menial jobs with the DTOs. These young people have few other options. This situation will persist until fundamental

3. William Finnegan, "Silver or Lead," *New Yorker*, May 31, 2010, 44–46.

4. Alma Guillermoprieto, "Poverty of Opportunity: Crime's Breeding Ground," *Americas Quarterly* (Spring 2010): 50–55.

5. GDP growth in Mexico is projected to be between 4 and 5 percent in 2010, but this estimate comes after 2009 when GDP fell by 6.5 percent.

reforms open other opportunities in Mexico. Those that make the political decisions in Mexico have not yet sufficiently opened these opportunities. They have failed to make the structural reforms that will stimulate the growth in GDP the country needs or to alter microeconomic practices that inhibit economic growth. Some of these reforms are now being considered, and perhaps it will be different this time, although past talk about basic reforms has come to naught.

The slogan that prevailed at the outset of Mexico current administration was that of "war." It might have been better to highlight "opportunity"—to focus on changes that would improve the social situation of almost half of all Mexicans.

13 SUMMARY FACTS

The following are the 10 main summary facts of this report:

1. Of the four illicit drugs highlighted in this report (marijuana, cocaine, heroin, and methamphetamines), marijuana is dominant. In the month prior to the survey in 2008, there were 15.2 million marijuana users in the United States, who made up 75.7 percent of all past-month drug users. Past-month users of the other three drugs in 2008 were 1.9 million for cocaine, 0.3 million for methamphetamines, and 0.2 million for heroin. The numbers of illicit drug users would change dramatically if marijuana production and use were legalized in the United States.
2. Caulkins and Sevigny, in appendix C, however, state that cocaine (including crack) accounts for two-thirds of the monetary value of the illicit U.S. drug market and the other three drugs combined account for the remaining third.
3. No reliable figures exist on the total gross wholesale proceeds that return to Mexico from the illicit drug trade in the United States, but the U.S. National Drug Intelligence Center estimated the number at between $18 billion and $39 billion, while Winer estimates it is between $10 billion and $39 billion.
4. The use of the four drugs has been relatively stable during the past decade.
5. In contrast, drug violence in Mexico, including killings, has increased each year since President Felipe Calderón declared his war on drugs in 2006. The numbers reported killed each year since then were 2,477 for 2007, 6,290 for 2008, 7,724 for 2009, and more than 5,000 up to June 2010—a total of about 22,000—with no letup in sight.
6. The violence associated with drug trafficking and the Mexican government's antinarcotics response has engendered considerable insecurity among the Mexican population. Consequently, public support for the government's antinarcotics policy has been diminishing.
7. The drug-trafficking organizations have been in constant flux as different drug-trafficking organizations (DTOs) gain and lose power. Most of persons killed were DTO workers who died as the various groups contended for *plazas*, or locations from which to enter the U.S. market. The DTOs, however, also target police and government officials, and innocent bystanders are often caught in the crossfire.
8. The DTOs are criminal organizations with sources of income in addition to illicit drug sales, such as money from kidnapping and extortion. If their narcotics income were to be reduced or eliminated, such as by legalization of drugs in the United States, the DTOs would continue to exist, perhaps under another name.
9. When Mexican authorities trace weapons captured from the DTOs, they find that most come from the United States. DTO firepower is frequently greater than that of the police in specific battles between them.

10. The Mexican authorities have identified four main arms-trafficking routes, which are described in the appendix by Nathan Jones.

Comments on Foregoing Summation

The main instrument for Mexican-U.S. antinarcotics cooperation is the Mérida Initiative launched in 2008, for which the United States promised $1.4 billion over three years in assistance for equipment and training. This sum is modest in comparison with the far higher Mexican expenditures for maintaining domestic security, plus the reality that killings in the conflict with the drug trafficking organizations take place almost exclusively in Mexico. The United States provides some additional funding to Central American countries under Mérida, because the route for most of the cocaine goes through that region into Mexico and then into the United States.

No evidence thus far suggests that the binational cooperation under Mérida is having any significant effect. Indeed, the DTOs are able to carry out their criminal activity largely with impunity. Some DTO officials have been killed in specific shootouts, but the legal system is not functional in dealing with them. The leading gubernatorial candidate in the state of Tamaulipas, Rodolfo Torre of the Institutional Revolutionary Party, was gunned down and killed on June 28, 2010, by DTO operatives. This was just days before the July 4 gubernatorial election. It was also the highest-profile political assassination in Mexico in 15 years.

Both the United States and Mexico have imprisoned many drug users (not the senior DTO officials) in the past, with little apparent effect on the narcotics trade, and imprisonment is no longer so extensive. The DTOs, in light of the billions of dollars at their disposal, are able to practice wholesale bribery of police and government officials; and there is no protection against this practice unless the profits from narcotics sales in the United were halted. Halting such sales would require legalization of the now illicit narcotics, and, except possibly for marijuana, the U.S. government and Congress are unwilling to take such as step. If the drugs were legalized in Mexico, the effect would be only modest because the profits come overwhelmingly from U.S. sales.

APPENDIX A
GOAT HORNS, BLACKBIRDS, AND COP KILLERS
U.S. GUNS IN MEXICO'S DRUG VIOLENCE
Nathan Jones

My joke in Texas is that Texans think we ought to have all of the guns in Texas and that we do not want to export them to Mexico.—U.S. Representative Gene Green[1]

It is impossible to miss the constant stream of reporting on drug-related violence in Mexico. The violence has affected Mexican society in a macabre fashion, inspiring the rise of a narco-vocabulary, including nicknames for the guns used most by drug traffickers.[2] AR-15s are known as Chanates (Blackbirds), for their black finishes; AK-47s are known as Cuernos de Chivos (Goat Horns), for their curved ammunition clips; and Belgian Five-SeveN pistols are known as Matapolicias (Cop Killers), for their armor-piercing rounds.[3] A common characteristic of all these guns is their easy availability on the U.S. market.

Much of the public debate has focused on the U.S. demand for drugs and thus U.S. culpability in providing the funding for Mexico's drug violence. Increasingly, the debate has included the U.S. responsibility for providing ready access to guns for Mexican cartels.[4] A recent report from

1. Representative Gene Green at a hearing on the proposed Merida Initiative October 25, 2007, *U.S. Security Assistance to Mexico* (Washington, D.C.: Foreign Affairs Subcommittee on the Western Hemisphere, U.S. House of Representatives, 2007).

2. David Shirk, "Drug Violence in Mexico: Data and Analysis from 2001–2009," January 17, 2010, http://justiceinmexico.files.wordpress.com/2010/04/drug_violence.pdf; David Shirk, "Crime Indicator Database for the Justice in Mexico Project at the Trans-Border Institute," December 21, 2009, http://www.sandiego.edu/peacestudies/tbi/; "Mexico under Siege: The Drug War at Our Doorstep," in *Mexico Under Siege*, November 29, 2009, http://projects.latimes.com/mexico-drug-war/#/its-a-war.

3. Ken Ellingwood, "Grim Glossary of the Narco-World: Average Words Aren't Sufficient for the Over-the-Top Violence of Mexico's Drug War, So New Ones Have Been Invented," *Los Angeles Times*, October 28, 2009, http://www.latimes.com/news/nationworld/world/la-fg-narco-glossary28-2009oct28,0,1009690.story; Ismael Bojorquez, "El 'Cuerno' y el 'Chanate,'" *RIO DOCE: Un Nuevo Periodismo Para Sinaloa*, October 18, 2009, http://www.riodoce.com.mx/content/view/3075/42/.

4. The term "cartel" may be a misnomer for Mexican drug-trafficking organizations, because they have not demonstrated the ability to control drug prices in the United States. The term "cartel," however, has become the common usage and will thus be used here. For excellent discussions on the problematic use of the term "cartel" for Mexican drug-trafficking organizations, see Colleen W. Cook, *CRS Report for Congress: Mexico's Drug Cartels* (Washington, D.C.: Congressional Research Service, 2007), www.fas.org/sgp/crs/row/RL34215.pdf; Marc Lacey, "Drug Wars: When a 'Cartel' Really Isn't," *Economix*, October 10, 2009, http://economix.blogs.nytimes.com/2009/09/21/drug-wars-when-a-cartel-really-isnt/?scp=1&sq=merida perce nt20initiative&st=cseID-526; and Jose Luis Velasco, *Insurgency, Authoritarianism, and Drug Trafficking in Mexico's Democratic Transition*, edited by David Mares (New York: Routledge, 2005). See also the discussion by Cook, *CRS Report*, note 1 on "cartels" versus drug-trafficking organizations (DTOs).

the U.S. Government Accountability Office (GAO) stated that 90 percent of guns recovered and traced from crimes in Mexico came from the United States. Though these numbers are debated, no reputable source suggests that anything less than the vast majority of guns involved in crimes in Mexico come from the United States. According to the Mexican government, more than 2,000 guns flow per day from the United States into Mexico, in an "iron river" of guns across the 2,000-mile border through 19 formal points of entry and innumerable "informal" crossing points.[5] According to William Hoover, assistant director for field operations for the Bureau of Alcohol, Tobacco, Firearms, and Explosives (ATF), "Mexican president Felipe Calderón and Mexican attorney general Eduardo Medina Mora have identified cartel-related violence as a top security priority and proclaimed the illegal trafficking of U.S.-source firearms to be the 'number one' crime problem affecting the security of Mexico."[6]

Both President Barack Obama and Secretary of State Hillary Clinton have acknowledged the U.S. responsibility for the flow of guns into Mexico and have pledged to work with the Mexican government to combat the problem. However, strengthening gun control legislation in the United States may be politically unfeasible. Thus, the United States' policy on the flow of guns into Mexico is likely to mirror its drug policy, with a focus on interdiction efforts, as embodied by programs like Project Gunrunner (ATF Houston Grupo de Coordinacion de Armas), Armas Cruzadas (an initiative of the U.S. Immigrations and Customs Enforcement Agency of the U.S. Department of Homeland Security), and bilateral partnership agreements like the Mérida Initiative.[7]

This appendix (1) assesses the "iron river" problem; (2) provides a history of the rise of drug violence in Mexico, using four of the most militarized cartels as identified by the Mexican government, Los Zetas, the Arellano-Félix Organization, the Pacific Cartel (Sinaloa Cartel), and the rising La Familia Michoacána; (3) provides policy options; and (4) assesses the viability of the recommended option of increasing bilateral interdiction efforts and funding.

The "Iron River"

The flow of guns into Mexico is a mirror image of the flow of drugs into the United States. Drugs flow north, while guns, bulk cash, and methamphetamine chemical precursors flow south along precisely the same routes (figure A1). According to the Mexican government, more than 2,000

---

5. Jess T. Ford, *Firearms Trafficking: U.S. Efforts to Combat Arms Trafficking to Mexico Face Planning and Coordination Challenges* (Washington, D.C.: U.S. Government Accountability Office, 2009), http://www.gao.gov/new.items/d09709.pdf.

6. It should also be noted that guns are not the only weapons used in the Mexican DTOs' conflicts with the government and other DTOs. Other weapons and weapon accessories are relevant; night-vision goggles and scopes, bullet-proof vests, armored cars, radios, surveillance equipment, radio jamming equipment and silencers also play a role in DTO violence in Mexico. The increased seizures of light weapons like anti-tank rockets and grenades will be discussed later in further detail. See "Statement of William Hoover, Assistant Director for Field Operations, Bureau of Alcohol, Tobacco, Firearms, and Explosives, United States Department of Justice, and Anthony P. Placido, Assistant Administrator for Intelligence Division, Drug Enforcement Administration, United States Department of Justice, before the United States Senate Committee on the Judiciary Subcommittee on Crime and Drugs Concerning Law Enforcement Responses to Mexican Drug Cartels," March 17, 2009, U.S. Senate Committee on the Judiciary and U.S. Department of Justice, 2009.

7. Bureau of Alcohol, Tobacco, Firearms, and Explosives, U.S. Department of Justice (ATF), "Project Gunrunner Success Statistics: Houston Field Division—Gun Runner Impact Team (GRIT) April 28–August 28, 2009," http://www.atf.gov/press/releases/2009/10/100109-doj-gunrunner-success-stats.pdf.

Figure A1. Four Arms-Trafficking Routes Identified by the Mexican Government

Source: Procuraduria General de la Republica (PGR), "USA-Mexico Firearms Smuggling: March 26, 2009," March 26, 2009, http://www.pgr.gob.mx/prensa/2007/docs08/trafico%20de%20armas%2026%20marzo%202009%20eng%20%282%29.pdf. Used with permission.

guns flow south into Mexico from the United States per day via *hormigas* (ant trails), people smuggling guns individually across the border, and through more sophisticated straw-purchasing rings (the practice of using a third party with a clean record to purchase guns on your behalf). These rings are often associated with Mexican drug cartels and operate throughout the United States.[8] Each cartel appears to have its own suppliers and supply chains. Anecdotally, the origins of traced guns tend to correlate with the presence of cartel drug distribution cells in the United States.

Straw Buyers

Mexican gun laws are very strict. Straw purchasers buy guns in the United States and smuggle them to Mexico, where they sell at a high markup, allowing enforcer squads of drug cartels to combat Mexican security services and each other with higher levels of violence. Some estimate that there is a 300 percent markup for guns smuggled from the United States into Mexico, and specific investigations have suggested a 500 percent markup.[9]

8. Mexican DTOs have been identified by the Department of Justice's National Drug Intelligence Center as operating in more than 195 American cities. See "Situation Report: Cities in Which Mexican DTO's Operate within the United States," April 11, 2008, http://www.usdoj.gov/ndic/pubs27/27986/27986p.pdf.

9. Vivian S. Chu and William J. Krouse, *Gun Trafficking and the Southwest Border* (Washington, D.C.: Congressional Research Service, 2009), internal-pdf://crs reportonflowofgunssouth-0291854872/crsreportonflowofgunssouth.pdf; Ford, *Firearms Trafficking.*

Typically, straw-purchasing rings recruit cash-strapped individuals with clean criminal records to buy guns legally and pass them on to the ring for transport into Mexico. Some rings are run by individuals, but many are loosely affiliated with Mexican drug cartels. Limited checkpoints going into Mexico make the transport of guns into Mexico a low-risk endeavor.[10]

Where Do the Numbers Come From?

The ATF is the lead U.S. law enforcement agency enforcing U.S. gun laws, and its eTtrace database provides the best data on U.S. guns in Mexico.[11] ETtrace allows for the identification of crime patterns involving guns and the development of leads for investigators to solve criminal cases. The ATF seized 11,568 firearms in fiscal year 2008 and 16,383 in fiscal year 2009. The most recent publicly available analysis of eTrace data comes from the GAO report *Firearms Trafficking: U.S. Efforts to Combat Arms Trafficking to Mexico Face Planning and Coordination Challenges*, from June 2009. On the basis of an analysis of guns seized in Mexico and entered into the eTrace System, the GAO was able to determine that 87 percent of guns recovered and traced in Mexico from January 2004 to December 31, 2008 (a five-year study), were of U.S. origin.[12]

The statistics on guns traced from Mexican crimes to the United States become more precise and accurate with each year. Numbers from more recent years provide a more accurate representation of the guns recovered from crimes in Mexico, because each year a higher percentage of guns from Mexico is entered for tracing. For example, in 2008 the Mexican government claimed that nearly 30,000 guns were seized in crimes, but only 7,200 were submitted for tracing. More guns were traced in 2008 than in 2007, and so forth.[13]

In "The Myth of 90 Percent," Fox News has claimed that this low percentage of total guns submitted for tracing produces biased results because Mexican law enforcement does not submit for tracing guns that "obviously" do not come from the United States. Factcheck.org attempted to verify this assumption with the ATF, but no such consistent biasing procedure could be identified. Fox News' claim that only 17 percent of guns recovered in Mexican crimes are traceable to the United States is thus highly implausible. The low percentage of guns entered for tracing has nothing to do with an intentional selection bias in the sample, but rather a lack of trained law enforcement officers capable of entering these guns into the database in Mexico.[14] Another hindrance to tracing

---

10. Chu and Krouse, *Gun Trafficking*.

11. The database eTrace is an ATF database that tracks guns recovered in crimes in the United States and Mexico to develop leads in criminal firearms cases. It is currently the best source of data on firearms recovered in crimes in Mexico. As is discussed below, eTrace data is often incomplete. ATF, "ATF Deploys Spanish eTrace to Mexico, Guatemala and Costa Rica," 2009), http://www.atf.gov/press/releases/2009/12/123009-atf-deploys-spanish-etrace.html; ATF, "ATF Expands Efforts to Combat Illegal Flow of Firearms into Mexico," December 13, 2009, http://www.atf.gov/press/releases/2008/01/011608-atf-expands-efforts-to-combat-firearms-trafficking.html.

12. Ford, *Firearms Trafficking*.

13. Ibid.; Jess T. Ford, *U.S. Assistance Has Helped Mexican Counternarcotics Efforts, but the Flow of Illicit Drugs into the United States Remains High* (Washington, D.C.: U.S. Government Accountability Office, 2007), http://www.gao.gov/new.items/d08215t.pdf.

14. D'Angelo Gore, "Counting Mexico's Guns: President Obama Says 90 Percent of Mexico's Recovered Crime Guns Come from the U.S.—That's Not What the Statistics Show," December 28, 2009, http://www.factcheck.org/2009/04/counting-mexicos-guns/; "Only a small fraction of guns in Mexico come from the U.S. While 90 percent of the guns traced to the U.S. actually originated in the United States, the percent traced to the U.S. is only about 17 percent of the total number of guns reaching Mexico." William La Jeu-

was that the eTrace software operated only in English until December 30, 2009. Later in 2010, the Spanish eTrace system will be introduced more widely throughout Mexico. With increased training for Mexican law enforcement officers on how to trace guns, a Spanish-language version of the eTrace system coming online in early 2010, and with increasing educational levels among police officers, eTrace data will become more precise each year.[15]

Where Do the Guns Come From?

Two factors influence from which state in the United States guns recovered from crimes in Mexico are sourced. The first is how lenient the gun laws are in that state. States that allow same-day purchasing and do not limit the number of guns purchased are more likely to be the sources of guns recovered in Mexico. The second important factor is proximity. Transporting guns over a shorter distance within the United States reduces costs, shortens the time to get the product to market in Mexico, and reduces the likelihood that the guns will be captured in routine road stops within the United States. Texas and Arizona are the border states with the loosest gun laws. California currently has more stringent laws and was a significant source state for guns recovered in crimes in Mexico. Texas, Arizona, and California account for 70 percent of all guns traced from Mexican government seizures from 2004 to 2008.[16]

According to the GAO analysis, which includes data from 2004 to 2008, of the guns recovered in crimes in Mexico and traced back to the United States, 39 percent came from Texas, 20 percent from California, 10 percent from Arizona, 17 percent from the other top 10 states, and 14 percent from other states.[17]

According to the GAO, there are 6,700 retail gun stores or pawnshops selling guns along the Southwest border and 55,000 federal firearms licensees throughout the United States. Mexican government estimates are roughly double, with more than 12,000 businesses selling firearms near the U.S.-Mexican border, and more than 100,000 gun stores and gun shows throughout the United States (factoring in gun shows may help to account for the divergent estimates).[18] Gun shows are also a boon for straw purchasers and firearms traffickers because they include undocumented sales from private collectors, which make it impossible to trace guns recovered in crimes in Mexico back to straw purchasers in the United States.[19]

According to the Associated Press, in 2007 there were 1,131 guns recovered in crimes in Mexico traced back to the state of Texas, 436 to California, 238 to Arizona, 35 to New Mexico, 38

nesse and Maxim Lott, "The Myth of 90 Percent," December 28, 2009, http://www.foxnews.com/politics/elections/2009/04/02/myth-percent-guns-mexico-fraction-number-claimed/.

15. It should also be noted that Mexican federal prosecutions do not need to successfully or completely document import markings, serial numbers, or model numbers. It is sufficient for federal prosecution under article 83 of the Mexican federal firearms law merely to show that the rifle or handgun was of a caliber that is for the exclusive use of the military. This further contributes to insufficient data entry into the eTrace system by Mexican law enforcement. ATF, "ATF Deploys Spanish eTrace."

16. Ford, *Firearms Trafficking.*

17. Ford, *U.S. Assistance Has Helped Mexican Counternarcotics Efforts.*

18. PGR, *Trafico de Armas: Mexico-USA* (Mexico City: PGR, 2008), http://www.pgr.gob.mx/prensa/2007/docs08/tr%C3%A1fico_d...pdf; PGR, *USA-Mexico Firearms Smuggling, March 26, 2009 (English)* (Mexico City: PGR, 2009), http://www.pgr.gob.mx/prensa/2007/docs08/trafico percent20de percent20armaspercent2026 percent20marzo percent202009 percent20eng percent20 percent282 percent29.pdf.

19. Ford, *Firearms Trafficking.*

to Colorado, 37 to Oklahoma, 25 to Louisiana, 26 to Nevada, 31 to Georgia, 24 to South Carolina, 28 to Ohio, 29 to Illinois, 19 to Indiana, 68 to Washington, 61 to Florida, and 31 to other states.[20]

Florida and Washington both demonstrate that despite distance, loose gun laws are an important factor in increasing the likelihood that a U.S. state will be the source of guns recovered in crimes in Mexico. In recent years, states that are both close to the border and have loose gun laws, like Texas and Arizona, are the most likely to be source states for guns used in drug-related crime in Mexico. It is often difficult for the ATF to stop straw buyers from transporting guns across country from states like Washington because a crime has not been committed until the straw buyers are crossing the Southwest border. Thus, running surveillance on straw buyers driving cross country is manpower and time intensive for this relatively small law enforcement agency. The ATF is capped by Congress on its maximum number of special agents, which limits the agency to fewer agents in 2010 than were authorized in 1926.[21]

Where Are the Guns Recovered in Mexico?

There are two available metrics for determining where guns from the legal U.S. market will be recovered Mexico. The first is to assess drug related homicides and assume U.S. weapons are used in those acts of violence. This is not an unreasonable assumption, given the percentage of guns traced back to the U.S. market using eTrace, but it is not direct data either. The second uses more direct data involving gun seizures. Both eTrace and Mexico's Center for National Planning, Analysis and Information to Combat Crime (CENAPI) have data on from which Mexican states guns are recovered. CENAPI data includes all 29,824 guns seized in 2008, while eTrace data includes only 6,854 of those which could be positively traced to a given Mexican state. Despite the different sample sizes, the GAO determined that there was a strong correlation between the two data sets. When the top 10 states were ranked, both lists included 8 of the same states. In no particular order, these 8 states are (1) Baja California Norte, (2) Chihuahua, (3) Michoacán, (4) the Distrito Federal, (5) Jalisco, (6) Oaxaca, (7) Tamaulipas, and (8) Guanajuato.[22] These states are recognizable for their levels of drug violence because they are disputed drug-trafficking territories like the state of Chihuahua. They are also recognizable as home base areas for major cartels; Tamaulipas is the home of the Gulf Cartel, for example. Geographically, they are concentrated on the Pacific Coast and on the U.S. border (figure A2).

What Types of Guns Are Recovered?

The types of guns recovered in crimes in Mexico tend to be legally available within the U.S. domestic market. Figure A3 is a list of the guns most frequently recovered in Mexico and traced, from the GAO.

It is commonly argued that the fully automatic versions of guns like the AR-15 and AK-47 are not easily available in the United States and that modifying these guns into fully automatic versions is very difficult, though not impossible. Thus, it logically follows that the weapons cartels in

---

20. "Mexican Cartels: Drug Organizations Extending Reach Farther into US," MSNBC, December 13, 2009, http://www.msnbc.msn.com/id/32049643/ns/world_news-americas/.

21. P. Metcalfe, *Whispering Wires: The Tragic Tale of an American Bootlegger* (Portland: Inkwater Press, 2007).

22. Ford, *Firearms Trafficking.*

Figure A2. Firearms Trafficking to Mexico

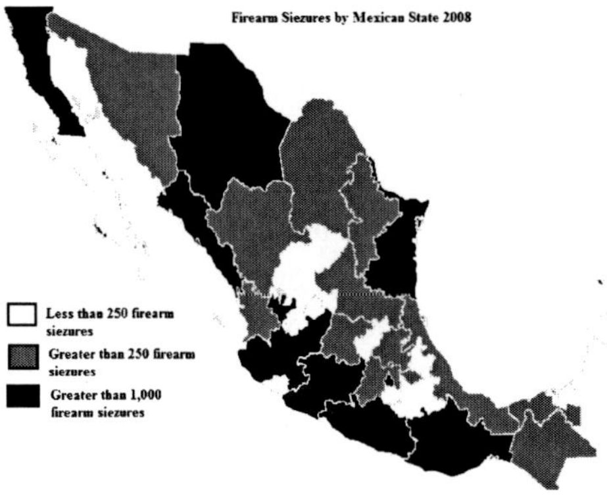

Source: Jess T. Ford, *Firearms Trafficking: U.S. Efforts to Combat Arms Trafficking to Mexico Face Planning and Coordination Challenges* (Washington, D.C.: U.S. Government Accountability Office, 2009), http://www.gao.gov/new.items/d09709.pdf.

Figure A3. Firearms Types Most Frequently Recovered in Mexico and Traced (2004–2008)

9 mm pistol
.38 caliber revolver
.22 caliber pistol
.38 caliber pistol
7.62 mm AK-47–type semiautomatic rifle
.22 caliber rifle
.223 caliber AR-15–type semiautomatic rifle
.45 caliber pistol
12 gauge shotgun

Source: Jess T. Ford, *Firearms Trafficking: U.S. Efforts to Combat Arms Trafficking to Mexico Face Planning and Coordination Challenges* (Washington, D.C.: U.S. Government Accountability Office, 2009), http://www.gao.gov/new.items/d09709.pdf.

Mexico are currently using come from the black market of Central America and not U.S. straw purchasers. But this argument is specious. On the basis of eTrace data, few machine guns are recovered in Mexico. Machine guns, or the fully automatic versions of the AK-47 and AR-15, represent a small proportion (0.3 percent) of guns seized and traced in Mexico from 2004 to 2008.[23] A well-trained cartel hit man would likely prefer a semiautomatic version of these guns because of the inaccuracy of the fully automatic version. The majority of machine guns recovered in drug cartel investigations in Mexico were sold or imported into the United States and converted in clandestine arms factories, which is actually a simple process given the level of technology in 1947 (AK-47).

The Rise of Drug Violence in Mexico: The Demand for Arms

Smuggling weapons across the United States–Mexico border has a long history stretching back to the nineteenth century.[24] The current increased demand for weapons in Mexico has been sparked by the militarization of the Mexican drug cartels. According to a recent U.S. State Department travel advisory, "Some recent Mexican army and police confrontations with drug cartels have resembled small-unit combat, with cartels employing automatic weapons and grenades. Large firefights have taken place in towns and cities across Mexico."[25] Military roadblocks have altered the tactics of drug-trafficking organizations. Instead of traveling openly in armed convoys, they avoid checkpoint interdiction by placing loads of ammunition, firearms, bulletproof vests, night vision goggles, and other criminal equipment in stash houses at key logistical locations to avoid checkpoints. Large arms seizures are evidence of this adaptation.

There have been more than 22,700 drug-related deaths (*ejecuciones*) in Mexico since Calderón took office in December 2006 and began his offensive against the Mexican cartels. He has responded by saturating 18 Mexican states with more than 45,000 federal troops, supplementing local and state law enforcement agencies widely viewed as corrupt.[26] This strategy has been combined with a five-pillar strategy for long-term reform: (1) recovery of public spaces, (2) law enforcement operations, (3) institutional reform, (4) recovery of social cohesion and trust, and (5) international cooperation.[27]

Despite the implementation of this five-pillar strategy, there has been a steady increase in drug-related homicides in Mexico. In 2006, there were 2,120 drug-related homicides; in 2007, 2,280; in 2008, 5,153; and in 2009, 6,587.[28] The most violent cities in Mexico are typically afflicted with intercartel warfare. The City of Nuevo Laredo was extremely violent until a truce was

23. Ibid.

24. George Grayson, *Mexico: Narco-Violence and a Failed State?* (New Brunswick, N.J.: Transaction, 2009).

25. U.S. Department of State, "Travel Advisory: Mexico—Security," December 13, 2009, http://travel.state.gov/travel/cis_pa_tw/pa/pa_4491.html?css=print.

26. "Mexico's Drug War: Stories, Photos, Videos—Mexico Under Siege—It's a War," *Los Angeles Times*, n.d., http://projects.latimes.com/mexico-drug-war/#/its-a-war.

27. Embassy of Mexico, *Mexico and the Fight against Drug Trafficking and Organized Crime: Setting the Record Straight* (Washington, D.C.: Embassy of Mexico, 2009), http://portal.sre.gob.mx/eua/pdf/SettingTheRecordStraightFinal.pdf.

28. Shirk, "Drug Violence."

Figure A4. Drug-Related Killings in Mexico

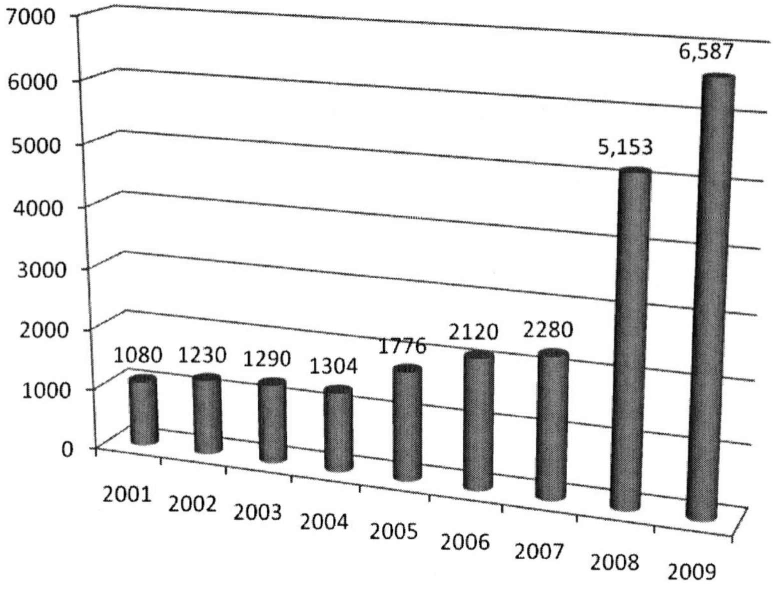

Source: Data are from the Transborder Institute, University of San Diego. David Shirk, "Drug Violence in Mexico: Data and Analysis from 2001–2009," January 17, 2010, http://justiceinmexico.files.wordpress.com/2010/04/drug_violence.pdf. Used with permission.

achieved between the Sinaloa Cartel led by Chapo Guzman and Los Zetas. Their turf war ended when the Sinaloa Cartel agreed to pay a *cuota* (tax) on drugs shipped through that *plaza*.[29] Once that truce was achieved in 2007, violence in Ciudad Juarez immediately increased as Chapo Guzman attempted to wrest control of Ciudad Juarez from the Juarez Cartel.[30] This has made Ciudad Juarez the most violent city in Mexico, on a par in danger with war zones like Iraq and Afghanistan. Figures A4 and A5 graphically demonstrate the rise in drug-related homicides.

The increase in violence should not necessarily be construed as a failure of Calderón's policy. It may indeed be a sign of long-term success, as is asserted by many Mexican government officials.[31] The spike in violence has been caused by the recent heavy government pressure on the cartels. It is, however, part of a larger story of the Mexican government pulling out of the business of drug trafficking. Cartels are today fighting with each other for fewer points of entry into the United States and responding to the government with violence. The increasing levels of violence will likely continue well into the next *sexenio* and will increase the demand for arms in Mexico from the United

29. The term *plaza* refers to territory or franchise area which a cartel can control and includes ports of entry, air, land, tunnels, and sea.

30. John Burnett, "Nuevo Laredo Returns to Normal as Violence Slows," January 23, 2009, http://www.npr.org/templates/story/story.php?storyId=99742620.

31. Ken Ellingwood, "Actually Violence Is Down—So Say the Numbers," *Los Angeles Times*, August 22, 2009, http://www.latimes.com/news/nationworld/world/la-fg-mexico-murder22-2009aug22,0,3018278.story.

Figure A5. Rate of Cartel-Related Killings per 100,000 Inhabitants

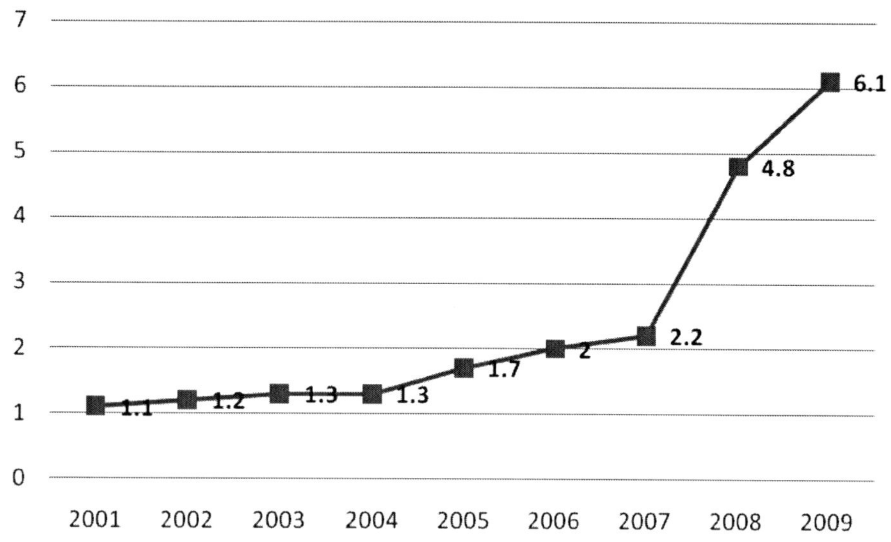

Source: Data are from the Transborder Institute, University of San Diego. David Shirk, "Drug Violence in Mexico: Data and Analysis from 2001–2009," January 17, 2010, http://justiceinmexico.files.wordpress.com/2010/04/drug_violence.pdf. Used with permission.

States and the international black market. Mexican drug cartels' distribution is also expanding beyond the United States, particularly in Europe, which increases their profitability and resilience.

How Did Mexico Get to This Point?

Although drug trafficking from Mexico to the United States dates back to the nineteenth century, drug-related violence increased in the 1990s and has ballooned in the first decade of the twenty-first century. There is one primary factor that led to this steady increase in drug-related violence: the removal of the state and state security institutions from involvement in drug trafficking. As Duran-Martinez and Snyder argue, when the Mexican state reduced its role in drug trafficking, it ceased to be a power broker among drug traffickers in the country. The Partido Revolucionario Institutional (PRI; Institutional Revolutionary Party) ruled Mexico for 70 years following the Mexican Revolution. Corruption was institutionalized under the PRI and included the protection of high-level traffickers in return for bribes. With increased democratization and transparency, dramatically marked by the election of President Vicente Fox of the Partido Acción Nacional (National Action Party) in 2000, the state's role in drug trafficking has slowly changed from one of participation to antagonism, epitomized by President Calderón's strong antitrafficking stance.[32] When this modus vivendi ended, the drug traffickers were left to defend their turf from each other

32. Many fear that when Fox's successor, Felipe Calderón, ends his term in 2012, a PRI candidate will be elected and will return Mexico to a modus vivendi with traffickers that will reduce violence in the short term but irrevocably damage Mexican governability and democratization over the long term. See Angelica Duran-Martinez and Richard Snyder, "Does Illegality Breed Violence? Drug Trafficking and State-Sponsored Protection Rackets," *Crime, Law and Social Change* (2009): 253–273.

and from the state. Without state protection, the traffickers steadily built up enforcer squads to meet the challenges of rival cartels and to intimidate/corrupt law enforcement officials.[33]

Three cartels have been most notable in this violent arms race and have been ranked by the Mexican attorney general's office as the most heavily armed cartels in Mexico: Los Zetas / the Gulf Cartel; the Arellano-Félix Organization / the Tijuana Cartel; and the Pacific Cartel, also known as the Sinaloa Cartel.[34]

The Arming of the Arellano-Félix Organization

The Arellano-Félix Organization (AFO), also known as the Tijuana Cartel, was the first of the cartels to begin the militarization process in the early 1990s. Its intense conflict with Joaquin Guzman-Loera (El Chapo) of the Sinaloa Cartel forced it to defend its territory by recruiting massive enforcer squads in the mid-1990s. As the lore goes, the Arellano brothers attempted to work out a truce with Chapo Guzman in Puerto Vallarta, but the meeting went poorly and later that night Guzman's enforcers attempted to kill the Arellano brothers in a nightclub. Their bodyguard, David Barron-Corona, saved their lives by providing suppression fire and directing them out an air-conditioning duct. It was at this point that the Arellanos realized they had to increase the size of their enforcement squads. They looked to Barron for enforcers, who were recruited from his San Diego Logan Heights street gang and his Mexican Mafia prison gang. These enforcers were trained by corrupted Mexican police and foreign mercenaries to use military-style weapons. One squad of enforcers waiting in Guadalajara for the arrival of El Chapo assassinated Juan Jesús Cardinal Posadas of Guadalajara in a case of mistaken identity in 1993. The assassination of a cardinal of the Catholic Church, the most respected institution in Mexico, forced the AFO to further increase its enforcement squads, while its leadership was forced into hiding.[35]

These enforcer squads required extensive arms, as evidenced by major drug and arms seizures. On March 7, 2008, the Mexican military had a two-hour shootout with elements of the AFO, which resulted in the arrest of three cartel members and one of the larger arms seizures in Mexican history. The seizure included 91 guns; 50,000 rounds of ammunition, grenades, explosives; and more than half a ton of marijuana.[36]

The intense government pressure on the AFO would culminate in the arrest or killings of its top leadership, including: the arrest of Benjamin Arellano-Félix in 2002, the killing of his brother and chief AFO enforcer Ramon in 2002, the arrest of Francisco Javier Arellano-Félix "El Tigrillo" in 2006, the October 2008 arrest of Eduardo Arellano-Félix "El Doctor," and the arrest of various high-ranking lieutenants.[37] The resulting leadership vacuum led to a split within the cartel

33. Ibid.

34. PGR, "USA-Mexico Firearms Smuggling."

35. Sam Dillon, "Mexican Traffickers Recruiting Killers in the U.S.," *New York Times*, December 4, 1997, http://www.nytimes.com/1997/12/04/world/mexican-traffickers-recruiting-killers-in-the-us.html?pagewanted=2&pagewanted=print; *Drug Enforcement Administration Lecture Series: Harrod, Scharf and Zieglar* (Washington, D.C.: U.S. Department of Justice, 2008), http://www.deamuseum.org/transcripts/Harrod_Scharf.pdf.

36. Chris Aspin, Lizbeth Diaz, and Noel Randewich, "Mexican Soldiers Make Huge Drug Gang Arms Seizure," Reuters, December 29, 2009, http://www.reuters.com/article/idUSN0739689820080308.

37. "Mexican Drug Cartels: Two Wars and a Look Southward"; "Mexican Drug Cartels: Government Progress and Increasing Violence," *Stratfor*, December 11, 2008, internal-pdf://STRATFOR--MEXICAN

between Fernando Sanchez-Arellano (El Ingeniero), the nephew of the Arellano brothers, and Teodoro Garcia-Simental (El Teo), an enforcer lieutenant of the organization. El Teo's faction paid for its large numbers of enforcers through kidnappings. Thus we have seen a dramatic increase in kidnappings, in Mexico City and Tijuana in particular.[38]

This process is indicative of another trend in Mexico's violent cartel situation, the decapitation strategy pursued by the Mexican government and U.S. law enforcement, has resulted in AFO leadership vacuums. These vacuums are filled by younger, more violent, and less experienced managers, like El Teo.[39] Internecine cartel violence led by these younger managers has increased not just kidnapping rates but also drug-related homicide rates. For example, in April 2008, AFO factions fought a massive gun battle on the streets of Tijuana, leaving 13 dead and 9 wounded. Over a 14-square-kilometer area, police recovered 11 bullet-ridden abandoned vehicles, 1,506 spent shell casings, and 60 guns.[40]

The AFO and Tijuana more generally are illustrative of the types of drug-related violence that have plagued Mexico. First, kidnappings have increased to cover the costs of enforcers as drug profits have dried up under government pressure on cartel leadership and on the border. Kidnapping, as a means to extort payment for drug debts, has long been a tool for drug-trafficking organizations. Second, decapitation or "kingpin" strategies targeting cartel leaders has resulted in internecine violence within cartels. Third, weakened cartels are often challenged by rival cartels attempting to expand their turf and profits. Fourth, as the government—in Tijuana, for example—takes affirmative steps to root out corruption in the police force, cartels target the officers who stand in their way.[41]

The Arming of Los Zetas / the Gulf Cartel

The story of the Gulf Cartel and Los Zetas exemplifies the increased demand for assault rifles from the United States into Mexico. It is considered by the Mexican government the most heavily armed cartel. In the late 1990s, the Grupo Aeromovil de Fuerzas Especiales (GAFES; Mexican Special Forces) were sent to the state of Tamaulipas to combat the Gulf Cartel led by Osiel Cardenas-Guillen. The GAFES were contacted by the Gulf Cartel and switched sides. They became known as Los Zetas, the armed wing of the Gulf Cartel. Although estimates vary on the original number of Los Zetas who were GAFES, the Zetas produced what was known as the "Zeta effect," in which the former GAFES have trained many lower-level enforcers for the cartels in more deadly tactics. They

---

percent2520Cartels percent25202008[1]-Copy-3654030605/STRATFOR--MEXICAN percent2520Cartels percent25202008[1]-Copy.pdf.

38. Richard Marosi, "Mystery Man Blamed for Gruesome Tijuana Deaths," *Los Angeles Times*, December 18, 2008, http://www.latimes.com/la-fg-tijuanadruglord18-2008dec18,0,5864824.story.

39. Vanda Felbab-Brown, "The Violent Drug Market in Mexico and Lessons from Colombia," Foreign Policy at Brookings: Policy Paper, September 30, 2009, internal-pdf://03_mexico_drug_market_felbab-brown-3168980493/03_mexico_drug_market_felbabbrown.pdf; Vanda Felbab-Brown, *Shooting Up : Counterinsurgency and the War on Drugs* (Washington, D.C.: Brookings Institution Press, 2009); Vanda Felbab-Brown, "Interview on Mexican Drug Cartels," interview by Nathan Jones, July 2009.

40. "Massive Gunbattles Break Out in Tijuana; 13 Dead, 9 Wounded," Fox News, December 29, 2009, http://www.foxnews.com/story/0,2933,352739,00.html. *El Mexicano*, April 27,2008.

41. Richard Marosi, "Tijuana's Security Chief Needs All of It He Can Get: Julian Leyzaola Lives with Threats and Worse, Plus the Accusations," *Los Angeles Times*, December 20, 2009, http://www.latimes.com/news/nation-and-world/la-fg-tijuana-police20-2009dec20,0,1484440.story.

have also been reinforced by Kaibiles, Guatemalan Special Forces trained in counterinsurgency tactics. Naturally, these highly trained military forces brought with them expertise in military weaponry like those imported from the United States.[42]

Los Zetas also learned the drug-trafficking trade under the tutelage of their Gulf Cartel leaders. Once Osiel Cardenas Guillen was arrested by the Mexican authorities in 2003 and extradited to the United States in 2007, it appears that Los Zetas have become their own cartel and no longer take their orders from the Gulf Cartel, though they continued to cooperate until very recently.[43] The success of Los Zetas has inspired imitations like Los Pelones of the Sinaloa cartel and other armed enforcer squads.[44]

The Zetas were the source of the largest arms seizure in more than 20 years in Mexico. On November 6, 2008, in Reynosa, Tamaulipas, the Mexican military and federal agents seized "540 rifles, 98 fragmentation grenades, 14 cartridges of dynamite, seven .50-caliber Barrett sniper rifles, 67 bulletproof vests, and a LAW [light anti-tank weapon] rocket." The day after the seizure, "El Hummer," Jaime Gonzales-Duran, one of the original Zetas members, was arrested by the Mexican government. STRATFOR analysts noted that the .50-caliber sniper rifle is capable of stopping a car, killing at more than 1.5 miles away, grounding a rotary-wing airplane, and piercing the strongest body armor.[45] According to the *Arizona Republic*, a Ciudad Juarez police officer was killed with a .50-caliber sniper rifle traceable to Phoenix in March 2008.[46] Also, .50-caliber sniper rifles are easily available on the U.S. domestic gun market.[47] This arms seizure demonstrates the heavy weaponry being used in Mexican drug cartel violence and its availability on the U.S. gun market.

Of the 383 guns seized and traced back to the United States in the Reynosa seizure, 120 of them had a "time-to-crime"[48] of 5 years or less. Of those 120 guns, 45 percent were 223 caliber (AR-15s use this type of ammunition), 27 percent were 7.62 millimeters (AKs use this type of round), 9 percent were 9 millimeters, 7 percent were 5.7 millimeters (Five-SeveN pistols and P90s use this round), 7 percent were .30 caliber, and 5 percent were other types of guns. A total of 80 percent of these guns were traced to back to Texas.[49] This seizure is a perfect demonstration of the types of weapons trafficked from the United States into Mexican drug cartel hands.

This seizure also demonstrates the unavailability of some weapons being used in Mexico on the U.S. market. Fragmentation grenades, LAW rockets, and dynamite are not available on the U.S.

---

42. Hal Brands, "Los Zetas: Inside Mexico's Most Dangerous Drug Gang," December 29, 2009, http://www.airpower.maxwell.af.mil/apjinternational/apj-s/2009/3tri09/brandseng.htm.

43. Recent reports suggest that Los Zetas and remnants of the Gulf Cartel are in a power struggle for control of the organization.

44. Brands, "Los Zetas"; Hal Brands, "Mexico's Narco-Insurgency and U.S. Counterdrug Policy," Strategic Studies Institute, 2009, internal-pdf://Readthisarticle!-0646374926/Readthisarticle!.pdf.

45. "Mexico Security Memo November 10, 2008," December 29, 2009, http://www.stratfor.com/node/126816/analysis/20081110_mexico_security_memo_nov_10_2008.

46. Sean Holstege, "Prosecutors in Ariz., Mexico Target Smuggling," *Arizona Republic* (Phoenix), March 14, 2008, http://www.azcentral.com/arizonarepublic/local/articles/0314borderagreement0314.html.

47. A Barret 50-caliber sniper rifle sells for $8,900 in Nevada and for $40,000 to $50,000 in Mexico.

48. "Time to crime" is defined as the time from which the gun was legally sold to the time it was recovered in a crime in Mexico. Investigators pay attention to this, because a shorter time to crime may be evidence of trafficking. People buying guns legally and for legal purposes tend to possess them longer.

49. Todd Bensman, "Most Guns from Raid Traced to Texas," *My San Antonio* (San Antonio, 2009), http://www.mysanantonio.com/news/mexico/Officials_say_most_weapons_from_raid_came_from_Texas_dealers.html.

domestic market. Unless they are the result of theft from the U.S. military, which is unlikely, these weapons most likely come from black market sources via Central America.[50]

The Pacific Cartel (Sinaloa Cartel)

The Mexican government has identified the Pacific Cartel as the third-highest-ranked cartel in terms of the use of heavy weaponry. The Pacific Cartel once included the Sinaloa Cartel of Chapo Guzman, the Juarez cartel, and the Beltran-Leyva Organization (BLO). They have since violently split with each other, and it no longer makes sense to describe it as a unified cartel. The largest and most successful remnant of the Pacific Cartel is the Sinaloa Cartel led by Chapo Guzman. This cartel has engaged in extreme violence in its competition with the Juarez Cartel over the Ciudad Juarez / El Paso *plaza*, but violence has not characterized the strategy of this cartel. Chapo Guzman is a sophisticated cartel leader who has survived since the 1980s, while other cartel leaders have been captured or killed. He is known for his bribes, contacts, and intelligence within the Mexican government. Thus, he is more likely to provide intelligence to the government on a rival cartel instead of resorting to violence. The split with the Beltran-Leyva Organization was the result of an arrest of one of the Beltran-Leyva brothers. The BLO leadership believed Chapo knew of the impending state action and did not inform them. That event led to a bloody split between the BLO and the Sinaloa Cartel. This cartel has always had its squads of enforcers, but in response to Los Zetas more gangs were formed and given names like Los Pelones and Los Negros.[51]

"Chapo" Guzman-Loera's organization continues to remain highly profitable by smuggling cocaine, to which cartels like the AFO have lost access. It may be that profitability explains the lower levels of armaments seized by the government from this cartel. Or it could be that the government is so corrupted by the Sinaloa Cartel that high-level seizures of drugs and armaments have been impossible. The success of the Sinaloa Cartel is contrasted by the weakening profits of the AFO / Tijuana Cartel remnants, which have been forced to diversify into criminal activities like kidnapping and extortion. Chapo, having more sophisticated managerial abilities and high profits, has relied less on weaponry and more on government intelligence than the militarily predisposed Zetas and the fragmented AFO remnants.

La Familia Michoacána

A fourth highly weaponized Mexican drug-trafficking organization has recently been elevated to "cartel" status by the U.S. and Mexican governments due to its size and scope of operations. La Familia Michoacána, based in President Calderón's home state of Michoacán, has been described as a cult-like drug cartel, which encourages its members to carry Bibles and is believed to have emerged originally as an anti-drug-trafficking vigilante group. Its ideology promotes the sale of methamphetamines to Americans, though not Mexicans. It is deeply embedded in the social networks of the state of Michoacán and is violent but careful to send messages that it only kills other rival traffickers and avoids killing civilians.[52]

---

50. "Mexico Security Memo November 10, 2008."
51. Brands, "Los Zetas."
52. U.S. Department of Justice, "DEA Announces Largest Single U.S. Strike against Mexican Drug Cartels: Project Coronado Results in 1,186 Arrests and Huge Drug and Money Seizures against One of the

Figure A6. A Photograph of Weapons Seized Resulting from Project Coronado

Source: U.S. Department of Justice, "DEA Announces Largest Single U.S. Strike Against Mexican Drug Cartels: Project Coronado Results in 1,186 Arrests and Huge Drug and Money Seizures against One of the World's Most Violent Drug Cartels," press release, February 26, 2010, http://www.justice.gov/dea/pubs/pressrel/pr102209a.html. Used with permission.

It is considered by the U.S. Drug Enforcement Administration to be a "heavily armed" cartel that utilizes "military grade weapons." Agency photos of weapons seizures resulting from Project Coronado, a 44-month multiagency operation against La Familia Michoacána operations in the United States, demonstrate that La Familia utilizes the same types of weapons as other Mexican cartels including, AR-15 and AK type guns (figure A6).[53]

"Light" Weapons Not from the United States

Seizures have revealed that Mexican cartels also use light weapons that are unavailable on the U.S. domestic market. Although these weapons would still be classified as infantry weapons, they have significantly greater firepower than the armaments used by the Mexican police and military. These weapons are sometimes referred to as "light weapons," and they include rocket-propelled grenades, antitank rockets, grenades and surface-to-air missiles.[54] None of these weapons are legally available for purchase in the United States. Table A1 gives the weapons known to be used by Mexican drug cartels based upon media and government reports on arms seizures in Mexico.

World's Most Violent Drug Cartels," press release, February 26, 2010, http://www.justice.gov/dea/pubs/pressrel/pr102209a.html; Grayson, *Mexico.*

53. U.S. Department of Justice, "DEA Announces Largest Single U.S. Strike."

54. Reports of Mexican Cartels possessing surface-to-air missiles are unverifiable at this time.

Table A1. Weapons Known to Be Used by Mexican Drug Cartels

Light Weapons Seized in Mexico	Availability on U.S. Legal Domestic Market
Fragmentation grenades	Unavailable on U.S. domestic market
Grenades	Unavailable on U.S. domestic market
50 cal machine guns	Parts available in the United States
RPG7	Unavailable on U.S. market
Anti-tank rockets M72	Unavailable on U.S. domestic market
Anti-tank rockets AT4	Unavailable on U.S. domestic market
MGL 37-millimeter grenade launcher	Unavailable on U.S. domestic market

Sources: Media and government reports on arms seizures in Mexico.

There are three possible sources for these weapons: U.S. military armories, Mexican military armories, and the international black market, especially via Central America. Data on guns traced from U.S. armories suggests that this is a minimal source of guns traced from crimes in Mexico, despite the sporadic cases of Mexican cartels recruiting from within the U.S. military and even joining the U.S. military for the purpose of stealing weapons from armories.[55]

There has been a steady increase in the number of these types of weapons used in Mexico. One telling statistic was reported by the *Los Angeles Times* in March 2009. "The Mexican government said it has seized 2,239 grenades in the last two years, in contrast to 59 seized over the previous two years."[56] It appears now that Mexican drug cartels are stockpiling increasingly powerful armaments in anticipation of conflicts with each other and the state. As the situation escalates, we are likely to see heavier weaponry used by Mexican cartels that are unavailable on the U.S. domestic market, in addition to more of the AK-47s, AR-15s, and P90s which are.

The Current U.S. Response

The United States and Mexico have experienced unprecedented levels of intergovernmental cooperation in recent years, a positive side effect of the increased in violence in Mexico. The current U.S.–Mexican response to the problem of arms trafficking has focused on interdiction and enforcement. The flow of arms from the United States into Mexico has been viewed by the U.S. government as one component of a larger threat to Mexico posed by organized crime and its

55. "According to ATF data for fiscal years 2004–2008, of the 23,159 guns seized in Mexico and traced, 160 firearms, or 0.70 percent, were found to be U.S. military arms." Ford, *Firearms Trafficking*.

56. Ken Ellingwood and Tracy Wilkinson, "Drug Cartels' New Weaponry Means War: Narcotics Traffickers Are Acquiring Firepower More Appropriate to an Army—Including Grenade Launchers and Anti-tank Rockets—and the Police Are Feeling Outgunned," *Los Angeles Times*, December 31, 2009, http://www.latimes.com/news/nationworld/world/la-fg-mexico-arms-race15-2009mar15,0,7843719,print.story.

Figure A7. Mexican Drug Trafficker's Advantage in Arms

Note: Mexican state police units, like those in the state of Jalisco, also carry AR-15 type weapons and 9-millimeter Glocks while SIGs are typically too expensive. There is also a lack of standardization among the weapons carried by the various Mexican law enforcement agencies. The Mexican Army utilizes the .308 NATO caliber H&K G-3 rifle and the similar FX-05 Xiuhcoatl. Captains and above utilize MP-5 H&K 9-millimeter machine pistol.

Source: Allan Wall, "The Mexican Army and its Controversial New Rifle," March 12, 2007, http://mexidata.info/id1289.html; Doug Stevens, "Trafficker's Advantage in Arms," Los Angeles Times, 2009, http://www.latimes.com/news/nationworld/world/la-031409-fg-2mexico_arms_race-g,0,2306703.graphic. Used with permission.

potential for "spillover" into the United States. There have been two prongs to the current U.S. response to organized crime in Mexico: increased law enforcement efforts; and the "Mérida Initiative," a bilateral partnership between the countries.

The Mérida Initiative

In mid-2007, Felipe Calderón met with President George W. Bush in the city of Mérida on the Yucatán Peninsula. There, Calderón and Bush discussed the shared problem of organized crime in Mexico and strategies to combat it. The plan that would eventually emerge from this process was the Mérida Initiative, a partnership sensitive to issues of Mexican sovereignty, providing funding and equipment to the Mexican government to combat organized crime. It also included the principle of shared responsibility of the United States as both a consumer of drugs and supplier of weapons and chemical precursors for methamphetamines. The United States is committed in principle to combating the flow of guns south into Mexico. The Mérida Initiative as originally conceived would provide $1.4 billion over three years to the Mexican government, although it is likely that the Mérida Initiative will provide less funding than planned. Most government officials in the United States believe that like Plan Colombia, the Mérida Initiative would become an annual funding package. It provides funding for immigration databases, surveillance planes, helicopters for drug interdiction, canines, ion scanners, and training for Mexican law enforcement.[57]

The U.S. Law Enforcement Response

There has been increased law enforcement effort on the issue of the flow of arms into Mexico. The lead agencies have been the ATF and the U.S. Immigrations and Customs Enforcement Agency of the U.S. Department of Homeland Security (ICE). The cooperation of these agencies has been hindered by

57. June S. Beittel and Clare Ribando Seelke, *Mérida Initiative for Mexico and Central America: Funding and Policy Issues* (Washington, D.C.: Congressional Research Service, 2009), available at www.crs.gov; Rebecca G. Rush and Colleen W. Cook, *Mérida Initiative: Background and Funding* (Washington, D.C.: Congressional Research Service, 2008), http://www.seguridadregional-fes.org/upload/4267-001_g.pdf.

numerous factors. Until recently, they operated under an outdated memorandum of understanding between the agencies. This resulted in redundant investigations including botched undercover investigations at gun shows.[58] Second, these agencies have fundamentally different characters and bureaucratic cultures; the ATF is under the Department of Justice, and ICE is under the new Department of Homeland Security.[59]

Project Gunrunner, which began in 2005 in cooperation with the Mexican government, has been the ATF's response to the flow of guns into Mexico. The project has increased the number of ATF agents working on the issue and has increased the training of Mexican law enforcement for tracing guns. It has also provided six ATF agents to the El Paso Intelligence Center to increase intelligence sharing on the United States–Mexico border.[60]

In 2008, ICE responded to the issue of the flow of guns into Mexico with its Operation Armas Cruzadas, which is designed to increase investigative leads and intelligence. ICE also has 10 Southwest Border Enforcement Teams (BEST teams), which facilitate interagency cooperation. ICE estimates it spends $15.1 million focused on disrupting the flow of guns into Mexico but notes that it spends over $1 billion in activities related to border enforcement.[61]

The Recent Mexican Government Response

Very recently, the Mexican government has also begun enforcing the border on its side. The added infrastructure—including "gates, cameras and vehicle scales—is meant to help curtail the flow of drug money and weapons to Mexican organized crime groups."[62] All cars crossing into Mexico will one day be checked at the border as they leave the United States. The stoppage times are intended to be short, at eight seconds per car, but that will translate into long lines of cars flowing across the border during peak traffic times. The Mexican government has begun this process at the Tijuana border crossing but has not thus far been effective in seizing arms and bulk cash shipments. On both sides of the border, smugglers are adept at avoiding checkpoints and corrupting border officers to wave them through. With spotters, the cartels and smuggling operations can identify and avoid checkpoints and searches. Mexico's SIAVE (System of Vehicle Control) program simply weighs the car as it enters Mexico and compares the weight with the profile of that car. The commonsense drug cartel countermeasure is to remove the spare tire, remove passengers, reduce fuel in the tank and add the equivalent weight in bulk cash or weapons.[63]

---

58. Ford, *Firearms Trafficking*.

59. The various agencies have different definitions of what a gun is; e.g., some agencies count scopes and various gun parts as entire guns.

60. Ford, *Firearms Trafficking*.

61. Ibid.

62. Richard Marosi, "Mexico Tightens Security at U.S. Border Crossings," *Los Angeles Times*, November 24, 2009, http://www.latimes.com/news/local/la-me-border-crossing25-2009nov25,0,3756431.story.

63. Ibid.; Tania Navarro, "Mexico's New Border Inspection System Has Business Leaders Worried," San Diego News Network, March 23, 2010, http://www.sdnn.com/sandiego/2009-11-17/mexico/mexicos-new-border-inspection-system-has-business-leaders-worried.

Policy Options

The flow of guns into Mexico from the United States must be viewed in the larger context of organized crime as a threat to the national security of both Mexico and the United States. It is funded by the U.S. demand for drugs in a symbiotic relationship. Ironically, Mexico's democratic consolidation and reductions in corruption and complicity with the drug trade have caused the increase in drug-related violence within Mexico. This has also increased "spillover" into the United States. Spin-off enforcer gangs of the AFO, like Los Palillos, have come to the United States and targeted for kidnapping members of the AFO in Southern California.[64] Also, Phoenix has become the kidnapping capital of the United States, as kidnapping cells from Mexican drug-trafficking organizations have moved there to enforce debt obligations owed to human traffickers by undocumented workers smuggled through Mexico.[65] Policy action on this issue is necessary to prevent the further spillover of violence into the United States and strengthen Mexico's state capacity during its democratic consolidation. This section provides policy options addressing the problem of the flow of guns from the United States into Mexico.

The first option is to strengthen domestic gun legislation. An effective strategy to eliminate the flow of arms from the United States into Mexico would be to increase gun control legislation at the federal level.[66] Unfortunately, this option is politically unfeasible due to the strength of the U.S. gun lobby and the low priority this issue will have for the Barack Obama administration as it grapples with issues like health care, job creation, terrorism, and major wars in Iraq and Afghanistan. Most gun legislation is the purview of the states, and states like Texas and Arizona are likely to have less support for gun control legislation than the American public as a whole. Although increased gun control could reduce the flow of guns from the United States into Mexico, it would likely only drive up the price of guns on the black market for Mexican drug cartels.[67]

The second option is to expand bilateral interdiction. The Mérida Initiative is the embodiment of the bilateral fight against organized crime for the United States and Mexico and should be regularized into an annual funding package. Central American countries like Guatemala, El Salvador, and Nicaragua are included with funding in the Mérida Initiative but are effectively an afterthought. They will need increased funding as Mexican traffickers, feeling the pressure in Mexico, push into Central America. Domestically, the United States should also increase funding for and expand ATF and ICE operations, especially Project Gunrunner. Mérida and Project Gunrunner have been the vehicles for bilateral cooperation on shared security issues between the United States and Mexico. To expand on the success of Project Gunrunner, the ATF would need

---

64. Solomon Moore, "War without Borders: How U.S. Became Stage for Mexican Drug Feud," *New York Times*, December 12, 2009, http://www.nytimes.com/2009/12/09/us/09border.html?_r=1&pagewanted=print.

65. Sam Quinones, "Phoenix, Kidnap-for-Ransom Capital," *Los Angeles Times*, February 12, 2009, http://www.latimes.com/news/nationworld/world/latinamerica/la-na-drug-kidnappings12-2009feb12,0,544773.story; "Mexico Security Memo November 10, 2008."

66. E.g., the United States could pass legislation to expand the reporting to the ATF multiple sales of rifles of AK and AR-15 clones/types preferred by Mexican drug cartels.

67. For a detailed description of proposed gun control legislation geared toward addressing this issue, see Violence Policy Center, "Iron River: Gun Violence & Illegal Firearms Trafficking on the US-Mexico Border," 2009, www.vpc.org/studies/indicted.pdf.

a dramatic increase in funding and an expansion of the number of agents and industry operation investigators to regulate U.S. gun sales and further reduce the flow of guns into Mexico.[68]

The third option is to ratify CIFTA. The Inter-American Convention against the Illicit Manufacturing and Trafficking of Firearms (CIFTA) would require all states belonging to the Organization of American States (OAS) to share information about illegal arms trafficking, properly document and share information on guns produced and sold within the hemisphere.[69] The United States is one of only 4 of 34 states in the OAS to sign, but fail to ratify, CIFTA. The treaty was signed in 1997 under President Bill Clinton but was never ratified in the Senate due to domestic gun lobby pressures. It is also unlikely to be ratified because gun control is a politically controversial issue which is likely to stir the passions of the Republican/libertarian base. The gun lobby views CIFTA as a backdoor means by which to enact domestic gun control legislation. Indeed, the success of CIFTA in addressing the issue of the flow of guns into Mexico is dependent upon the domestic legislation it would inspire for the United States to be in compliance with the terms of the treaty. As Johanna Mendelson-Forman describes in her piece on CIFTA (also part of this project), the ratification of CIFTA would be more of a moral victory for those who believe the United States is culpable for the flow of guns into Mexico, than it would be an effective means by which to prevent the flow of guns south.[70]

The fourth option is to legalize marijuana. In discussing the legalization of marijuana and its impact upon Mexican drug cartels and their demand for U.S. weapons, it is important to remember that legalization cannot be partial. A situation in which the ability to produce marijuana within the United States is so restricted as to prevent the sating of American demand will not eliminate the role of organized crime in the trafficking of marijuana. Only when large agribusiness has openly engaged in the U.S. production of marijuana will U.S. demand be sated and the role of organized crime in this market be eliminated.

The legalization of marijuana would have different effects upon the various Mexican drug cartels. The Arellano-Félix Organization (Tijuana Cartel) would likely be affected the most negatively because it is most dependent upon marijuana, having lost its Colombian cocaine connections.

The Sinaloa Cartel, led by Chapo Guzman, has maintained its profitable cocaine connections and thus would be least impacted by the legalization of marijuana. La Familia Michoacana would also be minimally affected because of its specialization in methamphetamine production and trafficking. The impact of the legalization of marijuana on the demand for arms from Mexican drug

---

68. It should also be noted that there have been American law enforcement agents working with vetted Mexican law enforcement teams since Operation United Eagles (2003). Also, U.S. intelligence agents may be embedding in Ciudad Juarez, according to the *Washington Post*, though this has been denied, probably due to Mexican sovereignty sensitivities. U.S. Department of Justice, *DEA History 2003–2008* (Washington, D.C.: U.S. Department of Justice, 2008), http://www.justice.gov/dea/pubs/history/2003-2008.pdf; William Booth, "U.S. to Embed Agents in Mexican Law Enforcement Units Battling Cartels in Juarez," *Washington Post*, February 24, 2010, http://www.washingtonpost.com/wp-dyn/content/article/2010/02/23/AR2010022305560_pf.html.

69. U.S. Department of State, Inter-American Convention against Illicit Manufacturing of and Trafficking in Firearms, 1997, http://www.state.gov/p/wha/rls/49907.htm.

70. Mendelson-Forman also describes how the passage of CIFTA would have important secondary effects. First, it would send a message to Latin American countries that the United States is committed to multilateralism and diplomacy on this issue. Second, it would create a deterrent effect by sending a message to gun merchants in the United States that the administration is committed to preventing the flow of guns south. Third, it would add another legal dimension (via an international treaty obligation) to U.S. gun laws.

cartels is difficult to predict. On the one hand, it would drive the profits and available gun money down for cartels like the AFO. On the other hand, it would further force them into a diversification of criminal activities like kidnappings and extortion. All these activities would increase their demand for weapons. The legalization of marijuana in the United States would certainly privilege the Sinaloa Cartel vis-à-vis the AFO in terms of its continued profitability and ability to purchase weaponry. The efficacy of the legalization of marijuana in reducing the demand for illegal guns in Mexico is difficult if not impossible to predict, given the myriad of relevant and changing factors.

Assessment of the Preferred Option: The Bilateral Interdiction Approach

Although domestic gun control legislation would be the most effective strategy for eliminating the flow of guns into Mexico, it is politically infeasible because of the strong lobby against it and the low priority of the issue domestically. It also would only serve to drive the prices of guns on the black market up for Mexican drug cartels. Conversely, the continuation of the Mérida Initiative into regular security assistance to Mexico and an expansion of ATF and ICE efforts to stop the flow of guns into Mexico, would be politically palatable and has demonstrated its potential effectiveness. It would also deepen the current and historic levels of institutional cooperation between the United States and Mexico. The Mérida Initiative also has the advantage of targeting organized crime generally, not just on the specific issue of arms trafficking.

With only approximately 5,000 total employees and 2,500 total agents, the ATF is stretched especially thin at its present level to meet this important challenge. Part of an effective interdiction approach would be to increase the number of ATF agents and industry operations investigators who monitor federal firearms licensee (FFL) compliance and identify suspicious trends in purchases. This would help to identify FFLs and straw purchasers operating deep in the United States that may be the source of the arms trafficked to Mexico. Regularizing the Mérida Initiative and providing funding for an increase in the number of ATF agents and Project Gunrunner would help to address the flow of guns south and further strengthen ties between Mexican and U.S. government officials.

The success of the ATF's Project Gunrunner Impact Teams (Grupo de Coordinacion de Armas, GRIT) is an example of what the ATF can do by enforcing existing legislation. As part of Project Gunrunner, the ATF sent 100 experienced agents and industry operation investigators in "GRIT" teams to the Houston area from April to August 2009. In that 120-day period, GRIT teams developed more than 1,100 leads that turned into 276 criminal cases.[71] In this period, GRIT teams were able to follow through on 87 percent of the leads developed. As a result of the efforts of these GRIT teams, the ATF seized 443 illegal firearms, 141,442 rounds of ammunition, 3 explosive devices, $165,234 in currency, 5 kilograms of cocaine, and 1,500 pounds of marijuana. The success

71. It should be noted that the 1,100 leads often led back to the same Mexican DTOs, which explains why those leads resulted in fewer cases. It should be further noted that the ATF is capped by Congress in the number of agents it can have. GRIT teams exhaust existing agents, and the travel cost for their testimonies is also not budgeted. Thus, an expansion of the ATF must come in the total number of agents allowed under the cap and not just the creation of GRIT teams, which pull agents from other locales. Interestingly, the current cap on the number of agents that the ATF can employ is lower than it was in 1926 during Prohibition, when it was at its peak of 2,600. Currently, the ATF has some 5,000 employees and 2,562 agents. Metcalfe, *Whispering Wires: The Tragic Tale of an American Bootlegger.*

of the GRIT teams demonstrates what the ATF can accomplish in cooperation with its Mexican counterparts when properly resourced.[72] With more, the ATF can do more.

Consequences of Choosing the Preferred Option

Expanding bilateral arms trafficking interdiction efforts and making the Mérida Initiative a long-term source of funding for Mexico is an expensive proposition. Interdiction efforts are always more expensive than addressing root causes like drug consumption. Unfortunately, it is often politically infeasible to choose to legalize and regulate the consumption of drugs. Although marijuana may be more socially acceptable—indeed, a proposition on the November 2010 California elections would potentially legalize it for recreational use in California—the devil is in the details of the legislation. Legalizing use without legalizing production in large quantities will not address the supply-and-demand factors that contribute to the drug war and violence in Mexico. Legalization of drugs would also have to include the legalization of production by large scale U.S. agribusiness to address its contribution to violence in Mexico.

Conversely, the Mérida Initiative provides the equipment and funding necessary to strengthen Mexican military and law enforcement institutions as Mexico struggles with drug cartels that are increasingly heavily armed. An expansion of the ATF and Project Gunrunner especially would further deepen these cross-border ties, strengthen the capacity of the Mexican state vis-à-vis organized crime, and allow the United States to better regulate the sale of guns here in the United States to prevent their illegal acquisition by drug-trafficking organizations. This institutionalization of bilateral cooperation with Mexico, in conjunction with Calderón's five-pillar strategy, will fortify the Mexican state through its struggle with the cartels and beyond.

72. ATF, "Project Gunrunner Success Statistics."

APPENDIX B
MEXICAN MONEY LAUNDERING
A STUDY IN CROSS-BORDER CURRENCY FLOWS, A PERMEABLE FINANCIAL SERVICES SECTOR, AND REGULATORY ARBITRAGE

Jonathan M. Winer

Wholly apart from the exacerbating factor of the cross-border drug trade, local conditions have long made Mexico vulnerable to domestic money laundering. These conditions include:

- a substantial underground economy, amounting to between 30 and 50 percent of its formal economy, in which off-the-books income is the norm;
- many communities without access to banks whose people rely on informal money services businesses when they need to move beyond hand-to-hand exchanges of currency for remittances or broader access to the formal economy;
- a historically weak system of financial institution supervision which resulted in the collapse of the entire domestic commercial banking system in 1994 and was then largely replaced by foreign-origin financial institutions primarily focused on serving upper-end commercial and affluent sectors of the population;
- weak enforcement of regulatory controls on financial institutions in general, with infrequent imposition of sanctions for failure to abide by formal rules of any kind, let alone those intended to control money laundering;
- minimal to nonexistent enforcement of anti-money-laundering laws on licensed financial institutions, and limited—and only recent—enforcement of such laws against unregistered *casas de cambio* (currency exchange houses);
- multiple sources for illicit funds to launder, including domestic drug production and trafficking, arms smuggling, people smuggling, stolen cars, kidnapping, corruption, and protection rackets.

These domestic money-laundering vulnerabilities provide an environment in which it has been easy for launderers to place the proceeds of the continual, massive flow of bulk currency generated and collected by the drug trade within the United States before moving south back to Mexico. Southern-bound bulk currency shipments to Mexico are estimated by the U.S. National Drug Intelligence Center as involving most of the $18 billion to $39 billion in annual gross wholesale proceeds from illicit drug distribution in the United States.[1]

---

1. "Testimony of William McMahon, Deputy Assistant Director for Field Operations, Bureau of Alcohol, Tobacco, Firearms and Explosives, U.S. Department of Justice, and Anthony P. Placido, Assistant Administrator for Intelligence, Drug Enforcement Administration, U.S. Department of Justice," U.S. House of Representatives, Committee on Homeland Security, Subcommittee on Border, Maritime, and Global Counterterrorism" July 16, 2009. The figure was produced by multiplying the total quantity of Mexico- and Colombia-produced drugs available at the wholesale level in the United States by the wholesale prices for those drugs.

Mexico's banking statistics provide indirect confirmation of the movement of funds south from the United States. As Mexican attorney general Eduardo Medina Mora told the Mexican Congress in October 2007, Mexican banks receive about $1 billion from their U.S. counterparts annually but return up to $16 billion, of which about $10 billion "does not have an explanation . . . and could be attributed to the flow of drug-trafficking money."[2]

Whether the actual amount is at the annual floor of $10 billion in drug money laundered from the United States or is near the annual ceiling of $39 billion, the total narcotics funds from the United States laundered in Mexico represents an important part of Mexico's domestic economy. For comparison, in 1995, Mexico's total revenue from tourism was $12 billion.[3] For a remarkably long period, it has been less costly, more efficient, and safer for drug traffickers to physically transport the proceeds of drug trafficking to Mexico than to deposit it in U.S. financial institutions by any means, direct or indirect. The bulk currency is transported by car and truck from wherever it is generated in the United States across the Mexican border and from there continues south to Panama and Colombia, is stored in stash hours, or is placed into Mexico's payments system.

Bulk currency movements are not the sole means by which funds are laundered to and within Mexico. Other mechanisms for laundering drug money from the United States to Mexico include remittances through U.S. money services businesses back to Mexico; the use of the Black Market Peso Exchange (BMPE) to purchase goods in the United States and elsewhere from drug money for resale in Mexico, and bulk purchases of stored value cards, preloaded with cash, which can then be used in automated teller machines in Mexico. Drug money launderers constantly innovate, seeking greater speed, efficiency, and safety. But the other techniques provide merely a steady stream of funds going south, compared with the river of bulk currency.[4]

To date, nothing has replaced the simple fact that the 2,000-mile U.S.-Mexican border is even less of a barrier for smugglers sending currency south then it is for those sending narcotics north. Mexican countersmuggling capabilities remain weak and, too often, corrupt. For its part, the United States focuses most of the customs resources on its southern border on keeping goods out of the United States as they go north, rather than inspecting southern-bound goods. For this reason, Mexico has long complained that it has been inundated with small arms smuggled into Mexico from the United States. Its officials have objected less loudly to the contemporaneous smuggling of endless truckloads of bulk currency at the same border crossings.

Most of the bulk currency generated by the drug trade leaves the United States through the four states bordering Mexico: Texas, Arizona, New Mexico, and California. From there, the currency goes to destinations in Mexico, which are only mysterious if one ignores the major cases that have been brought in recent years against certain businesses in the northern states of Mexico. Once these drug proceeds are successfully smuggled—usually by truck—into Mexico, one of several techniques is used to place the funds:

---

2. Economist.com, January 31, 2008, cited by Douglas Farah in International Strategy Center report, "Money Laundering and Bulk Cash Smuggling: Challenges for the U.S.-Mexico Border, June 19, 2009, http://www.strategycenter.net/research/pubID.203/pub_detail.asp.

3. International Monetary Fund, *Mexico: Detailed Assessment Report on Anti-Money-Laundering and Combating the Financing of Terrorism*, IMF Country Report 09/7 (Washington, D.C.: International Monetary Fund, 2009), paragraph 2.

4. See, e.g., "Testimony of Andrew Selee, Director of the Mexico Institute, Woodrow Wilson Center before the House Subcommittee on National Security and Foreign Affairs of the Committee on Oversight and Government Reform," March 12, 2009.

- The bulk currency is deposited into a *casa de cambio*. The *casa de cambio* then places the funds in a Mexican financial institution on the premise that the funds have been placed with it by its retail customers in Mexico. The Mexican financial institution then "layers" the funds to another bank, either in Mexico or elsewhere, where they can be used by the drug-trafficking organization.
- The currency is transported back into the United States by a *casa de cambio* through an armored car or courier service. These are often "precleared" because the funds are presented as generated from legitimate financial transactions and have documentation from the customer regarding the legitimacy of the funds. After the car or courier has moved the funds back through the United States–Mexico border, the cash typically is deposited in a U.S. bank account on behalf of a Mexican *casa de cambio* or financial institution. Those that are not cleared, but that involve the smuggling funds that have had no layering, are typically smuggled beyond false panels in trucks heading for the United States.
- The currency is placed in a cash-intensive business, such as a restaurant, bar, or consumer goods store, which then deposits it in a financial institution as the proceeds of the cash activity.

Deposits into the formal banking system that have been fully laundered through layering, thereby hiding the original ownership and treating the proceeds as the earnings of a legitimate business, are primarily made for one of two purposes—payoffs to others involved in trafficking in other countries or investment of profits. Immediate business needs, to pay those involved in the drug production or transit, are ordinarily taken care of in cash. Large amounts of currency for operating funds are retained in "stash sites," typically held in personal residences, not only in transit areas, but in urban areas or rural areas—wherever it is convenient and safe for the traffickers. Other quantities of currency leave Mexico to go south, through Panama, for placement into the world's financial system through Panamanian banks and shell companies, or used for purchasing goods in the Colon Free Zone through the BMPE. Still more currency goes even further south, into Colombia, where it has opportunities similar to those in Panama to be laundered through the purchase of goods in the BMPE or by deposit into legitimate banks. The funds remaining in Mexico are integrated into the country's economy and financial sector through the purchase of luxury cars and real estate and by being invested in a variety of small businesses.[5]

The persistence and volume of bulk currency smuggling from the United States to Mexico as the principal mechanism by which laundered drug money is placed into the payments system reflects a fundamental reality about the differences between the controls on financial institutions in the United States and those in Mexico. Rather than trying to deposit currency directly through any means in the United States, drug traffickers find it cheaper, safer, and more efficient to smuggle currency thousands of miles, despite checkpoints and a national border, to get bulk currency into Mexico, where it can be introduced into the payments system. This practice in turn reflects two other practical calculations for those laundering funds for the drug traffickers. The first calculation is that the southern border of the United States is readily permeable and involves few risks to smugglers. The second calculation is that Mexico's financial regulatory and enforcement system will be no more a barrier than are the law enforcement controls at the border.

The bulk currency phenomenon reflects regulatory and enforcement arbitrage in a very pure form. On the U.S. side of the border, laundering the currency proceeds of drug trafficking is

5. International Monetary Fund, *Mexico*, paragraph 54.

comparatively difficult. But on the Mexican side, it is still, even in 2010, comparatively easy. Ironically, it has also been easy for Mexican *casas de cambio* to enter into relations with U.S. banks that enable them to send back for deposit to these banks funds from drug traffickers that never would have been accepted by the banks without having first been laundered through the Mexican *casas de cambio*.[6]

This appendix summarizes how (and why) Mexico has become the largest launderer of U.S.-denominated bulk currency in the world; the major modalities of Mexican money laundering, and its relationship with cross-border drug-trafficking activity between Mexico and the United States. It summarizes Mexican regulation and enforcement of international money-laundering norms, reviews patterns of laundering revealed by U.S. and Mexican enforcement activities, and highlights emerging trends. Finally, it suggests possible indicators of change in Mexican money-laundering activity and possible policy options to increase the risks for drug money launderers to place their funds in Mexico.

Prevalence and Magnitude

The government of Mexico has told the International Monetary Fund that it can make no estimates of the level of money laundering in Mexico. Mexican officials have stated that they have not been able to develop an appropriate methodology to undertake such estimates, noting in particular the impossibility of distinguishing between legitimate remittances from Mexicans working in the United States and payments involving Mexico's informal economy and the proceeds of criminal activity.[7]

An Australian economist, John Walker, has undertaken global analyses of money laundering by country since the late 1990s, looking at the relative size of criminal proceeds from a set of different criminal activities that include narcotics smuggling, other forms of smuggling, frauds, and theft. As of 2002, his model estimated total Mexican money laundering involving narcotics and other criminal activity, but not including corruption, to be $26 billion a year.[8] In March 2009, the U.S. Department of State estimated that some $25 billion in funds generated by narcotics trafficking are circulating within Mexico's formal financial system at any time.[9]

---

6. E.g., the *Wall Street Journal* reported in 2008 that "internal emails and documents filed in federal courts in Miami, Chicago and New York describe former ties between Wachovia and money-changing firms. In a case in U.S. Court in Miami, federal agents seized more than $11 million in 23 Wachovia accounts belonging to Casa de Cambio Puebla, a Mexican chain. U.S. and Mexican prosecutors said they believed the money was being laundered, according to legal papers filed by Puebla. Mexican police raided Puebla offices last fall, alleging relationships with a major drug cartel." "Wachovia Is Under Scrutiny in Latin Drug-Money Probe," *Wall Street Journal*, April 26, 2008.

7. International Monetary Fund, *Mexico*, paragraph 50.

8. John Walker, "Estimating Illicit Flows: Asking the Right Questions," 2009, www.johnwalkercrimetrendsanalysis.com.au/Oslo.ppt.

9. U.S. Department of State, *State Department International Narcotics Control Strategy Report (INCSR) 2009, Volume 2, Mexico*, http://www.state.gov/p/inl/rls/nrcrpt/2009/vol2/index.htm (hereafter *INSCR 2009*). The State Department's *International Narcotics Control Strategy Report (INCSR) 2010, Volume 2, Mexico* (hereafter *INCSR 2010*), released on March 1, 2010, provides a range of estimates from $8 billion to $25 billion being repatriated to Mexico from the United States annually by drug-trafficking organizations, without specifying the basis for the estimate or its range (http://www.state.gov/documents/organization/137429.pdf). Volume 1 of *INCSR 2010* provides an estimate of $15 billion to $30 billion generated by Mexican drug traffickers in the United States, which it states is "mostly" repatriated to Mexico through bulk currency,

The U.S. National Drug Intelligence Center (NDIC) estimates that Mexican and Colombian drug-trafficking organizations generate, remove, and launder between $18 billion and $39 billion in wholesale drug proceeds from the United States annually, a large portion of which is bulk-smuggled out of the United States at the southwestern border. The NDIC derives these figures by multiplying the total quantity of Mexico- and Colombia-produced drugs available at the wholesale level in the United States by the wholesale prices for those drugs. The NDIC further analyzed the volume of repatriated U.S. banknotes and found that differences in volume indicate significant bulk cash smuggling along the United States–Mexico border. In 2009, the NDIC found that at least $17.2 billion in U.S. banknotes was transported to Mexico through illicit nonbank channels over a two-year period. Notably, no similar pattern was found with Canada.[10] Separately, the Mexico Institute of the Woodrow Wilson International Center for Scholars estimated the total amount of drug money laundered in Mexico as between $15 billion and $25 billion.[11] By comparison, Mexico is spending an estimated $11 billion on security across the board, suggesting that the traffickers have greater revenues to apply to smuggle drugs than the government of Mexico has to defend against them.[12]

The sums laundered from illicit narcotics probably represent 90 percent or more of the total money laundered in Mexico, apart from the proceeds of corruption. Other than narcotics, the major sources of funds for laundering include stolen cars, which are estimated to represent about $7.6 billion a year in total U.S. losses, only a portion of which is then transported through Mexico;[13] people smuggling, estimated to represent just $300 million a year by the Library of Congress as of 2002; and gun smuggling, which, due to the relatively low cost of firearms, appears to amount to millions of dollars rather than billions of dollars a year.[14]

Although other forms of criminal activity generate illicit proceeds that need to be placed, layered, and integrated in Mexico's financial system, Mexico's money-laundering problem is first, foremost, and fundamentally a drug-money-laundering problem. The vast preponderance of the proceeds of North American drug consumption are generated in the United States and repatriated to Mexico.

---

again with no explanation of the analytic basis of the range estimate, or the difference between that figure and the figure used elsewhere in the same report (http://www.state.gov/documents/organization/137411.pdf).

10. NDIC, "National Drug Threat Assessment," December 2008, http://www.justice.gov/ndic/pubs31/31379/31379p.pdf.

11. Mexico Institute, Woodrow Wilson International Center for Scholars, *The United States and Mexico: Towards a Strategic Partnership* (Washington, D.C.: Woodrow Wilson International Center for Scholars, 2009).

12. Manuel Suárez-Mier, legal attaché, Embassy of Mexico, provided the $11 billion total Mexican security spending statistic in his remarks at "Transnational Criminal Organizations in the Americas: Responding to the Growing Threat," colloquium, George Washington University, January 29, 2009. Of course, not all the funds spent by Mexico on security are to counter the drug traffickers, and not all the resources available to the drug traffickers are used to evade law enforcement.

13. See National Insurance Crime Bureau statistics at https://www.nicb.org/theft_and_fraud_awareness/brochures.

14. See, e.g., Violence Prevention Center, "Indicted: Types of Firearms and Methods of Gun Trafficking from the United States to Mexico as Revealed in U.S. Court Documents," April 2009, http://www.vpc.org/studies/indicted.pdf.

Inherent Vulnerabilities

Cash is inherently vulnerable to money laundering, as it can change hands leaving less of a trail than can electronic funds, thereby facilitating tax and regulatory avoidance.. For much of Mexico's population, for differing reasons in urban and rural areas, electronic transactions remain the exception, and those in cash are the norm.

A Large Informal Economy

Mexico's underground economy is among the highest in Latin America, estimated by academic experts at 40 to 60 percent during the 1990s,[15] with recent estimates ranging from a low of 27 percent to a high of 50 percent.[16] The informal sector has many components within Mexico's overall economy, of which some 70 percent is in the service sector, 26 percent in manufacturing, and just 4 percent in agriculture.[17] In urban areas, it includes as many as 1 million "street vendors" (*vendedores ambulantes*), who sell food and consumer goods, many of which are of uncertain or illicit provenance.[18] A detailed International Labor Organization (ILO) study published in 2002 found that informal employment accounted for 64 percent of total employment in Mexico in the late 1990s, and 55 percent of nonagricultural employment. The ILO found that informal employment outside agriculture was almost evenly divided between employment in informal enterprises and informal jobs outside informal enterprises and included both disguised workers and perennial temporary workers, who receive their payments in cash. The ILO found that Mexico's informal sector included the overwhelming majority of those employed in agriculture (94 percent), construction and trade (both 73 percent), and transportation (63 percent). The ILO found that 22 percent of all financial services industry activity also related to the informal economy.[19]

Vulnerability to money laundering is inherent in this labor structure. With a very large portion of the economy operating on a cash basis, the population is used to moving currency into and out of the formal sector for quotidian purposes. At the same time, the dividing line between licit and illicit is blurred, with a minimal visible difference between, for example, the sale of goods

---

15. Fredrich Schneider, "Shadow Economy," Linz University, June 2002, http://www.econ.jku.at/members/Schneider/files/publications/Encyclopedia.PDF.

16. See, e.g., Andreas Buehn and Friedrich Schneider, "Corruption and the Shadow Economy: A Structural Equation Model Approach, Linz University, May 2009, estimating the underground economy in Mexico to be 32.6 percent, http://www.econ.jku.at/members/Schneider/files/publications/CorrShadow_FirstDraft_WorkingPaper.pdf. Also see F. Schneider and D. Enste, "Shadow Economies: Size, Causes and Consequences," *Journal of Economic Literature*, 38 (2000): 77–114; and a study in which academics at the University of Denver used satellite images and electrical consumption comparisons to estimate Mexico's economy as about 50 percent higher than that officially reported: Tilottama Ghosh et al., "Estimation of Mexico's Informal Economy and Remittances Using Nighttime Imagery," 2009, http://www.mdpi.com/2072-4292/1/3/418/pdf.

17. International Monetary Fund, *Mexico*, paragraph 39.

18. See, e.g., John Cross, "Formalizing the Informal Economy: The Case of Street Vendors in Mexico City," American University in Cairo, 1995, http://www.cs.uwaterloo.ca/~alopez-o/politics/streetv.html. See also Sergio Solache, "Counterfeit Goods Market Explodes across Mexico," *Arizona Republic*, October 15, 2006, http://www.azcentral.com/arizonarepublic/business/articles/1015biz-mex-counterfeit1015.html.

19. International Labor Organization, "Women and Men in the Informal Economy: A Statistical Picture," 2002, http://www.wiego.org/publications/women percent20and percent20men percent20in percent20the percent20informal percent20economy.pdf, which includes a detailed case study on Mexican unemployment and underemployment.

that have been purchased legitimately from a manufacturer, and those that are purchased from a free zone as part of the BMPE. The substantial portion of the total financial sector associated with the informal economy further illustrates the permeability between the legitimate and the underground in Mexico, as informal money services businesses of any scope routinely move funds into the formal financial services sector for both transactions and deposits. The finding that the transportation sector is largely informal is consistent with the fact that Mexican truckers are typically paid in cash on a transactional basis, rather than paid salaries. Transactional, cash payments are also typical of arrangements for truckers involved in the transportation of narcotics north and currency south.[20]

Elements feeding the informal economy in Mexico include excessive labor regulation and taxes, which create incentives to remain off the books; recurrent inflation, which has destabilized the credit sector, injured small and medium-sized enterprises in the formal sector, and encouraged black markets; and stagnant salaries in much of the formal sector, which have risen at rates below inflation, creating incentives for employees to maintain their standard of living by avoiding taxation by staying in unreported jobs.[21] These conditions also breed corruption and encourage individuals to supplement their incomes with not only off-the-books activity but also complicity in criminal activity.

Unbanked Areas

Rural areas in Mexico have long had minimal involvement in the banking system, a tradition of tax avoidance, and an orientation toward keeping cash under the mattress. Private commercial banks have a presence in only about one-sixth of the country's political divisions—just 465 of its 2,439 municipalities. A government-owned development bank and a number of small financial intermediaries cover an additional 525 municipalities, leaving 1,449 municipalities and their total population of almost 14 million with little, if any access, to formal financial services.[22] In 2009, the IMF found that just 20 percent of Mexico's population had access to the country's banks.[23]

The result is that these areas rely on unlicensed money transmitters both to receive and to transmit funds. Such unlicensed firms in turn have relationships with licensed money transmitters or with banks in Mexico, depositing and withdrawing large sums of cash as needed. Again, this structure is exceedingly vulnerable to money laundering and contains essentially no inherent controls against it.

---

20. See, e.g., "Statement of Janice Ayala, Deputy Assistant Director Office of Investigations, U.S. Immigrations and Customs Enforcement, Department of Homeland Security, Hearing on 'Cargo Security at Land Ports of Entry: Are We Meeting the Challenge,' Committee on Homeland Security, Subcommittee on Border, Maritime, and Global Counterterrorism," October 22, 2009, finding Mexican drug-trafficking organizations using tractor-trailer trucks to smuggle bulk currency south following drug shipments north; www.ice.gov/doclib/pi/news/testimonies/091022ayala.doc. *A recent* anecdotal description is contained in "Along U.S.-Mexico Border, a Torrent of Illicit Cash," *New York Times*, December 25, 1999, http://www.nytimes.com/2009/12/26/world/americas/26laredo.html?pagewanted=all.

21. Brambila Macias and Jose Ca', "Modeling the Informal Economy in Mexico: A Structural Equation Approach," Foscari University, April 2008, http://mpra.ub.uni-muenchen.de/8504/1/MPRA_paper_8504.pdf.

22. *Economic Letter: Insights from the Federal Reserve Bank of Dallas* 3, no. 7 (July 2008), http://www.dallasfed.org/research/eclett/2008/el0807.html.

23. International Monetary Fund, *Mexico*, paragraph 68.

Remittances

Remittances have long been an important part of the Mexican economy, but their relative importance to Mexico has changed as a result of the long-term structural unemployment and lower wages that arose in the wake of the 1994 peso crisis. A 2005 World Bank study on U.S.–Mexican remittances found that following the 1994 peso crisis, worker remittances grew rapidly, becoming by 2003 Mexico's second-largest source of external finance after oil, eclipsing foreign direct investment and tourism receipts. The World Bank found that remittance flows received in Mexico during 2003 surpassed $13 billion, a number that the U.S. Department of State found had grown to $24 billion by 2007.[24]

Most of the funds that move through remittances are the proceeds of work by Mexican immigrants to the United States. However, the structure of the remittance business also makes that mechanism vulnerable to laundering illicit funds. Essentially, any Mexican can obtain an identification card issued by a Mexican consular office and then use that identification to execute a remittance without having to open a bank account. Although this system eases access for immigrants to licit remittances, it creates a system that is open to money laundering. As of 2007, electronic transfers accounted for 95 percent of all remittances to Mexico, but little of this involved large commercial banks on either side. Instead, funds tend to be deposited on the U.S. side with money transmitters and received on the Mexican side by *cajas populares* and *cajas solidarias* (cooperatives serving low-income populations). The lack of identification requirements on either side of the transaction creates laundering opportunities for bulk currency transactions at either or both ends.[25]

Unlicensed Money Services Businesses

Although currency exchanges have a major part of the Mexican financial services market overall, Mexico has licensed only 24 currency exchange and money remittance businesses (*casas de cambio*), as of 2009. Such licenses are required for a firm if it engages in currency exchanges in a "habitual manner," which is defined so as to exclude the 4,380 unlicensed money transmitters and foreign exchange centers operating in the country acknowledged by the Mexican authorities, of which only 3,069 are even registered with the Mexican authorities, according to Mexican statistics. The IMF reports that industry associations estimate that the actual number of unlicensed money transmitters in Mexico exceeds 7,000.[26] As of 2005, there were more than 1,000 unlicensed but registered *casas de cambio* located directly at Mexico's northern border with the United States.[27]

The large number of unlicensed and unregistered currency exchanges is a consequence of Mexico having defined its regulatory requirements with numerous exclusions. For example, a

---

24. Raúl Hernández-Coss, *The U.S.-Mexico Remittance Corridor: Lessons on Shifting from Informal to Formal Transfer Systems*, World Bank Policy Research Working Paper, 2005, http://www1.worldbank.org/finance/html/amlcft/docs/Rem_CS/US-Mexico_Remittance_Corridor_WP.pdf.
25. See the findings in ibid.
26. See International Monetary Fund, *Mexico*, paragraph 186.
27. "U. S. Money Laundering Threat Assessment," December 2005, http://www.ustreas.gov/offices/enforcement/pdf/mlta.pdf.

registered (and in practice, largely unregulated) funds transmitter does not have to be licensed if it limits transactions with any individual up to a threshold of $10,000 per customer per day. Although unregistered transmitters are illegal, there are thousands of them, who in turn have relationships with registered or licensed institutions. In practice, even the registered transmitters have little oversight in practice, making them highly vulnerable to being used to launder money, receiving and delivering cash as needed throughout the country with minimal documentation requirements.[28] Remarkably, currency exchange and money remittance services that are carried out in border areas, such as those adjacent to the United States, and in free zones, along with firms that "regularly conduct business with foreigners," are not required to be licensed.

The services provided by Mexican currency exchange houses allow money launderers to exchange large quantities of small-denomination bills for large-denomination bills of the same or different currency, which can then be easily bulk shipped or deposited in bank accounts. They are also used to layer funds through a series of transfers to hide their origin, as when a *casa de cambio* deposits the cash it has received from a customer into its own account at a commercial bank. Generally, these firms have no anti-money-laundering controls in place, and in 2005 the United States estimated that a typical *casa de cambio* on the U.S.–Mexican border launders as much as $5 million a month, primarily on behalf of drug traffickers.[29]

Legal, Regulatory, and Enforcement Vulnerabilities

In recent years, Mexico has put a national system of anti-money laundering regulations into place governing its financial institutions, but important components of the sector have remained outside the controls. While Mexico's various forms of depository institutions are directly subject to the regulations, they do not cover Mexico's thousands of small money exchange houses, many of which remain unlicensed.

Structural Limitations and the Unlicensed Exchange Houses

In 1992, Mexico completed privatizing its commercial banks, which became insolvent during the peso crisis just two years later. Mexico then opened itself up to allowing foreign banks full ownership of most of its major commercial lending institutions, retaining only a small market share for domestic banks. As of 2009, 80 percent of the country's total financial sector assets was controlled by foreign-based financial institutions.[30] Currently, there are 46 banks, including 6 development banks and 71 foreign financial representative offices, operating in Mexico, as well as 95 insur-

---

28. See International Monetary Fund, *Mexico*, paragraphs 77–78.

29. "U. S. Money Laundering Threat Assessment."

30. Before the North American Free Trade Agreement (NAFTA), individual foreign banks could hold no more than 5 percent of a Mexican bank, and total foreign ownership in any single bank was limited to 30 percent, except a branch of Citibank. NAFTA opened the Mexican banking system to foreign banks. Following the peso crisis, financial reforms allowed foreign investors to acquire all or part of most existing banks. The Mexican commercial banking system currently consists of 11 domestic and 19 that are foreign owned. The foreign banks include 9 U.S. institutions, 2 Spanish banks, 6 other European banks, 1 Canadian bank, and 1 Japanese bank. Foreign banks now hold nearly 79 percent of total commercial bank assets. Together, BBVA, Citigroup, and BSCH hold 66 percent of these assets. See Federal Reserve Bank of Dallas, "Beyond the Border: Financial Globalization: Manna or Menace? The Case of Mexican Banking," *Southwest Economy*, issue 1 (January–February 2002).

ance companies, 479 investment companies, 155 credit unions, and 24 *casas de cambio*. The large, mostly foreign-owned financial institutions are all subject to anti-money-laundering laws and to centralized financial institution supervision. But the formal anti-money-laundering coverage applicable to these institutions is undermined by the practical reality that the same rules do not apply to the funds or institutions that *feed* these regulated institutions.

Because most of the country is unbanked, the banks are fed with transfers from thousands of unlicensed *casas de cambio*.[31] Even those that are licensed are largely unsupervised, as limited staff resources have prevented Mexico's financial regulators from inspecting most of them. As of late 2009, only 800 anti-money-laundering inspections had been undertaken by Mexican regulators of the 7,000 or more institutions theoretically covered under Mexican law.[32] As the IMF found in 2009, the failure to adequately supervise these *casas de cambio* has consequences for the rest of the country's anti-money-laundering controls because, "there is a potential of contagion risk for other financial institutions, e.g., banks that transact with these businesses."[33]

As a result of their relationship with Mexican financial institutions, the U.S. Department of the Treasury in 2006 warned U.S. banks to be more careful to guard against being drawn into Mexican bulk money-laundering transactions. The analysis is a provocative one. It suggests that as U.S. financial institutions put more effective anti-money-laundering controls in place after the 9/11 attacks and the enactment of Title III of the Patriot Act, the drug traffickers found it was easier to launder the funds in Mexico, with the collusion of Mexican banks. As Treasury found:

> The combined efforts of U.S. financial institutions and U.S. law enforcement . . . have made it increasingly difficult for narcotics traffickers to place their illicit currency proceeds directly into U.S. financial institutions. As a result, U.S. law enforcement has observed a dramatic increase in the smuggling of bulk cash proceeds from the sale of narcotics and other criminal activities from the United States into Mexico. Once the U.S. currency is in Mexico, numerous layered transactions may be used to disguise its origins, after which it may be returned directly to the United States or further transshipped to or through other jurisdictions.[34]

Factors that Treasury found indicating collusion by Mexican banks included the sharp increase in the sale of large-denomination U.S. bank notes to Mexican institutions by U.S. banks; small-denomination U.S. bank notes smuggled into Mexico were being exchanged for large-denomination U.S. bank notes possessed by Mexican financial institutions. Treasury also found deposits of currency and third-party items by Mexican *casas de cambio* to their accounts at Mexican financial institutions, followed by direct wire transfers to the *casas de cambio*'s accounts at U.S. financial institutions.[35]

All these practices suggest that, while anti-money-laundering policies and procedures at Mexico's major banks may limit the ability of money launderers to maintain direct relationships with those institutions to place their funds, such direct relationships are unnecessary. They can be maintained by the *casas de cambio*, which then place the funds into the formal banking system with no apparent impediments. Notably, not only Mexican banks but also U.S. banks have main-

---

31. International Monetary Fund, *Mexico*, paragraph 22.
32. Ibid., paragraph 28.
33. Ibid.
34. U.S. Treasury Department, "Advisory, FIN-2006-A003, Issued April 28, 2006, Subject: Guidance to Financial Institutions on the Repatriation of Currency Smuggled into Mexico from the United States."
35. Ibid.

tained relationships with the *casas de cambio*, enabling them to place very large amounts of drug proceeds into the formal financial system.

For example, in a case involving Wachovia, in 2007, federal agents seized more than $11 million in apparent drug proceeds from 23 Wachovia accounts belonging to Casa de Cambio Puebla, which is a chain of Mexican funds transmission outlets. Wachovia reportedly provided the Mexican *casa de cambio* with lines of credit, overdraft privileges, and remittance-processing services, with unsecured lines of credit exceeding $100 million a day.[36] Such substantial amounts raise obvious questions about due diligence on the U.S. side, and whether know-your-customer controls are meaningful, even at large U.S. banks, so long as they are not exposed to drug money at the *placement*, rather than the *layering*, phase.[37]

The Lack of Regulation of the Informal Economy

Beyond the issues of inadequate licensing and regulation of Mexican money services businesses lies the reality of Mexico's large informal economy and cash generation. Because so much of Mexico's economy operates using physical currency rather than electronic payments, numerous local businesses, in what might otherwise be legitimate economic sectors, are available to gather up illicit funds and launder them through Mexico's banks as if they are generated by the licit activity of these businesses. These institutions—such as automobile dealers, restaurants, supermarkets, clothing stores, and even personal services purposes—are not covered by Mexico's anti-money-laundering laws and have no meaningful controls in place. In recent years, multiple U.S. and Mexican narcotics enforcement cases have found such commercial firms to operate as little more than fronts for drug traffickers, especially those near the U.S.-Mexican border.[38]

Minimal Enforcement in Practice

As the IMF found in its 2009 mutual assessment undertaken of Mexico, while Mexico has anti-money-laundering laws in place in theory, in reality, very few cases of money laundering are actually investigated. During a period of 20 years (1989–2009), Mexico obtained just 25 convictions for money laundering,[39] with 5 other cases ending in acquittals.[40] From 2003 through 2007, a period in which $100 billion or more was laundered overall in Mexico—based on gross estimates—the Mexican authorities provisionally seized a total of $253 million, representing about one-quarter of 1 percent of the total.[41] Of that amount, just $67.5 million represent seizures of cash, represent-

36. "Wachovia Is Under Scrutiny."

37. The three phases of money laundering are placement, which is when illicit proceeds are placed with a financial institution; layering, which is the process of moving the illicit funds through the financial system so that they are cleaned and can be reused; and integration, which is the process of disbursing the funds in a fashion where they appear to be clean and are used to purchase something.

38. See, e.g., "Organized Crime in Mexico," STRATFOR, March 11, 2008 http://www.stratfor.com/memberships/112710/analysis/organized_crime_mexico; and Drug Enforcement Administration, "DEA Money Laundering," summary, http://www.justice.gov/dea/programs/money.htm.

39. International Monetary Fund, *Mexico*, paragraph 4.

40. Ibid., paragraph 13.

41. See the chart on provisional seizures given by International Monetary Fund, *Mexico*, paragraph 322. In 2009, the U.S. Department of State found that Mexican law enforcement was able to attack 1 percent of what it estimated as $25 billion circulating illegally in the banking system. It is not clear what this assess-

ing about one-sixteenth of 1 percent of the total.[42] Few of these cases resulted from investigations based on an analysis of financial transactions at financial institutions. Instead, almost all of them resulted from cash seizures at the airports and borders, where the defendants were unable to explain the source of large amounts of cash.[43] Drug traffickers are used to paying 5 to 10 percent of the total value of the narcotics to have illicit proceeds laundered.[44] Against such commissions, the "law enforcement tax" represents a very minor part of the cost of doing business.

Drug money seizures reflect the overall enforcement situation, in which few cases of any type are made, not just those involving money laundering. Although Mexico has a financial intelligence unit to receive and analyze cases of suspicious activity, when it reports cases to Mexican prosecutors, they seldom are able to find evidence that there has been underlying criminal activity, due to resource constraints. According to the IMF, Mexican officials reported that of every 100 crimes reported to Mexico's judiciary, only 5 percent ever reach a judicial ruling.[45]

Banks and other types of financial institutions have had little to fear for failure to implement fully anti-money-laundering policies and procedures. There are four principal supervisory authorities responsible for anti-money-laundering / combating-the-financing-of-terrorism compliance supervision. Each has broad authority to inspect the institutions under its jurisdiction and to sanction for noncompliance. However, to date the only sanction that has been put into place against any financial institution in Mexico by the Mexican authorities has involved fines for noncompliance with the with anti-money-laundering and/or combating-the-financing-of-terrorism regulations, in amounts described by the IMF as "relatively low."[46]

Inadequate Laws and Regulations

Mexico cooperates well with the United States and other countries in sharing information relating to particular money-laundering investigations. Mexico's bank secrecy laws do not inhibit such sharing, and cooperation through Mexico's financial intelligence unit (FIU) with other FIUs through the Egmont Group is rated as excellent by the United States,[47] and by the IMF's Financial Action Task Force.[48] However, in many other respects, Mexico's anti-money laundering laws retain numerous gaps from best international practice.[49]

---

ment was based on, as the figures provided by the IMF show at best a percentage at half or a quarter of 1 percent, depending on the assessment of how much money is being laundered. See *INCSR 2009.*

42. International Monetary Fund, *Mexico*, paragraph 324.

43. Ibid., "Executive Summary," 9, key findings. "The figures suggest that $99.75 of every $100 the cartels ship south is getting through, money that is fueling a brutal war that has killed 14,000 people in three years"; cited in "US Drug War Crackdown Misses the Money," Associated Press, December 17, 2009.

44. For an older case, see, e.g., "U.S. Says It Uncovered a $100 Million Drug-Money Laundry," *New York Times*, December 1, 1994, http://www.nytimes.com/1994/12/01/nyregion/us-says-it-uncovered-a-100-million-drug-money-laundry.html?pagewanted=all; or for a more recent case, see "Prewett Convicted of Drug, Money-Laundering Charges," *Sarasota Herald Tribune*, March 27, 2008, http://www.heraldtribune.com/article/20080327/NEWS/378378008?Title=Prewett-convicted-of-drug-money-laundering-charges.

45. International Monetary Fund, *Mexico*, paragraph 265.

46. Ibid., "Executive Summary: Preventative Measures," 12.

47. *INCSR 2010*, vol. 2, *Mexico Country Report.*

48. International Monetary Fund, *Mexico*, "Executive Summary: National and International Cooperation," paragraphs 37–38.

49. This section addresses only anti-money-laundering gaps. The IMF Financial Action Task Force's assessment of Mexico found numerous gaps relating to terrorist finance. These are relevant to Mexico's overall

The offense of money laundering is narrowly described, focusing on the illicit origin of funds in the financial system. It does not cover the concealment or disguise of the true nature, source, location, disposition, movement, or ownership of or rights with respect to property.[50]

Corporations cannot be charged with money laundering, because the country's anti-money laundering laws do not cover legal persons.[51] Moreover, corporations and other legal entities do not have to disclose beneficial ownership, making it virtually impossible for the Mexican authorities to determine who owns them.[52]

Firms that are engaged solely in remittances, known as *transmisores de dinero*, are not required to be licensed at all. In theory, they are subject to anti-money-laundering requirements and subject to supervision. In practice, they are not supervised through meaningful controls, such as onsite inspections, and the anti-money-laundering requirements apply solely to transactions of greater than $3,000, allowing them the ability to structure transactions below the $3,000 amount and thereby escape even minimal customer identification requirements.[53]

There are no customer due diligence requirements for money transmitters and remittance houses that handle transactions structured to remain at $3,000 or less.[54] Money transmitters and remittance firms in Mexico who disperse funds to recipients are not required to maintain a list of the agents, or those from who they receive funds. They also are not required to immediately obtain customer documentation after a transfer is paid by their agents or payers.[55] Money transmitters and remittance firms are not required to maintain customer due diligence information on those for whom they send wire transfers.[56] Customer due diligence obligations do not apply to various types of limited-purpose financial institutions. For example, multipurpose lending institutions, known as *sociedad financiera de objeto múltiple* (*SOFOMES*), are mostly unregulated. They are in theory subject to anti-money-laundering requirements under the Law for Auxiliary Credit Organizations and Activities. But in practice, no anti-money-laundering regulations have been issued that apply to *SOFOMES* as yet. Because no regulations have been issued, *SOFOMES* have no specific anti-money-laundering obligations, such as requirements that they engage in any form of due diligence regarding their customers.[57]

Due diligence may not meaningfully limit customer transactions in financial institutions in Mexico, in any case. There is no requirement, for example, that financial institutions undertake further customer due diligence when they encounter indicators of false, erased, or altered identification documents. Nor is there an explicit requirement that they determine whether a business seeking to open an account is acting for itself or on behalf of others.[58]

---

compliance with international standards in combating illicit finance overall, but have little meaningful relationship to Mexico's drug-money-laundering issues. Accordingly, they are not discussed in this appendix, but can be found discussed seriatim in the assessment set forth by International Monetary Fund, *Mexico*.

50. International Monetary Fund, *Mexico*, "Ratings of Compliance with FATF Recommendation 1," 313.

51. Ibid., paragraph 12.

52. Ibid., paragraph 32.

53. Ibid., paragraph 186.

54. Ibid., table on 323, finding elements of noncompliance with Financial Action Task Force recommendations.

55. Ibid.

56. Ibid.

57. International Monetary Fund, *Mexico*, paragraph 833

58. International Monetary Fund, *Mexico*, table on 314, finding elements of noncompliance with Financial Action Task Force recommendations.

The Ministry of the Interior issues temporary licenses for national lotteries, casinos, horse races, and sport pools, make them regulated entities. But none of these types of firms—nor lawyers, accountants, real estate agents, dealers of precious metals and stones, or couriers—are subject to anti-money-laundering reporting requirements. They can be paid in cash without having the obligation to determine the source of funds, and then deposit that cash in connection with their businesses to regulated entities, making laundering through such businesses low risk.[59]

The opportunities these kinds of gaps provide for laundering money as a result of the placement of bulk currency into the financial system by those in front companies or businesses colluding with traffickers are essentially endless.

Similarly, the anti-money-laundering laws relating to the movement of funds across the border are also essentially toothless. Since 2000, Mexico has required anyone moving currency into Mexico in the amount of $10,000 or more to report it to the Mexican Customs authorities. In turn, Mexican Customs sends these reports to Mexico's FIU. But the IMF found that it is not an offense to make a false declaration about the amounts one is transporting. In practice, cases of cross-border transportation of cash or other bearer-negotiable instruments are seldom investigated, and customs, immigration, narcotics control, and prosecutors do not coordinate domestically on issues related to currency smuggling.[60]

In summary, Mexico maintains poor controls on the entry of funds into the country across the border, failing to enforce applicable regulations or to make them work even conceptually, and similarly maintains poor controls on the introduction of those funds into the formal financial system by launderers as a result of its largely meaningless system of due diligence.

U.S. law and regulations differ from their Mexican counterparts in all these areas, making the introduction of currency into the U.S. financial system by launderers far more difficult. The cross-border legal and regulatory arbitrage creates the regulatory equivalent of a gravitational force sucking bulk currency south for placement.

Exacerbating the draw of funds into Mexico arising from its inadequate regulations is the manner in which Mexican law makes it difficult to seize funds. Mexico's asset forfeiture laws require preexisting criminal convictions. Mexico lacks a mechanism for civil forfeiture. The result is that there is no mechanism to seize the assets *used* by organized criminals, only the proceeds they have *generated* from the crime. As a result, even in a case where a person is convicted of drug trafficking or money laundering, the assets used to carry out the activity cannot be seized by Mexican law enforcement, even after conviction.

Cross-Border Smuggling Patterns

The funds generated by drug trafficking are enormous and lead to the corruption of officials wherever they are laundered. Moreover, it is not merely that the same organizations launder money as traffic in drugs, but also that the very logistical mechanisms between the two activities are related, due to the use of the major Mexican money-laundering organizations of bulk currency as their predominant mechanism for repatriating drug proceeds from the United States. In the border

59. See *INCSR 2009*.

60. International Monetary Fund, *Mexico*, table on 325, finding elements of noncompliance with Financial Action Task Force recommendations.

area, drugs come north in trucks and automobiles; money goes south in trucks and automobiles. The drugs, like the funds, have complex transit routings along the way, but consolidation at the border of both narcotics and cash is the norm.

To deliver funds to the border-facing front companies, the robust transit networks established by the drug-trafficking organizations to move narcotics north are replicated in the corridors used to move currency south. The interrelationship of these two types of smuggling is well illustrated by the transit patterns used in the South Texas border and San Antonio areas of Texas. In particular, the South Texas area, which extends from Val Verde County to Willacy and Cameron counties along the Gulf of Mexico, is extremely rural, largely uninhabited, and dominated economically by transit activity across the border.[61] Seventeen border crossings are located within this area, with drugs moved up to the United States from the Mexican cities of Ciudad Acuna, Piedras Negras, Nuevo Laredo, Ciudad Aleman, Reynosa, and Matamoros. The NDIC describes how the drugs are moved as follows: "Traffickers transit the corridors using overland transportation methods such as private vehicles, commercial tractor-trailers, passenger buses, and trains."[62]

This description is mirrored in the NDIC's summary of the movement of bulk cash. Just as the drugs are stored in Mexico's northern border towns, the currency is stored in the United States' southern border towns of Brownsville, Edinburg, Mission, McAllen, Pharr, Roma, and Rio Grande City, having landed there after having been generated throughout the eastern half of the United States. What happens then is simple: "When funds are transferred to this area, they are often collected and then transported in bulk to Mexico."[63] Essentially, the same corridors and mechanisms apply to each side of the transaction.

The NDIC's descriptions for South Texas mirror those provided by the NDIC for Arizona, New Mexico, and California, with minor differences related to logistical differences. For example, drug traffickers and money launderers in the Arizona border area rely on heavily used interstate highways to smuggle drugs in hidden compartments in vehicles, sometimes moving the drugs (or currency) through tunnels for the "last miles" between, for example, Tucson and Nogales, Mexico. Smuggling out of California is similar in its use of interstate highways but lacks the tunnel feature.[64]

The most recent major case related to Mexican money laundering, announced in February 2010, involved Western Union, illustrates the focus on getting funds to the southwestern United States. In this case, which was largely investigated by the authorities in Arizona, Western Union agreed to pay $94 million to settle charges related to money laundering along the southwestern border in Arizona solely concerned with people smuggling, rather than drugs. The agreed-on facts found that Western Union had moved roughly $177 million in wire transfers from some 29 U.S. states that were the most frequent destinations for persons being smuggled from Mexico to the United States during the period from 2003 to 2005, and another $142 million in wire transfers from the same states from 2005 to 2007. The agreed-on facts provided little further information about how law enforcement officials knew the funds related to alien smuggling, or what happened to the funds after they reached Western Union's Arizona agents from the other 29 states. The

61. NDIC, "NDIC Market Analysis, South Texas Border and San Antonio Market Area," February 2009, http://www.justice.gov/ndic/pubs32/32791/markets.htm.

62. Ibid.

63. Ibid.

64. See NDIC, "NDIC Market Analyses for Arizona Drug Market and for California Border Alliance Group Drug Market," http://wwww.justice.gov/ndic/pubs32/3276/abuse.htm.

implication, however, is that the funds were sent from the other states to Western Union offices in Arizona to be paid out near to the U.S. border with Mexico, so that they could then be sent to Mexico as bulk currency for placement.[65]

Institutionalized Corruption and the Vicious Circle of Mexican Vulnerability

Corruption in Mexico was institutionalized as a result of the overly long, seven-decade tenure of a single party in power, the Partido Revolucionario Institutional (Institutional Revolutionary Party). Grand corruption through kickbacks and payoffs involving government contracts, especially for infrastructure at the top, merged into petty corruption of police at the local level. These activities became most visible in the corruption, murder, and money-laundering trial of Raul Salinas in 1995, which revealed his close ties to major trafficking organizations in addition to his procurement-related corruption.[66]

The U.S. Justice Department currently identifies Mexican drug-trafficking organizations as the greatest drug-trafficking threat to the United States worldwide. Yet, this phenomenon was only consolidated during the past decade as a result of more effective controls on Caribbean routes, which forced trafficking inward to land areas not subject to interdiction by the U.S. government. These controls caused Colombian traffickers to subcontract to those in Mexico to move the drugs into the United States. There, they were able to exploit the country's vulnerabilities to corruption to secure close ties to senior law enforcement officials throughout the trafficking corridors. Over time, the Mexican trafficking organizations became increasingly powerful, developing control over most of the domestic U.S. narcotics market, with direct oversight of distribution in some 230 major U.S. cities.[67] By the end of 2008, as much as 90 percent of the cocaine entering the United States transited through Mexico.[68] Most of these drugs leave Mexico from drug distribution operations maintained near the southern side of the U.S.-Mexican border.

In early 2007, President Felipe Calderón determined that drug-related crime, violence, and corruption threatened the Mexican state, and he thus intensified enforcement activity against Mexican drug-trafficking organizations. These actions further intensified drug-related violence. In 2008, more than 5,600 people in Mexico were killed in drug-trafficking violence, including 522 Mexican military and law enforcement officials. By early 2009, drug-related violence had reached the level of 500 incidents a month as a result of a battle for control over narcotics markets. The killings have included outright assassinations of high-level law enforcement officials, beheadings, an arsenal of high-power weaponry and wanton murders of innocent bystanders.[69]

One result of the corruption and/or intimidation of local law enforcement officials in Mexico is that the country's limited resources to combat narcotics trafficking and money laundering are

---

65. Statement of Admitted Facts, Western Union Co., Form 8-K, Exhibit 10-1, Settlement Agreement, February 11, 2010. http://222.faqs.org/se-filings/10216/Western-Union-CO_8-K/dex101.htm, 16.

66. See, e.g., "Mexico Frees Ex-Leader's Brother," BBC, June 10, 2005, http://news.bbc.co.uk/2/hi/americas/4079372.stm, describing Salinas' release from prison after serving 10 years of a 23-year sentence.

67. NDIC, "National Drug Threat Assessment."

68. *INCSR 2009*.

69. "Testimony of David T. Johnson, Assistant Secretary, U.S. Department of State, Bureau of International Narcotics and Law Enforcement Affairs, before the Subcommittee on State, Foreign Operations, Related Programs of House Committee on Appropriations, March 10, 2009."

further weakened by those who cannot be relied upon to meet their obligations to combat these activities. The increase in the number of money services businesses, including both *casas de cambio* and *centros cambiarios* remitters operating along the southern side of the U.S.–Mexican border, has presented obvious targets for law enforcement activity targeted at unduly prosperous automobile dealerships, retail stories, real estate companies, and restaurants in border towns. Yet, before early 2007, little enforcement activity was directed at these targets. The more aggressive efforts by the Mexican government over the last three years have included actions against border area front companies, which in turn have generated further retaliatory attacks on officials. Such attacks have not ended President Calderón's efforts. But they do have two major consequences. First, they remove law enforcement officials who have proven to be effective and willing to go after their assets; second, they send a message to third parties that cooperation with government is a lethal offense. That message is likely received by, among others, those in the financial services sector who are involved in accepting proceeds whose origin is at best uncertain.

The level of infiltration of the government by drug traffickers affects counter-money-laundering activities by compromising intelligence on the business holdings of traffickers. For example, as of October 2008, the Sinaloa drug cartel paid off personnel at both the Assistant Attorney General's Office Specializing in Organized Crime (Subprocuraduría de Investigación Especializada en Delincuencia Organizada, SIEDO) and the U.S. Embassy in Mexico City to obtain confidential information, which, when exposed, forced the resignation of the chief of Mexico's Federal Preventative Police. A month later, the Mexican authorities detained the former head of SIEDO on accusations of receiving monthly payments of $450,000 from the Pacifico drug cartel.[70] In 2009, arrests of corrupt officials included a former Mexican drug czar and the current mayor of Chiapas;[71] 10 other mayors, a judge, and a top police official from the state of Michoacan, home of the drug-trafficking group known as La Familia;[72] and the former head of Mexico's national liaison office to Interpol, who would have extensive, detailed knowledge of the targets of foreign law enforcement agencies.[73]

Separately, members of Mexico's Congress have also proven to have been working for the drug traffickers and are protected by the immunity against criminal prosecution Mexico gives to all its elected officials while they remain in office. The most recent and important case involved Julio César Godoy Toscano, the half-brother of Michoacán governor Leonel Godoy (of the Partido de la Revolución Democrática, Party of the Democratic Revolution, PRD), who was found to be linked to La Familia Michoacana by a recent federal Secretaría de Seguridad Pública investigation. Godoy Toscano won election as a member of the PRD for one of the 12 directly elected seats in the federal Chamber of Deputies and then went into hiding after charges were brought. Despite the drug charges, the Chamber of Deputies would not act to remove him or his criminal immunity as a member of the Mexican Congress.[74]

---

70. See http://jurist.law.pitt.edu/paperchase/2009/04/mexico-senate-approves-pre-conviction.php.

71. " Former Mexican Drug Czar Arrested on Corruption Charges," CNN, January 26, 2009, http://www.cnn.com/2009/WORLD/americas/01/26/mexico.drug.czar/index.html.

72. "10 Mayors, Other Mexico Officials Detained," *Los Angeles Times*, May 27, 2009, http://articles.latimes.com/2009/may/27/world/fg-mexico-mayors27.

73. "Ordenan arrestar a ex mandos de Interpol," *El Universal*, January 16, 2009, http://www.eluniversal.com.mx/nacion/165134.html.

74. Sylvia Longmire, "Official Immunity and Mexico's Fight against Corruption," September 14, 2009, http://www.mexidata.info/id2403.html.

It is not possible to show a one-to-one correspondence between, on the one hand, Mexico's inadequate anti-money-laundering laws, its failure adequately to regulate *casas de cambio* and other forms of money services businesses, its lack of transparency governing corporate ownership, its legal shields for corporations against liability, and, on the other hand, its drug-related corruption. However, it is obvious that too many interests in Mexico, not just those directly involved in drug trafficking and money laundering, have a stake in maintaining the system as it is without further needed reforms, and therefore are likely to resist President Calderón's efforts to secure meaningful change.

Strategies

Mexico's financial services sector has developed to serve a society that has had very large incentives for nondocumentation of individual assets, transactions in goods and services, and movements of funds, whether assessed from those at the top who profited by grand corruption or those at the bottom who sought to remain undocumented from the threat posed by taxes, regulations, and extortion.

The greatest testimony to the effectiveness of the heightened enforcement activity undertaken by the Calderón administration is the violent reaction from the traffickers that has attended it. Yet all the enforcement activity undertaken to date has not resulted in the seizure of more than a fraction of the funds that are trafficked each year. For example, during the five-year period from 2003 through 2007, the Mexican authorities seized a total of $253.6 million in narcotics traffickers' dollar assets. Yet $206 million of the funds seized came in a single, major bust, meaning that just $47 million was seized in all other enforcement activity during those five years.

The seizure numbers related to money-laundering prosecutions alone, as distinct from seizures relating to drug trafficking, are paltry in light of the sums actually laundered. Between 2004 and 2007, Mexico secured the forfeiture of a total of $4.5 million, most of which ($4.2 million) was generated in a single year. In 2007, the most recent year for which statistics were included by the IMF in its report, Mexico reported that all its money-laundering prosecutions nationwide secured total seizures of just $21,000.[75] These figures suggest something essentially indistinguishable from impunity for those involved in laundering the proceeds of narcotics, as opposed to those who were found to be directly involved in the trafficking themselves and caught red-handed with currency.

Changes to Mexico's money-laundering laws and regulations to address the specific vulnerabilities created by their gaps could attenuate the risks posed by particular gateways to the global financial services sector from Mexico. But much larger issues need to be addressed for such changes to have a fundamental impact, including the continuing collusion of participants in Mexico's formal economy with the wealth generated by its underground one.

The government of Mexico has announced a series of reforms, some of which were to have taken place in 2009 but did not, to close regulatory gaps and to improve enforcement capabilities.[76]

---

75. International Monetary Fund, *Mexico*, paragraph 287.

76. Mexican bank regulators drafted a "multifaceted reform" bill that was to have been approved in early 2009 aiming to harmonize regulations between the big bankers and other types of financial institutions in Mexico, including credit unions, *centros cambiarios*, and *SOFOLES* undergoing deregulation and transitioning to *SOFOMES*. The government also announced its intention to release in 2009 an anti-money-laundering / combating-the-financing-of-terrorism National Strategy in 2009 specifying short- and long-range

Pending the detailed articulation of those reforms by the government, a general overview of some of the most important reforms is provided in the following subsections.

Creating Evidentiary Trails

Mexico needs a strategy for securing the documentation of currency into the country's formal financial system on a comprehensive basis, involving relatively small amounts of currency and including every aspect of the economy. Such a strategy needs to include tactics to provide incentives for Mexicans in unbanked areas to use some form of financial institution, and all those to be not only registered but also licensed and required to provide more detailed documentation to comply with their anti-money-laundering obligations.

As one example, to begin to document those whose economic activities are mostly or entirely underground, the Mexican federal government could issue plastic smart cards to be used for providing government benefits, for health care, for insurance, or for other governmental purposes. Such cards can then be required to carry out financial transactions, regardless of the type of entity being used to move funds. The Mexican government could also provide incentives to the country's registered funds transmitters to establish operations in unbanked or underbanked areas, and require them to supply adequate documentation sufficient to enable tracing of suspect transactions.

To address the laundering of bulk currency and its use by front companies, the government could extend its anti-money-laundering controls to high-intensity cash trades and businesses, such as supermarkets, pharmacies, nightclubs and bars, restaurants, and beauty salons, and begin to inspect such facilities not only for anti-money-laundering compliance but also to compare cash revenues with actual economic activity.

Mexico could also lower the threshold for reporting deposits of currency and for customer due diligence in general. Both thresholds today start at $10,000 and should be reduced substantially, to a maximum of $1,000.[77]

Mexico needs to undertake fundamental change in its treatment of corporations, requiring transparency in the declaration of beneficial ownership of each and every legal person registered in the country, and tracing such ownership back to discourage layering activity involving the hiding of ownership through multiple jurisdictions of which Mexico is only one stop. In tandem with such changes, the country needs to require disclosure by customers when they are depositing or moving funds on behalf of others. Corporations and other forms of legal persons need to be subject to the threat of criminal sanctions and seizure for violations of Mexican law generally, and money-laundering and tax laws in particular.

There is no general auditing requirement applied to Mexican financial institutions subject to anti-money-laundering regulations. An independent audit should be required of all entities engaged in funds transmission or other money services business in Mexico.

Finally, the new 3 percent Impuesto sobre Depositos en Efectivo tax on cash deposits of 15,000 pesos or more could have a very substantial impact in revenue collection and in allowing analy-

---

objectives and strategies, and establishing an interagency coordination group to examine emerging money-laundering trends and identify and propose legal and regulatory measures to mitigate gaps, but this did not take place either. See *INCSR 2009*; and International Monetary Fund, *Mexico*, describing planned initiatives.

77. See International Monetary Fund, *Mexico*, paragraph 150.

ses of transactions that will lead to greater enforcement successes against money launderers. But these results would require the government finding legitimate businesses that have failed to pay the tax and financial institutions that have failed to enforce such payments, imposing meaningful sanctions on them, and then repeating such efforts until the government succeeds in changing behaviors. Evidence that this has taken place to date during the 18-month period of the tax's initial imposition (2 percent, 25,000 pesos per deposit) was not visible.

Greater Resources for Supervision

Anti-money-laundering rules and documentation requirements are only as good as the oversight and supervision capabilities of regulators. Creating meaningful regulatory capabilities would require the provision of far greater resources by the government of Mexico. Such resources should, if systematically applied, more than pay for themselves through reducing tax evasion and securing the seizure of some portion of the funds now being laundered.

For example, Mexico's Tax Administration Service (Servicio de Administración Tributaria, SAT) is today responsible for the supervision of foreign currency exchange centers (*centros cambiaros*) and money remitters. There are about 2,212 registered *centros cambiarios* and 857 registered money remitters, plus some 2,400 to 4,400 unregistered operators (the higher number is more probable), who do not have to register because they ostensibly do not transmit funds above $10,000 per customer per day. The SAT is also responsible for supervising some 850 *SOFOMES* for anti-money-laundering / combating-the-financing-of-terrorism compliance, but it has not yet begun doing so because the regulations have not been issued. The SAT currently has six persons in its anti-money-laundering / combating-the-financing-of-terrorism unit and has access to about 52 more inspectors from its local branches that can carry out onsite inspections. During the period 2005–2007, it initiated and conducted about 800 onsite visits. Thus, it visited perhaps a tenth of the total number of institutions it supervised over a three-year period, or a little more than 3 percent a year.

Mexico needs to complete assigning regulators to every component of its financial services infrastructure and provide them sufficient personnel to conduct onsite inspections of each entity on a regular basis—ideally, biannually—but in any case not less often than once every three years. Such inspections should extend to cash-intensive businesses. Ideally, these inspections would be carried out by the SAT, so that tax-related infractions, and also money-laundering infractions, are detected and appropriate sanctions are imposed. The imposition of meaningful sanctions could result in substantially large revenue collections, along with the closure of businesses that are owned by traffickers or businesses acting as little more than fronts for laundering.

Addressing Regulatory Arbitrage

Mexico suffers from two distinct forms of regulatory arbitrage that create vulnerabilities for money launderers. Domestic regulatory arbitrage arises from the country's decision to only apply meaningful anti-money-laundering controls to its large commercial banks. As discussed, regulation and supervision of other types of nonbank financial institutions have been minimal, with numerous cases of anti-money-laundering reporting requirements applied to them, and none at all for the thousands of nonregistered, nonlicensed institutions. Cross-border regulatory arbitrage arises from the willingness demonstrated throughout Mexico's financial infrastructure to accept deposits of bulk currency with, it appears, little meaningful due diligence in practice, regardless of the theoretical regulatory controls. The former issue requires changes in law. The latter issue requires changes in practice.

All *casas de cambio* should be required to obtain licenses, including those that declare they do not handle an equivalent of more than $10,000 per customer per day or are not engaged in the business "in a habitual and professional/specialized manner." *Centros cambiarios* reporting that they conduct transactions less than the equivalent of $10,000 per client per day should be required to obtain a license and be subjected to regular inspection by the SAT. Firms that fail to obtain a license should be closed after a transition period, with their assets subject to seizure. These changes would immediately force the registration and licensure for the first time of thousands of businesses located in border areas and free zones, along with firms that regularly conduct business with foreigners, such as hotels. The failure to put controls in place on all these types of businesses has created gaps large enough to drive trucks filled with bulk currency through. To discourage launderers shopping for less-controlled financial institutions, *SOFOMES*, multipurpose lending companies, and *SOFOLES* (*sociedad financieras de objeto limitado*), limited-purpose lending companies, should immediately be subject to licensing, supervision, and anti-money-laundering regulations, along with inspections. This would require them to screen customers under due diligence rules.

The entire array of anti-money-laundering controls should be brought to bear on courier services, which are today both informal and unregistered. Couriers should be licensed and registered, and systematically subject to reporting requirements on all funds they handle. Customer due diligence, which today is only required for transactions that equal or exceed $10,000, should be required of all persons with whom an institution has a customer relationship (i.e., an account), and should apply to transactions of $500 or more.

Comprehensive know-your-customer requirements should be put in place at all forms of Mexican financial institutions at the level at least equivalent to the United States, where some form of official document providing customer identification is required for any transaction made through a money transmitter. Detailed information should be required for all customer (account) relationships, not just banks and *SOFOLES*, as is currently the case, with lower standards required in other types of account relationships.

Asset Seizures, Border Control, and Attacking the Corridors

In recent years, cases involving asset seizures and Mexico have become increasingly frequent, and can involve tens of millions of dollars at a time, as exemplified in the U.S. Operation Firewall against bulk currency laundering, which resulted in the seizure of more than $124.7 million in U.S. currency and monetary instruments along with the criminal arrest of 191 individuals in 2009. But other than the $207 million seized from traffickers in a single bust in Mexico City in 2007, asset seizures by the Mexican authorities have generally been small. Seizures of funds related to laundering through the financial system, as opposed to being stashed at a physical location, have been, compared with the volumes laundered, infinitesimal.

To date, the occasional raids on financial institutions engaged in laundering by Mexican authorities have come largely (or entirely) in response to, and in tandem with, asset forfeitures and investigations undertaken by U.S. officials. Mexican officials have been able to seize little themselves. A few dramatic enforcement cases could change the current perception of Mexican launderers—which is that, at worst, if the Americans target you, a particular operation may be shut down, but domestic enforcement activity against assets hidden in Mexico is unlikely.

Mexico's cross-border declaration laws contain a fundamental gap: They do not make it a crime to make a false declaration. False declarations must be criminalized and cases of cross-border transportation of cash or other bearer-negotiable instruments must be investigated, which is seldom the case today.

Control of the borders and the corridors is mostly a case of applying enforcement strategies through an approach called defense in depth. The principle of defense in depth means, in practice, that the border cannot be treated as a crossing but must instead by treated as a region, with checkpoints used to inspect and check goods in transit before they arrive at the crossing. The same organizations have their assets on both sides of the border, making them potentially susceptible to intelligence-based operations involving close cooperation between U.S. and Mexican officials. One major difficulty in making such cooperation work is the lack of trust between the two sides, which has been fueled by corruption on both sides, but especially on the Mexican side.

Another element of defense in depth means enhanced oversight of businesses operating in the major cities adjacent to the U.S. border, through toughened licensing regimes, onsite inspections, bookkeeping requirements, and overall oversight on the Mexican side. Such an approach could make a difference, as has been evident on the United States' southwestern border, where enforcement activity that involves federal–local collaboration and dramatically increased inspections of southern-bound goods has successfully targeted a number of front companies during the past few years.[78] It would also be physically dangerous, especially in its start-up phase, to those responsible for implementation. Moreover, even with the enhanced effort on the U.S. side, seizures of currency remain a fraction of that which moves through the region.

Enhanced Tax Reporting Requirements

At its core, to apply defense in depth on the laundering side, Mexico would have to require any business in the country that handles meaningful amounts of currency to maintain detailed records on its sources of cash. In theory, they should be doing that in any case for the purposes of taxation. As a 2002 study found, Mexico's tax collection rate is among the lowest in Latin America, amounting to at least 30 percent of the total funds due. The study found that one-third of the population pays no taxes, and another third underreports its earnings.[79]

A strategy on the part of the Mexican government to intensify documentation, bookkeeping, auditing, and reporting requirements on cash-intensive businesses would likely both generate revenue and reduce the disparity between U.S. and Mexican anti-money-laundering norms. One potentially important initiative in this area is President Calderón's policy of imposing a 2 percent tax on any business that deposits more than 25,000 pesos ($1,991) per deposit as of July 1, 2008, which was raised to 3 percent on deposits of 15,000 pesos ($1,553) as of January 1, 2010. The Impuesto sobre Depositos en Efectivo (IDE) was an effort by President Calderón to push people in the informal economy into the formal economy. In 2007, the IDE was initially named the Impuesto contra la Informalidad, or "tax against informality." In its preamble, the IDE explicitly stated that its goal was not revenue generation but countering tax evasion, by only taxing those who have

78. Testimony of Secretary Napolitano before the Senate Committee on the Judiciary, "Oversight of the Department of Homeland Security," May 6, 2009, http://www.dhs.gov/ynews/testimony/testimony_1241706742872.shtm.

79. Phyllis Lai Lan Mo, *Tax Avoidance and Anti-Avoidance Measures in Major Developing Countries* (Westport, Conn.: Praeger, 2003).

not reported income, because the 2 percent IDE payments would be credited toward income-tax payments.[80]

In principle, this kind of tax could have several different effects, depending on how it is enforced. The 2 percent / 3 percent tax could provide a mechanism whereby money launderers are free to deposit funds with no questions asked in legitimate financial institutions because they are raising revenue for the government. Alternatively, it could provide a mechanism whereby the government has much more information and documentation on where cash is entering the economy, and what it represents, making it easier to initiate enforcement cases. Or in another alternative, money launderers could seek to collude with financial institutions to cause the funds to be reported as having been made in small deposits (structured) below the threshold. In yet another alternative, the currency would not be deposited in Mexico but shipped somewhere else, such as to Panama's Colon Free Zone, where it could be used to purchase goods for the BMPE. But it is not possible to assess the comparative prevalence of these behaviors in practice in the absence of documentation of how the 2 percent tax on currency has worked in its first 18 months of operation.

Punishing Financial Institutions with Meaningful Sanctions

Although the United States first put basic anti-money-laundering requirements in place on banks in 1970 with the adoption of the Bank Secrecy Act, meaningful compliance by U.S. financial institutions, with the entire array of customer due diligence obligations, was limited before the decision of the Office of the Comptroller of the Currency to force out the management of Riggs Bank and sell the institution under congressional pressure in 2003. After the crackdown on Riggs, U.S. federal regulators began regularly imposing multi-million-dollar fines on U.S financial institutions, causing them to dramatically tighten their domestic anti-money-laundering compliance in practice and to ask more of their foreign correspondent banking institutions. By 2007, tighter standards began to be imposed by federal regulators on U.S. banks doing business with Mexican institutions, in response to federal perceptions that they were of high money-laundering risk. But such controls have not immediately had an impact on banking practices in Mexico itself.

All four of Mexico's principal supervisory authorities responsible for anti-money-laundering/combating-the-financing-of-terrorism compliance have broad powers to obtain access to and inspect the businesses under their jurisdiction and to sanction them for noncompliance. To date, they have applied minor administrative sanctions in the form of fines for noncompliance, totaling less than $1.3 million (15.6 million Mexican pesos) for all Mexican financial institutions combined during the period 2005–2007.[81] The average fine applied to date to money transmitters for infractions of anti-money-laundering regulations is about the equivalent of $525.[82] Although the Mexican authorities have told the IMF that recent fines are in higher amounts, the fines that have been reported to date would be unlikely to deter any institution choosing to undertake a cost/benefit analysis between the risks to date of noncompliance with anti-money-laundering obligations and with handling portions of the ocean of available drug proceeds. By contrast, seizure and closure or a forced sale of a significant financial institution for noncompliance, as happened in the United States in the Riggs case, might get the attention of financial institutions that may otherwise be comfortable with the status quo.

80. "Mexico's New Tax on Cash Deposits and Its Creditability under IRC Section 901," *Procopio*, June 2, 2008, http://www.procopio.com/assets/009/6208.pdf.

81. See sanctions graph, International Monetary Fund, *Mexico*, paragraph 908.

82. Ibid., paragraph 910.

The United States could take further unilateral action to force Mexico's hand in sanctioning financial institutions. Regulators could follow the past warnings that relationships with *casas de cambio* are high risk by intensifying scrutiny during inspections of U.S. financial institutions of those relationships, and imposing materially large fines on domestic banks found to have handled proceeds of uncertain provenance for *casas de cambio*. Such an approach would make it increasingly difficult for *casas de cambio* to have banking relationships with U.S. financial institutions, and thereby make laundering back to the Unite States less efficient and more costly.

Addressing Corruption

Current Mexican anticorruption efforts associated with the drug wars are visible and produce shocking revelations on a recurrent basis. Mexico has a number of mechanisms in place to address corruption, including a disclosure regime applicable to public officials. Its anti-money-laundering laws comprehensively require financial institutions to engage in enhanced due diligence related to "politically exposed persons" (PEPs), or persons associated with the government who are of higher risk of generating proceeds of corruption. In theory, the financial institutions are reporting PEPs-related suspicious transactions to the authorities, and Mexico has reported to the IMF Financial Action Task Force team assessing Mexico that it currently has investigations of PEPs under way. According to the IMF task force's assessment, these investigations include cases against former Mexican government officials accused of corruption who have invested large sums of money in the coastal zone of Baja California Sur and the Mayan Riviera, using front men and trusts to hold their property. But indictments and seizures are not visible.[83]

The composition, scope, and efficacy of Mexico's array of anticorruption efforts are beyond the reach of this appendix.[84] It should be sufficient to note the following statement in the IMF's anti-money-laundering assessment of Mexico: "It is also striking to note the absence of convictions for corruption offenses, given that corruption is one of the underlying offenses most commonly prosecuted in Latin America as a predicate offense for money laundering."[85]

Mexico is a signatory to essentially all of the world's relevant conventions regarding corruption and has adopted an extensive set of anticorruption measures. Comprehensive laws and regulations are useful; visible enforcement against notorious offenders is essential.

83. Ibid., paragraph 17.

84. A useful if slightly dated assessment is available from Transparency International, "Country Study Report on Mexico," 2001, http://www.transparency.org/policy_research/nis/nis_reports_by_country.

85. International Monetary Fund, *Mexico*, paragraph 473.

APPENDIX C
THE EFFECTS OF DRUG ENFORCEMENT & IMPRISONMENT ON TRANSIT COUNTRIES
THE CASE OF THE UNITED STATES AND MEXICO
Jonathan P. Caulkins and Eric L. Sevigny

U.S. and Mexican drug markets are deeply intertwined, and Mexico suffers substantial damage, particularly from drug-related violence and corruption, as a result of being the source or conduit of most illegal drugs consumed in the United States. The salient characteristic of U.S. drug policy is toughness—a willingness to incarcerate extraordinary numbers of drug law violators. Indeed, of the 336,000 people imprisoned in the United States in 2004 for drug law violations, 13,000 were Mexican nationals and another 28,000 were U.S. citizens of Mexican ancestry. The juxtaposition of these two facts raises questions as to whether a softening of U.S. drug policy might benefit Mexico. However, a more detailed analysis suggests that this is not the case. Short of outright legalization of drugs or intentionally allowing drugs to enter the United States via a different route, no simple changes to U.S. policies would greatly ameliorate the consequences that U.S. drug users' demand creates for Mexico. In general, Mexican American drug inmates look very much like their fellow citizens of other ancestries. The foreign nationals, in contrast, were typically involved with much greater quantities of drugs, although not more likely to be in large organizations or report weapons involvement. Precisely because they represent fewer than 10 percent of all drug law violators in prison, it would be possible to change policies toward them without having to make a dramatic change in overall U.S. drug policy.

Introduction

Most of the world's illegal drugs are exported across international boundaries. That is, most illegal drugs are consumed in a country other than where they were produced.[1]

A considerable literature has developed asking how interventions in drug source and/or transit (also called "transshipment") countries affect drug use and drug-related problems downstream.[2] With the partial exception of border interdiction, particularly for relatively isolated coun-

1. Afghanistan produces more than 90 percent of the world's supply and consumes less than 10 percent. Likewise, essentially all cocaine is produced in South America, but North America and Europe dominate consumption. The Netherlands is thought to play a prominent role in ecstasy manufacture, but is itself much too small to account for more than a small share of global consumption. Domestic production is a significant source of cannabis in many final market countries, and marijuana is the most prevalent illegal drug, but it accounts for a modest share of black market revenue, drug-related crime, and drug-related social cost. United Nations Office on Drugs and Crime, *2008 World Drug Report* (New York: Oxford University Press, 2009).

2. Peter Reuter, "Eternal Hope: America's International Narcotics Efforts, *The Public Interest*, February 1985; Peter Reuter, "Quantity Illusion and Paradoxes of Drug Interdiction: Federal Intervention into Vice Policy," *Law and Contemporary Problems* 51, no. 1 (1988): 233–252; P. Reuter, G. Crawford, and J. Cave, *Sealing the Borders: The Effects of Increased Military Participation on Drug Interdiction* (Santa Monica, Calif.:

tries such as Australia,[3] the consensus is "not much"; it is quite difficult to intervene in source and transit countries in ways that materially affect drug availability and use in final market countries.

This appendix asks the opposite question. How do drug policies in final market countries affect problems upstream in source and transit countries? The particular focus is on how the United States' policies—notably its heavy reliance on incarceration—affect Mexico.

We set the context by briefly reviewing the important characteristics of the market relationship between Mexico and the United States. Then we proceed from general principles to particular facts, starting with the implications of the overall regime choice (prohibition vs. legalization vs. decriminalization) and moving through to explore data from the Survey of Inmates in State and Federal Correctional Facilities concerning who the United States incarcerates for drug law violations.

Our conclusion is that the United States and Mexico are linked through international drug trafficking, so U.S. policy certainly affects outcomes in Mexico. However, with the exception of across-the-board legalization—which is a nonstarter for both political and practical reasons—there are no quick fixes. It is not the case that Mexico's drug problems would disappear if the United States unilaterally adopted more modest policies.

Mexico's Role in U.S. Drug Supply

Mexico's role in U.S. drug supply varies by substance.[4] The market for cocaine (including crack) is by far the most important drug market in the United States. It accounts for on the order of two-thirds of both black market revenues and drug-related social costs.[5] Mexico has nothing directly to do with cocaine production, which occurs almost entirely in South America.[6] However, for the last 20 years Mexico has been the most important transit country.

The most common way for cocaine to reach U.S. markets is that it is produced in Colombia (even if the coca leaf is grown in Peru or Bolivia), smuggled into Mexico either directly or through another Central American country, and then moved across the Mexico–United States land border using an array of smuggling methods.

RAND Corporation, 1988); C. P. Rydell and S. S. Everingham, *Controlling Cocaine: Supply versus Demand Programs* (Santa Monica, Calif.: RAND Corporation, 1994); Jonathan P. Caulkins, *Evaluating the Effectiveness of Interdiction and Source Country Control*, RAND RP-410 (Santa Monica, Calif.: RAND Corporation, 1994); Letizia Paoli, Victoria Greenfield, and Peter Reuter, *The World Heroin Market: Can Supply Be Cut?* (New York, Oxford University Press, 2009).

3. Michael Hawley, "Heroin Shortage: The Cause," *Platypus Magazine*, no. 76 (2002): 43–48; Louisa Degenhardt, Peter Reuter, Linette Collins, and Wayne Hall, "Evaluating Explanations of the Australian Heroin Drought," *Addiction* 100 (2005): 459–469; M. Smithson, M. McFadden, and S. Mwesigye, "The Impact of Federal Drug Law Enforcement on the Supply of Heroin in Australia," *Addiction* 100 (2005): 1110–1120.

4. U.S. Drug Enforcement Administration, *Mexico: Country Profile for 2003* (Washington, D.C.: U.S. Government Printing Office, 2003).

5. Jonathan P. Caulkins, Rosalie Pacula, Susan Paddock, and James Chiesa, *School-Based Drug Prevention: What Kind of Drug Use Does It Prevent?* (Santa Monica, Calif.: RAND Corporation, 2002); Office of National Drug Control Policy, *The Economic Costs of Drug Abuse in the United States, 1992–2002* (Washington, D.C.: Executive Office of the President, 2004).

6. United Nations Office on Drugs and Crime, *2008 World Drug Report*.

In the 1980s, more cocaine moved through the Caribbean region, with countries such as the Bahamas playing a larger role in transit.[7] Smuggling routes evolve over time,[8] so it is not inconceivable that at some future point Mexico could once again be relegated to a secondary role. However, at this point Mexico offers three important advantages as a transit country: (1) a very long land border with the United States; (2) extensive legitimate cross-border commerce, within which contraband can be hidden; and (3) a large community of people with a common culture (language, ethnicity, etc.) on both sides of the border. In fact, the United States has more Mexican immigrants than any other nation in the world has *total* immigrants.[9]

Heroin, methamphetamine, and marijuana represent the second tier of illegal drug markets in the United States. All have black markets of roughly comparable dollar value and generate roughly comparable levels of social harm. Each individually is only about one-sixth as important as cocaine/crack, but all three are much more important than whatever substance is ranked fifth. Indeed, all other illegal drugs combined are of almost no consequence when analyzing U.S.–Mexican drug market connections.[10]

Clearly, these are broad generalizations. Marijuana differs in important ways from heroin and methamphetamine by being quite inexpensive. Not coincidentally, it is also by far the most widely used drug and is the one illegal drug that is not linked in important ways to nondrug crime or violence. Therefore, the black market for marijuana is very different from the markets for heroin or methamphetamine, even though all three are valued at roughly $10 billion a year. Nevertheless, in very round terms, one can think of U.S. drug markets as being two-thirds cocaine (including crack) and one-third heroin, methamphetamine, and marijuana combined.

From Mexico's perspective, heroin, methamphetamine, and marijuana collectively are more than one-third of the problem because these three substances are all produced in Mexico, whereas Mexico is only a transit country for cocaine. How much more important is unclear, because there are not good data describing the proportion of Mexican trafficking revenue or trafficking-related violence and corruption that is generated by each of these four drugs. Indeed, there is not even a consensus or precision in estimates of what proportion of the U.S. market for these substances is supplied by Mexican production.[11] (For a recently released analysis of these issues, see Kilmer et al. [2010]).[12] The U.S. Office of National Drug Control Policy estimates that Colombian heroin

---

7. Bonnie Dombey-Moore, Susan Resetar, and Michael Childress, *A Systems Description of the Cocaine Trade* (Santa Monica, Calif.: RAND Corporation, 1994).

8. Reuter, Crawford, and Cave, *Sealing the Borders.*

9. Pew Hispanic Center, *Mexican Immigrants in the United States, 2008* (Washington, D.C.: Pew Hispanic Center, 2009).

10. The one other category of drug that stands out for the United States is diverted pharmaceuticals, which account for a startlingly large share of all overdoses but not necessarily of black market revenues. However, diverted pharmaceuticals are not, to the best of our knowledge, importantly implicated in Mexican drug trafficking. U.S. Substance Abuse and Mental Health Services Administration, Office of Applied Studies, *Drug Abuse Warning Network, 2006: National Estimates of Drug-Related Emergency Department Visits*, DAWN Series D-30, DHHS Publication SMA 08-4339 (Rockville, Md.: U.S. Substance Abuse and Mental Health Services Administration, 2008).

11. Drug Availability Steering Committee, *Drug Availability Estimates in the United States*, Document NCJ-197107 (Washington, D.C.: U.S. Government Printing Office, 2002).

12. Beau Kilmer et al., *Reducing Drug Trafficking Revenues and Violence in Mexico: Would Legalizing Marijuana in California Help?* Occasional Paper (Santa Monica, Calif.: RAND, 2010).

accounted for more of the U.S. market than did Mexican heroin, and domestic production is significant for marijuana.[13]

At one time, cocaine transiting Mexico was controlled by Colombians, and Mexicans earned only a smuggling fee. Today, however, this balance of power has shifted. Mexican organizations buy cocaine from Colombia—at relatively low prices—and retain all the net revenues from selling the cocaine at the much higher import prices commanded in the United States[14] Hence, it would appear that Mexican organizations make more per kilogram of cocaine consumed in the United States than do Colombian organizations. Cocaine trafficking revenues for Mexican organizations may be on the order of $2.5 billion a year (250 metric tons x $10,000 per kilogram).

The amount of $2.5 billion could account for a large proportion of Mexican organizations' net revenues, even though it is a small proportion of the total U.S. retail market of roughly $65 billion.[15] The reason is that Mexican exporters do not sell directly to U.S. users, and prices are marked up by a factor of six as the drugs change hands multiple times between export and retail sale. Hence, even though high-level traffickers may individually generate substantial profits, the vastly larger number of lower-level sellers collectively retain the great bulk of the $65 billion as compensation for their time and the risks they incur.[16] How much of the $65 billion finds its way abroad is unclear, depending in part on how vertically integrated the higher levels of domestic distribution are with the cross-border smuggling. The analysis below of numbers of imprisoned drug law violators by nationality and organizational role gives some hints in that regard.

Despite these uncertainties, it is clear that all four substances generate substantial revenues for Mexican traffickers. The consequences for Mexico of these large black markets include very high rates of drug-related violence and corruption and also the availability of drugs at lower prices. Around the world and over time, many transit countries have suffered from high rates of drug abuse caused by high availability at moderate prices. Mexico and Turkey have been among the most conspicuous exceptions to this general rule. Rates of drug abuse in Mexico are reported to be increasing, but from a low base.[17] It is not clear what has made Mexico so resistant to drug abuse or how long that exception will persist.

---

13. U.S. Office of National Drug Control Policy, *Drug-Related Crime*, Document NCJ-181056 (Washington, D.C.: U.S. Government Printing Office, 2000).

14. Whereas Colombian organizations once used Mexican organizations to help with smuggling, it appears that Mexican organizations now outsource production to Colombians. Hence, the mere fact that the cocaine is not physically produced in Mexico does not necessarily mean that cocaine trafficking is not the main source of profits for Mexican traffickers.

15. U.S. Office of National Drug Control Policy, *Drug-Related Crime*.

16. Peter Reuter and Mark Kleiman, "Risks and Prices: An Economic Analysis of Drug Enforcement" in Michael Tonry and Norval Morris, eds., *Crime and Justice: An Annual Review of Research*, vol. 7 (Chicago: University of Chicago Press, 1986), 289–340; Thomas Babor, Jonathan Caulkins, Griffith Edwards, David Foxcroft, Keith Humphreys, Maria Medina Mora, Isidore Obot, Jurgen Rehm, Peter Reuter, Robin Room, Ingeborg Rossow, and John Strang, *Drug Policy and the Public Good* (New York: Oxford University Press, 2009).

17. K. C. Brouwer, P. Case, R. Ramos, C. Magis-Rodríguez, J. Bucardo, T. L. Patterson, and S. A. Strathdee, "Trends in Production, Trafficking, and Consumption of Methamphetamine and Cocaine in Mexico," *Substance Use and Misuse* 41 (2006): 707–727; M. E. Medina-Mora, G. Borges, C. Fleiz, C. Benjet, E. Rojas, J. Zambrano, J. Villatoro, and S. Aguilar-Gaxiola, "Prevalence and Correlates of Drug Use Disorders in Mexico," *Review of Panamerican Salud Publica* 19 (2006): 265–276.

(Only) The Regime Choice Is Decisive

The first and most consequential choice in drug policy is whether the substance in question can be legally produced and distributed for unsupervised consumption by a substantial segment of the population—for example, adults.[18] We refer to this choice as "legalization versus prohibition."

If the drug is legalized, there follow choices about who is allowed to produce and sell it (e.g., a government monopoly, as with lotteries, or private companies, as with tobacco), whether advertising is restricted (which is difficult to do in the United States, given free speech protections, but is more common elsewhere), what if any excise taxes will be assessed, and so forth. However, those refinements matter little for present purposes. Any form of drug legalization in the United States would most likely all but eliminate the corresponding black market in Mexico.

Likewise, if the substance is prohibited, there remain many choices. What sanctions will be enforced against both users and distributors? What should the sentence length be for various violations? Which prevention curricula should be endorsed? How should drug treatment be financed? However, almost any form of prohibition will generate a black market roughly as large as the current market and thus create problems roughly comparable to those of today; a frustrating reality of drug policy is that drug control programs have a fairly limited ability to dramatically reduce the scale of drug use and drug markets.[19]

Often, drug policy regime selection is described as a trinary rather than a binary choice, with decriminalization given as a third option. This makes sense when focusing on consequences for the final market country (the United States, in this case) but not from the perspective of drug source and transit countries.

Decriminalization means substantially reducing or even eliminating criminal sanctions for drug users, while continuing to prohibit production and distribution. Thus, supply continues to be provided by criminal enterprises. Furthermore, demand should if anything be greater under decriminalization because decriminalization eliminates important risks for buyers.[20] Hence, from the perspective of source and transit countries, decriminalization is a pure loss relative to prohibition. The black markets remain, but if anything they are even larger.

Unfortunately from the perspective of source and transit countries, with the possible exception of marijuana, it is decriminalization, not legalization, that is politically plausible. The implications of this are terribly important and often misunderstood. A sloppy reasoning would argue, "Legalization would clearly solve the problem of black markets in source and transit countries. Decriminalization is in some sense halfway to legalization. So it would benefit source and transit countries half as much as legalization." Such reasoning is simply misguided. Relative to prohibi-

18. Mark A. R. Kleiman, *Against Excess: Drug Policy for Results* (New York: Basic Books, 1992).

19. Babor et al., *Drug Policy.*

20. In practice, marijuana decriminalization seems to have relative modest effects on drug use, both because prices remain high and because typically enforcement risks for users were modest even before the decriminalization; Robin Room, Benedikt Fischer, Wayne Hall, Simon Lenton, and Peter Reuter, *Cannabis: Moving beyond the Stalemate* (Oxford: Oxford University Press, 2010). Only a few jurisdictions have formally decriminalized one or more of the hard drugs. Data concerning those natural experiments are disappointingly weak, so a degree of humility is in order. Nevertheless, it does not appear effects on use have been substantial; Robert MacCoun and Peter Reuter, *Drug War Heresies* (New York: Cambridge University Press, 2001).

tion, decriminalization is much more likely to exacerbate rather than ameliorate the problems posed by black markets in source and transit countries.[21]

A Caution Concerning Legalization of Drugs

Legalization of drugs might solve two salient aspects of Mexico's drug problem—the crime and corruption associated with large black markets. However, legalization in the United States could also adversely affect price and availability for Mexican users. If Mexico also legalized those drugs, prices would fall and availability would increase. If Mexico retained its prohibition, Mexico would no longer be a producer or transit country. However, the Mexico–U.S. border is relatively porous in both directions, not just one way, so if prices were much higher in Mexico than in the United States, that might induce smuggling from north to south. Prices matter because there is now an extensive empirical literature showing that drug use varies inversely with price; lower prices induce greater use and greater use-related types of harm, such as emergency room visits.[22]

There is some debate in the literature as to how much lower legal prices would be, but the most likely scenario is that untaxed prices would fall precipitously and it would not be possible for excise taxes to make up for more than a tiny part of the fall. Cocaine and heroin are available in source countries in ready-to-use form at roughly 1 percent of their current retail price in the United States, and their transportation costs are negligible. For example, a kilogram of cocaine that would sell for more than $100,000 at retail in the United States can be purchased in Colombia for $1,500 and—if legal—could be delivered by express mail for less than $50. Some commentators have observed that there are enormous markups for other agricultural products between farm-gate and retail shelves.[23] However, that misses two fundamental points. The cocaine and heroin that sell for so little in source countries are already in finished form; they are not like the corn that will become cornflakes only with additional processing. Furthermore, the ratio of value to weight is spectacularly different. It would make no sense to ship corn by overnight express at $50 per kilogram; even at retail, cornflakes cereal sells for only a few dollars per kilogram. However, shipping costs of $50 per kilogram are negligible, even compared with a price of $1,500 per kilogram (or $1.50 per gram). Hence, untaxed legal cocaine and heroin would cost at most a few dollars per gram.

Some suggest that excise taxes could be used to keep prices high,[24] but excise taxes of even $10 per gram seem unrealistic; they would invite smuggling to evade the taxes. Indeed, Canada's cigarette tax of $3 per pack (roughly $0.15 per gram) provoked a rapid expansion in black market

21. One potential exception would be marijuana decriminalization that extended to legalizing production for one's own use, as once was the case in Alaska. The net effects of increased use and increased domestic production on the demand for imported marijuana are ambiguous. There is no practical analog for cocaine, heroin, or methamphetamine.

22. For reviews, see M. Grossman, "Individual Behaviours and Substance Use: The Role of Price," in *Substance Use: Individual Behaviour, Social Interactions, Markets, and Politics—Advances in Health Economics and Health Services Research,* Vol. 16, edited by B. Lindgren and M. Grossman (Amsterdam: Elsevier, 2005), 407–439; and Babor et al., *Drug Policy.*

23. Jeffrey A. Miron, "The Effect of Drug Prohibition on Drug Prices: Evidence from the Markets for Cocaine and Heroin," *Review of Economics and Statistics* 85, no. 3 (2003): 522–530.

24. Michael R. Caputo and Brian J. Ostrom, "Potential Tax Revenue from a Regulated Marijuana Market: A Meaningful Revenue Source," *American Journal of Economics and Sociology* 53, no. 4 (1994): 475–490.

sales and so had to be repealed.[25] Excise taxes on gasoline and alcohol are far, far lower per unit weight.[26]

Drug Policy Choices within a Prohibition Regime

We have examined elsewhere the effectiveness of various options for controlling drug problems in the United States, especially those pertaining to drug use,[27] and drug-related crime,[28] and with a particular emphasis on enforcement and incarceration.[29] Those assessments marry judgments about the effectiveness of the interventions themselves with an analytic framework for translating those direct effects into overall implications for the market equilibrium and associated outcomes.

Here we retain the same judgments about effectiveness and analytic framework but shift outcomes, asking how these U.S. programs would affect outcomes in Mexico. In the interest of space, we give capsule summaries of the program's effectiveness in the narrow sense, rather than repeating the reviews of the relevant primary literature offered by Babor and colleagues, Caulkins, Caulkins and Kleiman, and Caulkins and Reuter.[30] This allows us to focus on how the findings differ when considering outcomes upstream in drug transit countries.

Reducing Demand

Any intervention that reduces the demand for illegal drugs in the United States will bring benefits to Mexico. Shrinking demand will tend to reduce the quantity that Mexico produces and transships. Furthermore, one typically expects declines in demand to reduce the price along with the quantity consumed. To the extent that this pattern holds here, the reduction in revenues of Mexican trafficking organizations might be even greater, in percentage terms, than the reduction in quantities supplied. So, just as the United States has an incentive to subsidize supply reduction programs in Mexico, Mexico has an incentive to subsidize demand reduction programs in the United States.

The bad news, from Mexico's perspective, is that conventional demand control programs are not particularly effective. Primary prevention in particular achieves nothing even close to the preventive effect of routine vaccination for childhood diseases. Even the very best primary prevention

25. John W. Galbraith and Murray Kaiserman, "Taxation, Smuggling, and Demand for Cigarettes in Canada: Evidence from Time-Series Data," *Journal of Health Economics* 16 (1997): 287–301.

26. A tax of $0.47 per gallon on a 2.8-kilogram gallon of gasoline is only $0.00017 per gram. Alabama's spirits tax of $18.78 per gallon works out to $0.0054 per gram of whiskey.

27. Babor et al., *Drug Policy*; Jonathan P. Caulkins, "Illicit Substance Abuse and Addiction," in *Investing in the Disadvantaged: Assessing the Benefits and Costs of Social Policies*, edited by David L. Weimer and Aidan R. Vining (Washington, D.C.: Georgetown University Press, 2009), 83–102.

28. See, e.g., Jonathan P. Caulkins and Mark A. R. Kleiman, "Drugs and Crime," in *The Oxford Handbook of Crime and Criminal Justice*, edited by Michael Tonry (New York: Oxford University Press, forthcoming).

29. Jonathan P. Caulkins and Peter Reuter, "How Drug Enforcement Affects Drug Prices," in *Crime and Justice: A Review of Research*, Vol. 39, edited by Michael Tonry (Chicago: University of Chicago Press, forthcoming).

30. Babor et al., *Drug Policy*; Caulkins, "Illicit Substance Abuse"; Caulkins and Kleiman, "Drugs and Crime"; Caulkins and Reuter, "How Drug Enforcement Affects Drug Prices."

programs will probably reduce participants' lifetime consumption by single-digit percentages.[31] Furthermore, to an important degree, the horse is already out of the barn. During the next decade or even two, the vast majority of U.S. drug demand will come from people who are already older than 13 or 14 years, the typical target ages for school-based prevention programs. Hence, even if prevention programs magically became 100 percent effective, so that not a single person from that generation ever touched an illegal drug, the impact on drug demand would be minimal for the next 5 years and very modest even 10 years hence.[32]

Treatment does not suffer from such delays, but there is still a catch. The familiar mantra that "treatment works" hides the fact that treatment works well only with respect to certain criteria. Many studies find that treatment's social benefits exceed its costs,[33] but this is not because treatment succeeds at reducing drug use by a large percentage. In fact, a number of studies conclude that treatment can be a good social investment even if there is no effect on drug use whatsoever,[34] because it reduces the amount of harm associated with use, notably HIV transmission.[35]

Rydell and Everingham offer one of the most-cited analyses of treatment's cost-effectiveness, famously finding treatment to be seven times more cost-effective than law enforcement.[36] However, one of their equally important but less-cited conclusions was that even if every dependent cocaine user enrolled in treatment every year, it would still take 15 years for cocaine use to fall by 50 percent, and this conclusion was based on treatment effectiveness estimates that have been criticized for being potentially too optimistic.[37]

The resolution of this apparent paradox is simple. Treatment's claim to be a good investment stems more from the fact that dependent users generate spectacularly high social costs per year of

---

31. T. Miller and D. Hendrie, *Substance Abuse Prevention Dollars and Cents: A Cost-Benefit Analysis,* DHHS Publication SMA 07-4298 (Rockville, Md.: U.S. Substance Abuse and Mental Health Services Administration, 2009).

32. Jonathan P. Caulkins, C. Peter Rydell, Susan S. Everingham, James Chiesa, and Shawn Bushway, *An Ounce of Prevention, a Pound of Uncertainty: The Cost-Effectiveness of School-Based Drug Prevention Program*, MR-923-RWJ (Santa Monica: RAND, 1999); J. P. Caulkins, S. Paddock, R. Pacula, and J. Chiesa, *School-Based Drug Prevention: What Kind of Drug Use Does it Prevent?* -1459-RWJ (Santa Monica: RAND, 2002).

33. Dean R. Gerstein, Robert A. Johnson, Henrick Harwood, Douglas Fontain, Natalie Suter, and Kay Malloy, *Evaluating Recovery Services: The California Drug and Alcohol Treatment Assessment* (Chicago: National Opinion Research Center, 1994); Andrew S. Rajkumar and Michael T. French, "Drug Abuse, Crime Costs, and the Economic Benefits of Treatment," *Journal of Quantitative Criminology* 13 (1997): 291–323; William S. Cartwright, "Cost–Benefit Analysis of Drug Treatment Services: A Review of the Literature," *Journal of Mental Health Policy Economics* 3 (2000): 11–26; Henrick J. Harwood, Deepti Malhrota, Christel Villarivera, Connie Liu, Umi Chong, and Jawaria Gilani, *Cost-Effectiveness and Cost-Benefit Analysis of Substance Abuse Treatment: A Literature Review* (Washington, D.C.: U.S. Department of Health and Human Services, 2002); Steven Belenko, Nicholas Patapsis, and Michael T. French, eds., *Economic Benefits of Drug Treatment: A Critical Review of the Evidence for Policy Makers*, 2005, http://www.nsula.edu/laattc/documents/EconomicBenefits_2005Feb.pdf.

34. E.g., Harold Pollack, "Methadone Treatment as HIV Prevention," in *Quantitative Analysis of HIV Prevention Programs*, edited by Edward Kaplan and Robert Brookmeyer (New Haven, Conn.: Yale University Press, 2001), 118–142.

35. Cf. Greg S. Zaric, Paul G Barnett, and Margaret L. Brandeau, "HIV Transmission and the Cost-Effectiveness of Methadone Maintenance," *American Journal of Public Health* 90 (2000): 1100–1111.

36. Rydell and Everingham, *Controlling Cocaine.*

37. Charles F. Manski, John V. Pepper, and Yonette F. Thomas, eds., *Assessment of Two Cost-Effectiveness Studies on Cocaine Control Policy* (Washington, D.C.: National Academy Press, 1999).

active use than from treatment having high effectiveness in any absolute sense.[38] The most common outcome of drug treatment is nearly immediate relapse. The situation is notably better with regard to opiates, where there are pharmacotherapies that can effectively substitute for the illegal drugs.[39] However, stimulants are the larger problem in the United States, and even after a generation of concerted effort, there is still no such thing as an effective pharmacotherapy for cocaine, crack, methamphetamine, or any other stimulant.

Reducing Supply

The United States, like most developed nations, devotes the greatest share of its drug control resources to law enforcement, and it is particularly zealous in the use of imprisonment. U.S. incarceration rates exploded from 1975 to 2000, far surpassing those in other Western countries.[40] There are many reasons why the United States is an outlier,[41] but increasing drug-related incarceration is a major driver.[42]

Most imprisonment of drug law violators in the United States falls on people who were involved in supplying drugs, albeit sometimes in minor roles. Users who had no involvement in drug distribution or any other nondrug crime make up a very small proportion of the prison population.[43]

The conventional theory of how this enforcement affects drug markets suggests that it accounts for an important share of the very large markup in prices between the U.S. border and retail.[44] Higher retail prices help suppress the quantity consumed,[45] and so also the demand the United States places on international drug markets. Hence, overall, Mexico should be happy that the United States is so energetic in its pursuit of domestic drug dealers.[46]

---

38. A. Thomas McLellan, James R. McKay, Robert Forman, John Cacciola, and Jack Kemp, "Reconsidering the Evaluation of Addiction Treatment: From Retrospective Follow-up to Concurrent Recovery Monitoring," *Addiction* 100 (2005): 447–458.

39. L. Amato, M. Davoli, C. A. Perucci, M. Ferri, F. Faggiano, and R. P. Mattick, "An Overview of Systematic Reviews of the Effectiveness of Opiate Maintenance Therapies: Available Evidence to Inform Clinical Practice and Research," *Journal of Substance Abuse Treatment* 28 (2005): 321–330.

40. A. Kuhn, "Incarcerations Rates across the World," in *Penal Reform in Overcrowded Times*, edited by M. Tonry (New York: Oxford University Press, 2001).

41. E.g., M. Tonry, "Why Are Incarceration Rates So High?" *Crime and Delinquency*, 45, no. 4 (1999): 419–437.

42. A. Blumstein and A. J. Beck, "Population Growth in U.S. Prisons, 1980–1996," in *Crime and Justice*, edited by M. Tonry and J. Petersilia (Chicago: University of Chicago Press, 1999), 17–61; M. Mauer, "The Causes and Consequences of Prison Growth in the United States," *Punishment and Society* 3 (2001): 9–20.

43. Eric Sevigny and Jonathan P. Caulkins, "Kingpins or Mules? An Analysis of Drug Offenders Incarcerated in Federal and State Prisons," *Criminology and Public Policy* 3, no. 3 (2004): 401–434.

44. Reuter and Kleiman, "Risks and Prices"; Jonathan P. Caulkins and Peter Reuter, "What Price Data Tell Us about Drug Markets," *Journal of Drug Issues* 28 (1998): 593–612; Caulkins and Reuter, "How Drug Enforcement Affects Drug Prices."

45. Grossman, "Individual Behaviours."

46. Indeed, one could argue that Mexico should be happy that the United States is so extraordinarily aggressive in its incarceration of nondrug offenders as well. Some burglars, robbers, and murderers are drug users, and incarcerating them incarcerates some portion of U.S. demand. (Contrary to cynics' claims, drug use in U.S. prisons occurs at rates far, far below the rates of use for those same individuals when free.)

The extent to which the United States' embrace of incarceration actually helps Mexico is limited, however, by fact that incarcerating typical drug dealers is not a terribly effective strategy for suppressing drug use. Kuziemo and Levitt estimate that the 1985–1996 increase in the number of drug law violators behind bars drove up cocaine prices by only 5 to 15 percent above what they otherwise would have been.[47] That is, to the extent that punishing suppliers affects drug markets at all, it affects markets in ways that Mexico should like. However, the effects of expanded incarceration on drug demand are not dramatic.

The crucial point is that the effect of being tough on suppliers has on drug prices and use is highly nonlinear. Shifting from legalization to prohibition with enough enforcement to achieve the structural consequences of product illegality has enormous effects, driving prices far above the legal price and thus greatly reducing use. However, expanding incarceration further, beyond this baseline, has much more modest incremental effects.[48] So the United States could cut its incarceration by 50 percent without severe adverse effects on Mexico, even though cutting incarceration by a second 50 percent would lead to dramatic changes.[49]

In general, therefore, Mexico should be pleased with the massive expansion in U.S. drug-related incarceration since 1980,[50] but the benefit is not enormous because the effects on U.S. drug use have not been enormous. But there are two or three very important exceptions to this general rule. First, to the extent that aggressive enforcement within the United States pushes the production of marijuana and methamphetamine out of the United States, that is clearly a loss for Mexico.[51] To be more precise, Mexico should be pleased with the United States' tough domestic enforcement against cocaine and heroin suppliers, but it should wish that the United States would go easy on marijuana cultivation and methamphetamine production, making it easier for suppliers to produce those drugs in the United States rather than carrying them across the Mexico–United States border.

Second, and of potentially greater consequence, seizing drugs in the United States is generally bad for Mexico, even if incarcerating the owner of the seized drug would be good. The reason is that supplying drugs that are seized further down the distribution chain in the United States is just as profitable as supplying drugs that are used in the United States. In a very real sense, seizing drugs in the United States increases demand for drugs produced in or shipped through Mexico.

Seizing 1 kilogram in the United States does not increase U.S. imports by 1 kilogram because seized drugs are not replaced one for one. Seizing drugs increases the cost to suppliers of successfully providing a gram for purchase at retail, and the suppliers pass those increased costs along to users in the form of higher prices. Those higher prices suppress use. The amount by which use

---

47. Ilyana Kuziemko and Steven D. Levitt, "An Empirical Analysis of Imprisoning Drug Offenders," *Journal of Public Economics* 88 (2004): 2043–2066.

48. Caulkins and Reuter, "How Drug Enforcement Affects Drug Prices."

49. Jonathan P. Caulkins and Peter Reuter, "Reorienting U.S. Drug Policy," *Issues in Science and Technology* 23 (2006): 79–85.

50. Jonathan P. Caulkins and Sara Chandler, "Long-Run Trends in Incarceration of Drug Offenders in the US," *Crime and Delinquency* 52, no. 4 (2006): 619–641, DOI: 10.1177/0011128705284793.

51. Short of legalization, no plausible easing of enforcement against cocaine or heroin would make their production practical in the United States because they are derived from plants that must be grown outdoors and so are easy to detect. Methamphetamine is manufactured, not derived from plants, and marijuana can profitably be grown indoors because it can generate more than $1,000 in retail value per square foot of growing area, vs. more like $5 per square foot for coca bushes and poppy plants as conventionally cultivated.

goes down per kilogram seized depends on many particulars, including the elasticity of demand and the replacement cost of drugs at the point seized. (As Reuter notes,[52] replacement costs are higher per unit seized when the seizures occur near the retail end of the distribution chain than when the seizures are made further up the chain.) Space limitations preclude a detailed analysis.[53] However, it is likely that on average, drug seizures in the United States increase demand for drugs produced in or shipped through Mexico. Unfortunately, seizures are appealing from a purely U.S. perspective because they do not involve the many costs of incarceration while still imposing costs on drug suppliers.

The third potential exception is the possibility that incarcerating suppliers creates violent competition about the chance to supply the incarcerated person's customers. If the person incarcerated in the United States operated in Mexico, that collateral violence could exacerbate drug-related violence in Mexico.

Interventions in Colombia and Afghanistan

U.S. drug policy also includes counterdrug activities in drug source countries, notably Colombia but also in Afghanistan. By and large, these interventions have no direct effect on Mexico. The primary reason is simply that interventions in source countries have little effect on retail prices or consumption in final market countries,[54] and any drugs seized or destroyed upstream from Mexico do not increase the volume that is shipped through Mexico the way that drugs seized in the United States do.

In the case of Afghanistan, there is the additional fact that there is not so much one global market for illegal opiates but two hemispheric markets. Most of what is consumed in the Western Hemisphere is produced in Colombia and Mexico.[55] Thus, at present, Afghanistan is not a noteworthy supplier of heroin to the United States.[56]

In theory, there could be exceptions to this general rule. In particular, if United States–supported law enforcement efforts in Colombia somehow made it very hard for Colombians to ship cocaine to Mexico, while making it very easy for Colombians to ship directly to the United States or through some other transit country, that might shift smuggling routes so they bypassed Mexico. By some cold calculus, it might be in the United States' interest to play favorites, condemning some less important country to being a narco-state in order to siphon trafficking away from Mexico, but such realpolitik has rarely entered the drug policy discourse, which is more often dominated by unrealistically optimistic commitments to eradicate, not merely relocate, drug trafficking.

---

52. Reuter, "Quantity Illusion and Paradoxes of Drug Interdiction."

53. E.g., see Caulkins and Kleiman, "Drugs and Crime."

54. Babor et al., *Drug Policy.*

55. This traditional view has been challenged; see Paoli, Greenfield, and Reuter, *World Heroin Market.* The counterargument is that estimated U.S. consumption (22 tons) greatly exceeds estimated South and Central American production (perhaps 10 tons). However, given the frailty of both consumption and production estimates, we remain persuaded by the fact that heroin seized in the United States rarely displays the chemical "signature" of Southwest or Southeast Asian production.

56. Afghanistan plays no role whatsoever in supplying U.S. cocaine/crack markets, the largest and most damaging in the United States, or, for that matter, any other U.S. illegal drug market.

Coerced or Mandated Abstinence

The discussion above suggests that none of the conventional U.S. drug policy pillars is likely to offer much help to Mexico. The better chance of achieving a larger, more immediate effect comes from so-called coerced or mandated abstinence programs that apply the stick of enforcement to users, not suppliers, but do so in an intelligent way.[57]

Like drug courts, these programs couple frequent drug testing with immediate and certain but modest sanctions for failed tests (e.g., one or two days in jail, starting immediately after the failed test). Incremental enhancements to conventional sanctions do not produce powerful deterrent effects,[58] but the more modern approach tries to "get deterrence right" by designing environments grounded in realistic models of human decisionmaking.[59] Notably, they stress certainty and celerity (swiftness) over severity. Furthermore, coerced or mandated abstinence is more scalable because it does not make such extensive use of a judge's scarce time.

Perhaps the most famous example is Hawaii's Opportunity Program with Enforcement (HOPE) for probationers. HOPE has cut failed or missed drug tests by 80 percent relative to regular probation and cut by more than half both new arrests and days of incarceration.[60] South Dakota's 24/7 Sobriety Program is another example.[61] Originally conceived as a response to repeat drunk driving offenders, the program achieved a better than 99 percent rate of testing clean and led South Dakota to expand it to most forms of community release, including pretrial release, probation or parole, and suspended sentences.

The idea is not that every single dependent user can achieve abstinence through these programs but that most can, and starting everyone with coerced abstinence achieves a form of "behavioral triage" that allows scarce treatment resources to focus on the subset of dependent individuals with the greatest need.[62] What makes coerced or mandated abstinence so important from Mexico's perspective is the observation that most cocaine, heroin, and methamphetamine consumed in the United States is used by people who are nominally under criminal justice supervision (e.g., are on probation), so they are subject to frequent testing with consequences for failed tests.

Summary

Illegal drug markets in the United States create enormous costs for Mexico. Legalizing these drugs would largely eliminate these costs. Tough or "hawkish" drug policies are in some sense the opposite of legalization, so one might expect that moving "closer" to legalization by enforcing a more

---

57. M. A. R. Kleiman, *When Brute Force Fails: Strategy for Crime Control* (Princeton, N.J.: Princeton University Press, 2009).

58. Daniel S. Nagin, "Deterrence and Incapacitation," in *The Handbook of Crime and Punishment*, edited by Michael Tonry (New York: Oxford University Press, 1998), 345–368.

59. David M. Kennedy, "Pulling Levers: Chronic Offenders, High-Crime Settings, and a Theory of Prevention," *Valparaiso University Law Review* 31(1997): 449—484; David M. Kennedy, *Deterrence and Crime Prevention: Reconsidering the Prospect of Sanction* (New York: Routledge, 2008).

60. Angela Hawken and Mark Kleiman, "HOPE for Reform: What a Novel Probation Program in Hawaii Might Teach Other States," *American Prospect Online*, April 10, 2007.

61. Jonathan P. Caulkins and Robert L. DuPont, "Is 24/7 Sobriety a Good Goal for Repeat DUI Offenders?" *Addiction*, forthcoming.

62. A. Hawken, "A Behavioral Triage Model for Identifying and Treating Substance-Abusing Offenders," submitted to *Journal of Drug Policy Analysis*.

"dovish" prohibition would at least partially ameliorate drug-related costs in Mexico. However, though it seems that Mexico would benefit from the United States expanding demand reduction measures—whether in the form of prevention, treatment, or coerced abstinence—an across-the-board easing of supply control efforts would not necessarily help, and could plausibly exacerbate, Mexico's problems.

However, the choices with regard to drug enforcement and associated incarceration are not only "how much" but also "what kind" and "against whom"? Presumably, the effects on Mexico of the United States imposing a five-year prison term are different when the individual convicted is a European American selling Colombian heroin at retail in Boston instead of a Mexican American cocaine kingpin whose smuggling organization spans the Mexico–United States border. Therefore, the next section gives an empirical investigation of who it is that the United States imprisons for drug law violations.

The Imprisonment of Drug Law Violators in the United States and Effects on Mexico

We examine some of the effects of U.S. incarceration on Mexico using data from the 2004 Survey of Inmates in State and Federal Correctional Facilities (SISFCF), a nationally representative survey of imprisoned individuals administered every five to seven years.[63] We begin by briefly discussing these data and our methods, as well as important limitations and delimitations of our analysis.

Data and Methods

The 2004 SISFCF, which is the most recent in a series that extends back to 1974, was conducted between October 2003 and May 2004.[64] The survey employed a two-stage sampling design, completing interviews with 14,499 inmates from 287 state facilities and 3,686 inmates from 39 federal

63. Bureau of Justice Statistics, *Survey of Inmates in State and Federal Correctional Facilities, 2004*, computer file ICPSR04572-v1 (Ann Arbor, Mich.: Inter-University Consortium for Political and Social Research, 2007).

64. Even though the 2004 SISFCF is the most recent available, one caveat is that the data are already five years old and may not reflect the current situation. For one, the Mexican drug trade has become particularly violent in recent years with a record 7,600 drug-related deaths in 2009 (Arthur Brice, "Deadliest Year in Mexico's War on Drugs," CNN.com, 2009), whereas a 2003 Drug Enforcement Administration report states that "the precise number of drug-related murders in Mexico is difficult to estimate, but drug-related violence accounts for hundreds of murders each year"; U.S. Drug Enforcement Administration, *Mexico*, 22. Some of this violence has spilled over into the United States, although 2009 produced a record low year for homicides in the United States as a whole. Significant changes in the drug trade and drug policy on both sides of the border have also occurred after 2004. For example, since President Felipe Calderon took office three years ago, Mexico has ramped up its efforts against the cartels and nearly doubled the rate of extraditions to the United States; Marc Lacey, "Mexico's Drug Traffickers Continue to Trade in Prison," *New York Times*, August 11, 2009. And on the U.S. side, the Drug Enforcement Administration–led Project Coronado targeting major Mexican DTOs has alone resulted in nearly 1,200 arrests and the seizure of almost 12 tons of drugs and $33 million in U.S. currency since 2005; U.S. Department of Justice, "Press Release: More Than 300 Alleged La Familia Cartel Members and Associates Arrested in Two-Day Nationwide Takedown," Office of Public Affairs, 2009. Thus, interpretation of our results must be made with the understanding that the data were collected prior to these recent market and policy shifts.

institutions. The total response rates were 89 percent and 85 percent, respectively.[65] Our analyses and point estimates are weighted to account for this nonresponse and other sampling design elements. These estimates have estimable confidence intervals, but, for ease of presentation, we do not report them here. Also, the data are self-reported, which introduces a degree of nonsampling error that cannot be estimated.

Our results generalize to the imprisoned population of federal (N = 129,299) and state (N = 1,226,171) inmates, as of January 2004. Thus, our analyses and ability to generalize exclude inmates held in local jails (generally, pretrial detainees and offenders sentenced to less than one year) and juvenile lockups.

For our purposes, we define the subpopulation of drug offenders in the SISFCF as those with a controlling drug offense. The combined sample of federal and state drug inmates (n = 4,707) includes n = 4,572 respondents with a primary drug offense plus an additional n = 135 "nondrug" cases (e.g., conspiracy, racketeering, weapons) that were clearly drug-related according to supplemental incident characteristic information. For certain analyses, we also define a smaller analytic subsample of drug offenders (n = 4,211) because n = 496 respondents with a controlling drug offense were erroneously never asked the survey's questions on drug offense incident characteristics (which collect information on drug type and quantity, role in the offense, and organizational involvement).[66]

Ethnic/National Identity and Imprisonment for Drug Crimes

To center our investigation on United States–Mexico drug policy and to provide a backdrop for subsequent analyses, we first examine the ethnic/national origin of drug law violators incarcerated in U.S. prisons. In total, we estimate that there were 335,550 drug offenders imprisoned in the United States in 2004, representing one-quarter (24.8 percent) of the 1.36 million federal and state inmates.[67] By jurisdiction, proportionately more federal inmates (57.3 percent) than state inmates (21.3 percent) were incarcerated for a drug crime, but because state prisons incarcerate roughly 10 times as many inmates as the federal prison system, the great majority of imprisoned drug law violators are in state (78 percent) rather than federal (22 percent) prisons.

Deciding how best to categorize people by ethnic/national background is tricky in the best of circumstances, and we were limited in our effort by the questions asked in the SISFCF. We were also guided by our analytic focus on United States–Mexico drug policy. Thus, with these constraints in mind, we were able to reliably distinguish between (1) U.S. citizens with no Mexican ancestry (i.e., "non–Mexican Americans"), (2) U.S. citizens of Mexican ancestry (i.e., "Mexican Americans"), (3) citizens of Mexico who are not also U.S. citizens (i.e., "Mexican nationals"), and (4) others who are citizens of neither Mexico nor the United States (i.e., "other foreign nationals"). About 7 in 10

---

65. Bureau of Justice Statistics, *Survey of Inmates.*

66. Interestingly, the additional 135 "nondrug" respondents in our subsample were all asked the drug incident characteristics. Personal communication with Bureau of Justice Statistics representatives suggest these discrepancies are likely explained by miscategorization of the controlling offense type, which can occur at any of three related and sequential offense classification points involving computer, interviewer, and, as a last resort, respondent identification of offense type. An error at any of these points can, and apparently did in a nontrivial number of cases, misdirect the interview.

67. There were also upwards of 150,000 drug offenders detained in U.S. local jails, but, as noted above, we do not focus on this population in our present analysis.

Table C1. Conviction Offense by Ethnic/National Identity, Federal Inmates, 2004

Conviction Offense	Non–Mexican Americans	Mexican Americans	Mexican Nationals	Other Foreign Nationals	Total
Drug offense	55.5	68.9	50.0	68.4	57.3
Trafficking/sales	77.6	79.1	70.8	68.8	76.3
Possession with intent	13.8	11.9	14.0	12.8	13.5
Simple possession	3.6	4.2	12.4	8.9	4.8
Other/unknown	5.0	4.9	2.8	9.4	5.3
Nondrug offense	44.5	31.1	50.0	31.6	42.7
N	99,682	8,705	8,831	12,081	129,999

Source: Created by author.

people in this latter group were citizens of just four countries: the Dominican Republic, Colombia, Cuba, and Jamaica. Collectively, here we refer to the first two groups as U.S. citizens and the second two as foreign nationals. We caution the obvious, however, in noting that these groups are not monolithic, especially non–Mexican Americans—a group that includes blacks, whites, and other non-Mexican Hispanics, among others.

Clearly, by our accounting, the majority of people in prison are non–Mexican Americans (84.7 percent). Notably, for our more homogenous ethnic/national groups, the distribution among inmates closely parallels the broader U.S. population in 2004. Overall, for example, 9.0 percent of prisoners reported being Mexican American, compared with 9.1 percent of the household population.[68] Mexican nationals (3.2 percent) and other foreign nationals (3.1 percent) were imprisoned in roughly equal numbers, which is also congruent with the Census Bureau's estimate for the number of foreign-born noncitizens (7.0 percent) in the United States in 2004.

Turning to our main analyses, we find that both the proportion of inmates convicted of a drug offense and the seriousness of the conviction offense differ by ethnic/national identity. As shown in table C1, the proportion of *federal* inmates incarcerated for a drug law violation ranges from half for Mexican nationals to nearly 7 in 10 for Mexican Americans. Moreover, among drug offenders, U.S. citizens on the whole were relatively more likely to be incarcerated for drug trafficking and/or sales, whereas a greater percentage of (both Mexican and other) noncitizens were incarcerated for simple possession. This is especially true of Mexican nationals, who proportionately were 3.5 times more likely to be incarcerated for simple possession than non–Mexican Americans. In comparison, other foreign nationals were relatively more likely to be incarcerated for other drug offenses, which at the federal level mainly include drug-related conspiracy and racketeering.

68. U.S. Census Bureau, *The American Community: Hispanics, 2004* (Washington, D.C.: U.S. Government Printing Office, 2007).

Table C2. Conviction Offense by Ethnic/National Identity, State Inmates, 2004

Conviction Offense	Non–Mexican Americans	Mexican Americans	Mexican Nationals	Other Foreign Nationals	Total
Drug offense	21.4	19.9	24.3	21.8	21.3
Trafficking/sales	57.5	51.7	58.1	71.3	57.3
Possession with intent	12.7	10.5	13.8	9.3	12.4
Simple possession	26.4	33.4	27.0	19.4	26.8
Other/unknown	2.5	4.4	1.1	0.0	3.4
Nondrug offense	78.6	80.1	75.7	78.2	78.7
N	1,048,703	112,929	34,144	30,395	1,226,171

Source: Created by author.

The *state*-level data reveal a contrary, if somewhat less distinct, offense by ethnicity and/or nationality distribution. As table C2 shows, the proportion of inmates incarcerated for a drug offense ranged from about one-fifth of Mexican Americans to one-quarter of Mexican nationals. Moreover, in contrast to federal inmates, Mexican Americans in state prisons had the least severe drug conviction profile, with about one-half sentenced for trafficking and/or sales and one-third for simple possession. In comparison, other foreign nationals were proportionately most likely to be sentenced for trafficking and/or sales and least likely to be sentenced for simple possession.

These observations give rise to two important policy questions. First, between the United States and Mexico, what percentage of Mexican nationals incarcerated for a drug offense is held in U.S. prisons? Second, how does the U.S. incarceration rate for Mexican nationals compare to the incarceration rate for non–Mexican Americans and for Mexican Americans? The answer to the first question will provide evidence on the relative cross-border use of incarceration for Mexican drug law violators, whereas the answer to the second question will provide some insight into whether or not the U.S. drug incarceration burden falls disproportionately on Mexican nationals and/or Mexican Americans. We treat each of these questions in turn.

The Proportion of Incarcerated Mexican Nationals Who Are in U.S. Prisons

In answering our first question, we derive two figures: the proportion of Mexican nationals incarcerated for (1) all crimes and (2) drug crimes only.[69] As detailed in table C3, we find that almost one-fifth (18.4 percent) of the Mexican nationals who were in prison for any crime in 2004 were incarcerated in the United States. For drug offenses, the share of Mexican nationals in U.S. prisons is even larger, at about one-quarter (25.9 percent). By way of comparison, the similar proportion

69. These figures naturally exclude Mexican Nationals incarcerated outside of either the United States or Mexico.

Table C3. Estimating the Proportion of Incarcerated Mexican Nationals Held in U.S. versus Mexican Prisons, 2004

Location of Prison	Number of Mexican Nationals in Prison for All Crimes	Percentage of Mexican Nationals in Prison for a Drug Crime (percent)	Number of Mexican Nationals in Prison for a Drug Crime
United States			
Federal	8,831	50.0	4,418
State	34,144	24.3	8,309
Total	42,975	29.6	12,727
Mexico			
Federal	49,442	51.0	25,215
State	140,721	8.0	11,258
Total	190,163	19.2	36,473
Total U.S. share	18.4 percent	—	25.9 percent

Source: Created by author.

of Canadian nationals incarcerated for any crime in U.S. (versus Canadian) prisons was a scant 1.8 percent. Although expatriate Mexicans far outnumber Canadians in the United States, it is no less striking that one in every four Mexicans behind prison bars for a drug offense is serving that time in a U.S. prison.

For the interested reader, we further explicate the underlying basis and assumptions supporting the calculations presented in table C3. First, from the SISFCF, we directly estimated the number of Mexican nationals held in U.S. prisons for all crimes to be 42,975. We then derived the overall number of Mexican nationals held in Mexican prisons by multiplying the total year-end 2004 Mexican prison population reported by Walmsley by the proportion of convicted inmates who were Mexican citizens as reported by the United Nations, that is, (191,890)(99.1 percent) = 190,163.[70] It follows that roughly 42,975/(42,975 + 190,163) = 18.4 percent of all incarcerated Mexican nationals were held in U.S. prisons.[71]

We similarly estimated from the SISFCF the number of Mexican nationals held in U.S. prisons for drug offenses to be 12,727. Deriving the comparable number for Mexico required several steps,

70. Roy Walmsley, *World Prison Population List*, 6th ed. (London: International Centre for Prison Studies, King's College, 2005); United Nations Office on Drugs and Crime, *Eighth United Nations Survey of Crime Trends and Operations of Criminal Justice Systems, Covering the Period 2001–2002* (New York: United Nations, 2005).

71. Since Mexico notoriously incarcerates a large population of pretrial detainees (Amnesty International, 2007), one could also contrast the *sentenced* population in prison. Azaola and Bergman (2007) report, for instance, that 43 percent of Mexico's prison inmates are unsentenced, a ratio that has remained steady over the past decade. In contrast, less than 1 percent of U.S. prisoners are unsentenced. Nevertheless, given that unsentenced inmates in Mexico commonly spend months and even years in prison, we feel the most important comparison to make is with total prison risk, not just post-sentencing prison risk.

because detailed data on the characteristics of Mexican inmates are not readily available. First, we located two estimates in the literature reporting the proportion of Mexico's inmates who were incarcerated for a drug crime: 51 percent for federal inmates,[72] and 8 percent for state inmates.[73] Second, we estimated the respective federal (N = 49,442) and state (N = 140,721) inmate populations by multiplying the total number of Mexican nationals held in Mexican prisons (N = 190,163) by 0.26 and 0.74, the federal-to-state inmate ratio that has remained steady during the last decade.[74] Third, multiplying across table C3, we estimated the number of Mexican nationals held in Mexican prisons for a drug offense to be (49,442)(0.51) = 25,215 at the federal level and (140,721)(0.08) = 11,258 at the state level. Finally, after summing the federal and state numbers, we determined that 12,727/(12,727 + 36,473) = 25.9 percent of Mexican nationals incarcerated for a drug crime were held in U.S. prisons.

Imprisonment Rates for Mexican Nationals vs. Other Groups

We estimate the drug and nondrug incarceration rates for four groups: non–Mexican Americans and Mexican Americans in the United States, and Mexican nationals in both the United States and Mexico. For each group, we divide the number of inmates incarcerated for each crime type by the group's 2004 population. The number of drug and nondrug inmates is based on the SISFCF and our analysis in table C3. The U.S. population counts are calculated from U.S. Census Bureau estimates of the household populations,[75] and the Mexico population is from the *CIA World Factbook 2004*.[76]

As shown in table C4, Mexican Americans and Mexican nationals are incarcerated at an equal rate for drug offenses (159 per 100,000), a figure that is about 1.4 times as large as the non–Mexican American drug incarceration rate (113 per 100,000). In contrast, Mexico's drug imprisonment rate of 35 per 100,000 is roughly one-quarter to one-third the rates of the three U.S. groups. Among nondrug offenders, the incarceration rates are considerably larger, ranging from a low of 146 per 100,000 for Mexican nationals in Mexico to 521 per 100,000 for Mexican Americans in the United States.

Two things are obvious from table C4. First, the United States is (no surprise) much more aggressive than Mexico when it comes to the use of prison, especially for drug crimes. Mexican

72. Dave Bewley-Taylor, Chris Hallam, and Rob Allen, *The Incarceration of Drug Offenders: An Overview* (London: Beckley Foundation Drug Policy Programme, 2009).

73. Elena Azaola and Marcelo Bergman, "The Mexican Prison System," in *Reforming the Administration of Justice in Mexico*, edited by Wayne Cornelius and David Shirk (San Diego: Center for U.S.-Mexican Studies, 2007), 91–114. In the absence of additional data, we made the following assumptions. First, Bewley-Taylor, Hallam, and Allen, *Incarceration of Drug Offenders*, report their 51 percent figure in reference to *sentenced* federal inmates. We assumed that this figure applies equally to both sentenced and unsentenced inmates. Second, Azaola and Bergman based their 8 percent figure on a 2002 survey of inmates from three central Mexican districts (the range across the three districts was 5–22 percent). We assumed that this average applies to Mexico as a whole.

74. Azaola and Bergman, "Mexican Prison System."

75. U.S. Census Bureau, *American Community: Hispanics*, table 1 and figure 7.

76. U.S. Central Intelligence Agency, *CIA World Factbook 2004* (Langley, Va.: U.S. Central Intelligence Agency, 2004).

Table C4. Overall Drug and Nondrug Imprisonment Rates per 100,000 by Ethnic/National Identity, 2004

	United States			Mexico
Measure	Non–Mexican Americans	Mexican Americans	Mexican Nationals	Mexican Nationals
Group population	247,799,815	17,893,281	8,001,482	104,959,594
Number imprisoned for a drug offense	279,442	28,493	12,727	36,473
Drug incarceration rate per 100,000	113	159	159	35
Number imprisoned for a nondrug offense	868,943	93,142	30,248	153,690
Nondrug incarceration rate per 100,000	351	521	378	146

Source: Created by author.

nationals living in the United States have an imprisonment rate for nondrug crimes that is 2.6 times greater than the rate for Mexican nationals living in Mexico, a ratio that swells to 4.5 to 1 for drug law violations.[77]

Second, Mexican Americans and Mexican nationals living in the United States face higher rates of imprisonment than do other U.S. citizens. What is not clear is what causes this difference. There are many possibilities: discrimination, socioeconomic status, different rates of offending, and overrepresentation in states with particularly tough enforcement and punishment policies (e.g., the South vs. the Northeast). There is no way to distinguish among these possibilities with the data at hand. It may be instructive, however, to contrast the relative rate of imprisonment for drug offenses with that for other offenses. If one believed that the relative imprisonment rates for nondrug offenses controlled for all the factors mentioned above, then the ratio of the rates might give an indication of whether Mexican Americans and/or Mexican nationals participate in drug-related criminal activity more or less than any greater or lesser tendency to participate in crime generally, relative to non–Mexican Americans.

By this (admittedly somewhat strained) logic, we would observe that the extent to which Mexican Americans are "overimprisoned" for drug crimes relative to non–Mexican Americans (159 being 41 percent higher than 113) is actually less than the 48 percent (521 vs. 351) extent to which they are overimprisoned for nondrug crimes. So one might speculate that Mexican Americans' higher rates of imprisonment for drug-related offenses may be due to other factors (discrimination, living in tough states, etc.) not a tendency to specialize criminal offending in drug crimes.

In contrast, the same 41 percent overimprisonment rate Mexican nationals suffer for drug-related offenses stands out relative to their much smaller 8 percent (378 vs. 351) rate of overim-

77. To be sure, the imprisonment rate of Mexican Nationals in the United States is *not* being driven up by the extradition of Mexican Nationals to serve time in U.S. prisons. Between 1995 and 2003, Mexico extradited only 133 fugitives to the United States for *all* crimes (Embassy of Mexico, 2004).

prisonment for nondrug crimes. Hence, one might guess that Mexican nationals but not Mexican Americans focus their offending on drug distribution as opposed to other, nondrug criminality. That would not be surprising if, as seems possible, Mexican nationals in the United States maintain stronger connections to colleagues in Mexico than do Mexican Americans, many of whom have been in the United States for generations.

However, we close by noting that these data can be looked at from either of two perspectives, like a glass half empty or half full. Although Mexican nationals and Mexican Americans may be overrepresented relative to non–Mexican Americans, they represent only 4 percent and 8 percent, respectively, of all people imprisoned in the United States for drug law violations. So, in one sense, though Mexican nationals and Mexican Americans may play a special role in drug trafficking in the United States, they do not in any sense appear to play a dominant role. Certainly, those proportions of drug law violators imprisoned in the United States are far, far smaller than the proportion of drugs consumed in the United States that are produced in or pass through Mexico.

Characteristics of Drug Law Violators Incarcerated in U.S. Prisons

The previous section found that Mexican nationals and Mexican Americans are somewhat but not dramatically overrepresented among drug law violators in U.S. prisons. That is perhaps surprising, given that a sizable share of illegal drugs consumed in the United States is trafficked through Mexico. This might suggest that Mexican drug organizations do not vertically integrate very far down into domestic U.S. drug distribution networks. However, those imprisoned for drug law violations in the United States are a heterogeneous group, and most are not kingpins.[78] So, it could also be that Mexican nationals and/or Mexican Americans play a substantially disproportionate role in the highest-level, most organized, and/or most violent aspects of drug distribution in the United States, even if their aggregate numbers in prison are not overwhelming.

To explore these possibilities, we turn to an examination of the types of drug offenders incarcerated in U.S. prisons, focusing on ethnic/national group differences in the type, quantity, and purity of the illegal drugs involved; participation in a drug-trafficking organization; the role played in the offense; weapons involvement; and southwestern border region drug trafficking. As noted above, for certain analyses, we focus on the subset of drug offenders ($n = 4{,}211$; $N = 299{,}913$) who were asked the SISFCF's questions on drug-related incident characteristics.

Market Indicators: Drug Type, Quantity, and Purity

In this section, we examine ethnic/national differences in drug market characteristics, focusing on the type and quantity of drugs involved in the offense for heroin, methamphetamine, powder cocaine, crack cocaine, and marijuana. In addition, we examine data on purity for heroin and powder cocaine (the SISFCF does not ask about purity for other drugs).

Several themes are evident from the results presented in table C5. First, although all groups are to some extent involved with each of the drugs investigated, our findings confirm well-recognized links between ethnic/national identity and trafficking in particular drugs: non–Mexican Americans with crack cocaine, Mexican Americans with methamphetamine and marijuana,

---

78. Sevigny and Caulkins, "Kingpins or Mules?"

Table C5. Select Drug Market Indicators by Ethnic/National Identity, Federal and State Drug Inmates, 2004

Drug Market Indicator	Non–Mexican Americans	Mexican Americans	Mexican Nationals	Other Foreign Nationals	Total
Heroin offender (percent)	9.6	13.5	13.4	17.2	10.4
Heroin quantity (median)	3.5	3.0	2.0	207.0	3.5
Heroin purity (median)	60	50	50	98	60
Methamphetamine offender (percent)	17.5	31.5	30.3	3.8	18.6
Methamphetamine quantity (median)	10.0	28.4	453.6	32.0	15.6
Powder cocaine offender (percent)	29.2	34.9	42.7	60.1	31.6
Powder cocaine quantity (median)	29.9	28.4	498.0	1,000.0	56.0
Powder cocaine purity (median)	67	79	80	85	70
Crack cocaine offender (percent)	37.8	9.9	8.5	13.4	33.3
Crack cocaine quantity (median)	4.0	14.0	907.2	90.0	5.0
Marijuana offender (percent)	12.5	18.4	10.5	10.2	12.8
Marijuana quantity (median)	28.9	2,722	90,718	153,000	99.0
N	250,601	25,454	10,718	13,140	299,913

Note: Percentages for drug type may sum to greater than 100 because multiple drugs could be reported. Drug quantities are expressed in grams. All calculations are based on nonmissing data, the amount of which varies by indicator.

Source: Created by author.

Mexican nationals with methamphetamine and powder cocaine, and other foreign nationals with heroin and powder cocaine.[79]

79. Admittedly, our aggregate ethnic/national groups mask additional variation. For example, were we dig deeper into the non–Mexican American group, we would see that 48.6 percent of whites vs. 0.4 percent of blacks were involved with methamphetamine and, conversely, that 7.0 percent of whites vs. 54.7 percent of blacks were involved with crack cocaine. That 58 percent of the non–Mexican Americans were black and only 30 percent white explains why the crack cocaine link appears more strongly in the aggregate analysis. Similarly, among other foreign nationals, Dominicans drive the heroin connection (with their relatively large numbers [21 percent] and substantial involvement with heroin [31 percent]), and Colombians drive

However, there is at least one small puzzle in these data: Whereas Mexican Americans and Mexican nationals were similarly more or less likely to be involved with heroin, methamphetamine, and both powder and crack cocaine relative to the larger population of offenders, this pattern did not hold for marijuana. Perhaps the relatively smaller proportion of Mexican national (10.5 percent) to Mexican American (18.4 percent) marijuana offenders might be due to the unfavorable logistics of smuggling bulky marijuana shipments combined with a strong domestically produced marijuana market and, to a degree, long-standing practices in some border jurisdictions of deferring prosecution of small-quantity Mexican marijuana offenders in favor of outright deportation.

The second point to draw from table C5 is that, in terms of quantity and purity of product, foreign nationals sit atop the distribution hierarchy, followed in turn by Mexican Americans and non–Mexican Americans. Indeed, with certain predictable exceptions, foreign nationals tended to traffic in pounds and kilograms of product that was (for heroin and cocaine) upwards of 80 percent pure. Conversely, U.S. citizens tended to deal in grams and ounces with purities less than 80 percent. These findings are consistent with the data on inmates' individual role in the offense presented next.

Inmates' Individual Role in the Offense

The inmate survey asks respondents a series of questions about their individual role in the offense at the time of arrest. From these questions, we constructed a single measure of the most serious role reported based on a generally accepted hierarchy of culpability.[80] The results are presented in table C6. Although enforcement pressure and prison risk vary by level of involvement in the drug trade, overall, the role in the offense of incarcerated drug offenders follows a classic pyramidal distribution, with relatively few high-level traffickers (10.4 percent being importers, producers, or financiers), more midlevel distributors (13.0 percent being wholesalers), and a far greater numbers of low-level sellers/handlers (35.0 percent being retailers, couriers, mules, etc.). The exception to this is that possessors were not incarcerated in numbers sufficient to support the distributional hierarchy above them (especially because a nontrivial number report "possessing" very large quantities that belie this low-level status). Last, quite a few offenders failed to identify a specific role, so we examine this subgroup on other characteristics below.

Not surprisingly, a person's role in the offense varies by ethnic/national identity. Several points from table C6 are worth mentioning. First, non–Mexican Americans are much less likely than the

---

the powder cocaine connection (with their large relatively numbers [20 percent] and heavy cocaine involvement [73 percent]).

80. Sevigny and Caulkins, "Kingpins or Mules?"; U.S. Sentencing Commission, *Special Report to Congress: Cocaine and Federal Sentencing Policy* (Washington, D.C.: U.S. Sentencing Commission, 2007). Specifically, we constructed this measure, first, by taking the highest level role indicated on the survey's primary role in the offense question (S5Q14a). These six roles, in order of seriousness, were importing, producing, money laundering, wholesaling, retailing, and possessing. Second, respondents who answered 'no' to all six roles (n = 701) as well as those with complete missing data (n = 24) were categorized as having an "unspecified role." (Unfortunately, the survey did not employ a sorely needed "other—specify" option for this question.) Third, we used the survey's contingent role question (S5Q14b) to identify offenders with certain mitigating characteristics, such as being a courier or mule. In particular, respondents who acknowledged serving in a low-level role of money runner, courier, mule, or loader were categorized as the lowest level distributors in our hierarchy (just above possessors).

Table C6. Role in the Offense at Time of Arrest by Ethnic/National Identity, Federal and State Drug Inmates, 2004

Highest Role in the Offense	Non–Mexican Americans	Mexican Americans	Mexican Nationals	Other Foreign Nationals	Total
Importer	1.7	5.6	4.0	9.9	2.5
Producer	7.8	2.2	2.8	0.2	6.8
Money launderer	1.1	1.1	0.1	0.8	1.1
Wholesaler	13.1	11.0	14.9	13.3	13.0
Retailer	32.3	18.2	19.2	12.2	29.8
Courier/mule/loader	4.1	8.0	12.9	15.2	5.2
Possessor	24.2	38.1	20.3	14.5	24.8
Unspecified role	15.6	15.8	25.9	34.0	16.8
N	250,601	25,454	10,718	13,140	299,913

Source: Created by author.

other ethnic/national groups to be directly involved in importing drugs into the United States, whereas the opposite is true regarding the production or manufacturing of illegal drugs. In other words, these data show that relatively few non–Mexican Americans directly facilitate the cross-border movement of drugs into the United States; conversely, relatively few foreign nationals (and Mexican Americans, for that matter) set up illegal growing, cooking, or manufacturing operations in the United States.

Second, U.S. citizens are more likely than foreign nationals to be money launderers. Indeed, Mexican nationals are rarely directly involved with laundering drug proceeds. Perhaps it is the Mexican Americans who are primarily responsible for repatriating these funds back to their Mexican counterparts.

Third, all groups are involved in U.S. wholesale distribution to an important degree. Though hardly noteworthy for U.S. citizens, the sizable share of Mexican and other foreign national wholesalers suggests that they maintain some important degree of command and control over large-quantity drug transactions within U.S. borders.

Fourth, although non–Mexican Americans dominate retail drug distribution both in relative and absolute numbers, the fact that 1 in 5 of the imprisoned Mexican national drug offenders and 1 in 8 other foreign nationals were involved in retail drug selling indicates some penetration into U.S. retail markets, even if together they account for just 4 percent of all retailers.

Table C7. Distribution of Drug Quantity for Offenders Reporting an Unspecified Role by Ethnic/National Identity, Federal and State Drug Inmates, 2004

Quintile of Quantity	Non–Mexican Americans	Mexican Americans	Mexican Nationals	Other Foreign Nationals	Total
First (smallest)	13.5	13.5	1.0	3.0	11.9
Second	11.0	8.2	4.1	6.1	10.0
Third	12.5	17.0	15.4	12.3	13.0
Fourth	12.4	19.4	27.8	31.3	15.5
Fifth (largest)	13.1	17.2	26.5	29.1	15.6
Unknown	37.5	24.7	25.1	18.1	34.1
N	38,113	3,758	2,675	4,317	48,864

Source: Created by author.

Fifth, though 1 in 4 other foreign nationals were directly involved with transporting drugs into the United States either as high-level importers or low-level movers/handlers, Mexican nationals and Mexican Americans were also involved in relatively large numbers in the cross-border transit of drugs (16.9 percent and 13.6 percent, respectively). However, Mexican nationals were more likely to be employed as low-level couriers/mules/loaders.

Sixth, Mexican Americans were much more likely than other groups to report being simple possessors of drugs. Notably, Mexican American possessors look more like their American than their Mexican counterparts with respect to quantities possessed. For example, both Mexican Americans and non–Mexican Americans possessed a median quantity of 2 grams of methamphetmine, compared with 1 ounce for Mexican nationals.

Finally, from one-quarter to one-third of foreign nationals did not identify a specific role among those asked, which is greater than the 15–16 percent figure among U.S. citizens. To provide some sense of who these offenders are, table C7 examines them by quintiles of the drug quantities involved in their offense.[81] Although we can say nothing about the one-third of these unspecified role offenders with unknown quantities, it is nevertheless notable that foreign nationals, and to a lesser extent Mexican Americans, were involved with relatively substantial drug quantities.

Organizational Involvement

In this subsection, we investigate reported involvement with a drug-trafficking organization (DTO) in the year before arrest and, if so, the nature of that involvement. These results are presented

81. Between the first and fifth quintiles, median quantities ranged from 0.1 g to 31.4 kg for heroin, 0.3 g to 3.2 kg for methamphetamine, 1.0 g to 46 kg for powder cocaine, 0.2 g to 300 g for crack cocaine, and 1.0 g to 153 kg for marijuana.

Table C8. Drug-Trafficking Organizations' Involvement in the Year Before Arrest by Ethnic/National Identity, Federal and State Drug Inmates, 2004

Organizational Involvement	Non–Mexican Americans	Mexican Americans	Mexican Nationals	Other Foreign Nationals	Total
Drug group member	8.1	9.4	4.8	10.5	8.2
Leader/organizer	27.0	19.5	34.9	16.1	25.8
Middleman	21.0	16.8	21.5	12.1	20.1
Seller	29.9	15.6	18.8	13.4	27.4
Underling	12.4	28.5	3.2	51.3	16.0
Other role	9.7	19.7	21.6	7.2	10.8
No drug group involvement	91.0	90.2	94.0	88.6	90.0
Missing data	0.9	0.4	1.1	1.0	0.9
N	250,601	25,454	10,718	13,140	299,913

Source: Created by author.

in table C8, which shows that no more than 1 in 10 drug offenders viewed themselves as being part of a DTO in the year before their arrest. What is more, Mexican nationals were about half as likely to report an association with a DTO as the other ethnic/national groups—an unexpected finding given their prominent role both as couriers/mules/loaders and large-quantity traffickers. It is also contrary to media and government reports of violent and large-scale DTOs controlling the Mexican drug trade. What this might suggest is that, rather than being run primarily by corporatized cartels, drug trafficking is more of "cottage industry" with its many individual entrepreneurs and small, fleeting groups of traffickers networking and cooperating as needed.[82] The alternative story is that DTOs, and particularly Mexican DTOs, are adept at avoiding the reach of law enforcement, which, given the extent of corruption in Mexico, is not implausible.

With respect to their organizational role, overall, about one-quarter of DTO members were leaders or organizers of the group and one-fifth were intermediaries facilitating the group's operations. Most, however, were sellers (27.4 percent) and relatively few were underlings (16.0 percent) such as drug carriers or money runners or those with other roles (10.8 percent). Given the scarcity of the data for Mexican national ($n = 6$) and other foreign national ($n = 22$) drug group members, we caution against any strong conclusions by ethnicity/nationality. Nevertheless, with this caveat

82. John Eck and Jeffrey Gersh, "Drug Trafficking as a Cottage Industry," in *Illegal Drug Markets: From Research to Prevention Policy*, edited by Mangai Natarajan and Mike Hough (Monsey, N.Y.: Criminal Justice Press, 2000), 241–271.

Table C9. Weapon Involvement by Ethnic/National Identity, Federal and State Inmates, 2004

Weapon Involvement Indicator	Non–Mexican Americans		Mexican Americans		Mexican Nationals		Other Foreign Nationals		Total	
	Drug	Non-drug	Drug	Non-drug	Drug	Non-drug	Drug	Non-drug	Drug	Non-drug
Possessed gun during offense	7.1	19.2	8.9	18.8	5.8	12.5	2.5	21.3	7.0	19.0
Illegal weapon seized at arrest	6.3	8.5	7.2	9.6	6.4	7.8	2.9	10.5	6.3	8.6
(Con)current weapon conviction	4.5	8.4	4.6	7.9	3.7	3.0	2.3	10.8	4.4	8.3
Received firearm sentence enhancement	6.7	13.0	7.6	13.3	8.1	12.6	5.8	16.7	6.8	13.1
Any of the above	14.0	27.4	16.3	26.6	13.1	22.0	8.0	33.7	13.9	27.4
N (thousands)	279.4	868.9	28.5	93.1	12.7	30.2	14.9	27.6	335.6	1,020

Note: Calculations are based on nonmissing data, the amount of which varies by indicator.

Source: Created by author.

in mind, it bears mentioning that incarcerated members of both non–Mexican American and Mexican national DTOs tended to operate in the upper echelons of these organizations, whereas incarcerated members of Mexican American and other foreign national DTOs tended to fill the lower echelons. Given the uncertainty of these estimates, we do not speculate further.

Weapon Involvement

Media accounts and government reports have emphasized the recent spate of drug-related violence in Mexico.[83] Fueling this violence is a flood of guns and money heading south, just as illegal immigrants and drugs flow north. Recent data reveal that 87 to 90 percent of the guns seized in Mexico and submitted for tracing to the Bureau of Alcohol, Tobacco, Firearms, and Explosives originate in the United States.[84] Although the 2004 SISFCF predates both the recent trends in violence and the stepped-up enforcement of gun trafficking along the southwestern border, the data might provide an early or baseline assessment of the United States–Mexico drug–gun connection.

83. June Beittel, *Mexico's Drug-Related Violence* (Washington, D.C.: Congressional Research Service, 2009).

84. Vivian Chu and William Krouse, *Gun Trafficking and the Southwest Border* (Washington, D.C.: Congressional Research Service, 2009); U.S. Government Accountability Office, *Firearms Trafficking: U.S. Efforts to Combat Arms Trafficking to Mexico Face Planning and Coordination Challenges* (Washington, D.C.: U.S. Government Accountability Office, 2009.

Toward this end, table C9 presents data on several indicators of weapon involvement by ethnic/national identity. However, because gun trafficking is prosecuted under different statutes than drug trafficking, gun activity might be missed if we just focused on drug offenders. Therefore, we investigate the gun–crime link for both drug and nondrug offenders.

The first thing to notice from table C9 is that, overall, Mexican national drug offenders are no more likely than non–Mexican American drug offenders to be involved with firearms. Moreover, although Mexican Americans are somewhat more likely to be involved with weapons than these two groups, the differences are slight. Interestingly, whereas other foreign national drug offenders were the least likely to be involved, when convicted of nondrug offenses, they were the most likely to have a criminal connection to firearms.

Following from this, a second point is that Mexican nationals convicted of nondrug crimes were less likely overall than the other groups to be involved with weapons (22.0 percent vs. 26.6 percent to 33.7 percent). Particularly notable is the finding that they were less than half as likely as the other groups to be convicted of a weapon offense (3.0 percent vs. 7.9 percent to 10.8 percent). In other words, Mexican nationals were rarely convicted of crimes indicative of gun trafficking (i.e., nondrug offenders with a current weapon conviction). Rather, it appears that weapon involvement among Mexican nationals, like the other groups, is more a product of their general criminality than any major involvement with gun trafficking.

In short, based on these inmate survey data, Mexican nationals' involvement with firearms generally and gun trafficking in particular is no greater, and even quite limited, relative to that of non–Mexican Americans. To a lesser extent, this is also true of Mexican Americans. From Mexico's perspective, this is not good news. Mexico would like to see lots of gun runners and gun-involved drug offenders locked up in U.S. prisons as a deterrent to the southern flow of weapons that end up in the hands of the Mexican DTOs. Recent U.S. efforts such as the Bureau of Alcohol, Tobacco, Firearms, and Explosives' Project Gunrunner may change this dynamic, but such an assessment using the SISFCF will have to await a future release in the series.

The Southwest Border Region

Although U.S. intelligence agencies report that Mexican DTOs and their gang affiliates have sprouted up in at least 230 U.S. cities,[85] the true extent and nature of their penetration into the United States remains unclear. One view is that Mexican DTOs hand over United States–landed drugs to their Mexican American gang affiliates in the border region for delivery throughout the United States. Another view holds that Mexican DTOs maintain ownership of the drugs until they are distributed to low-level wholesalers and retailers in U.S. population centers.

Although we cannot fully explore these possibilities, we examine in table C10 the geographic distribution of drug and nondrug offenses by ethnic/national identity to provide some insight. For our analysis, we divided the United States into two regions based on the state in which the offense occurred: the Southwest border region (including Arizona, California, New Mexico, and California) and the rest of the United States. The results show that, as measured by the geographic distribution of crime types, Mexican national drug offenders have substantially diffused their activities into U.S. nonborder regions. Indeed, 45 percent of Mexican national drug offenders committed

85. National Drug Intelligence Center, *National Drug Threat Assessment, 2009* (Johnstown, Pa.: National Drug Intelligence Center, 2008).

Table C10. Geographic Distribution of Offenses by Ethnic/National Identity, Federal and State Inmates, 2004

Region Where Offense Committed	Non–Mexican Americans		Mexican Americans		Mexican Nationals		Other Foreign Nationals		Total	
	Drug	Non-drug	Drug	Non-drug	Drug	Non-drug	Drug	Non-drug	Drug	Non-drug
Southwest border state[a]	18.4	22.0	70.7	82.2	52.5	77.4	11.0	28.1	23.8	29.3
Rest of United States	80.6	76.1	28.3	16.2	44.7	20.8	82.5	65.2	74.9	68.7
Missing data	1.0	1.9	1.0	1.7	2.8	1.8	6.5	6.7	1.3	2.0
N (thousands)	279.4	868.9	28.5	93.1	12.7	30.2	14.9	27.6	335.6	1,020

[a] Includes Arizona, California, New Mexico, and Texas.

Source: Created by author.

their crime in nonborder regions—sizably greater than either Mexican national nondrug offenders (21 percent) or both Mexican American drug (28 percent) and nondrug (16 percent) offenders. Notably, relatively few other foreign national drug offenders (11 percent) operated in the Southwest border region. This observation is consistent with the *National Drug Threat Assessment, 2009*, which shows the Dominican, Colombian, and Cuban DTOs are the dominant groups in Florida and the Northeast.[86]

Summary

Most illegal drugs consumed in most countries around the world are imported. Perhaps not surprisingly, given geographic and cultural proximity, Mexico plays a large role in producing and transshipping the drugs that are consumed in the United States, roles that generate considerable amounts of harm in Mexico.

Legalizing drugs in the United States would solve most of these problems, albeit at the price of introducing a few others. However, policy changes that might in some sense be construed as steps in the "direction" of legalization would mostly not make steps toward solving Mexico's problem. For example, though some might informally think of decriminalization as being "halfway" between prohibition and legalization, decriminalizing drugs in the United States would not solve half the problems Mexico suffers because of U.S. drug demand; indeed, it would as likely as not make things worse. Furthermore, though Mexico has a vested interest in seeing the United States expand its demand control efforts, Mexico would not necessarily benefit from scaling back supply control.

Incarceration is a particularly pronounced component of U.S. drug policy, and both Mexican Americans and Mexican nationals living in the United States are exposed to this heightened risk of

86. Ibid.

imprisonment. Indeed, both groups are somewhat overrepresented in American prisons for drug law violations, but this overrepresentation of approximately 40 percent is very modest compared with the overrepresentation of African Americans (roughly 700 percent). Hence, more than 90 percent of the burden of imprisonment for violating U.S. drug laws falls on U.S. citizens, and the share falling on Mexican Americans (9 percent) is not highly inconsistent with Mexican Americans' share of the U.S. population.

We also compared various characteristics of drug inmates across four ethnic/national groups: non–Mexican Americans, Mexican Americans, Mexican nationals, and other foreign nationals. Predictably, non–Mexican Americans were overrepresented among those who grew or manufactured drugs within the United States, whereas the other groups were overrepresented among importers. However, in most other respects Mexican American drug inmates looked much like their fellow citizens who were not of Mexican ancestry, except for predictable association by drug (e.g., Mexican Americans had lower rates of crack involvement). In contrast, noncitizens, whether nationals of Mexico or other countries, were much more likely than American citizens to be involved with larger quantities and higher purities.

Large-scale drug importation is often associated with large and violent drug-trafficking organizations. However, the noncitizen inmates—both Mexican nationals and others—did not report rates of organizational membership or weapons involvement that stood out from those of U.S. citizens. That is, only a small minority (roughly 10 percent) reported being part of an organization, and comparably small proportions answered affirmatively to any of four weapons-related questions. One interpretation of this would be that some of the worst behaviors of Mexican drug-trafficking organizations stay primarily on the Mexican side of the United States–Mexico border, but it could also reflect the age of the data (collected in 2004), unwillingness to report, or success of the largest and most violent organizations at avoiding incarceration.

From a Mexican perspective, this analysis could be construed as a double dose of disappointment with respect to hopes that U.S. actions will greatly ameliorate the damage that U.S. drug demand causes for Mexico. The one thing that would make a substantial difference—legalization, particularly of the expensive illegal drugs, cocaine/crack, heroin, and methamphetamine—is not politically plausible. Scaling back on the extreme levels of imprisonment for drug law violations may be a more plausible reform; after all, letting 90 percent of drug law violators out of prison would still leave imprisonment rates at the levels of the drug war during the first term of the Ronald Reagan administration, which no one thought of as being soft on drugs. However, it is not clear that reducing incarceration would help Mexico—and, at any rate, most of the inmates are American citizens, so American policymakers could be excused for thinking of drug-sentencing laws as primarily a domestic issue to be determined by domestic imperatives.

To close on a more hopeful note, precisely because such a relatively modest proportion of U.S. drug inmates are foreign nationals and/or were directly involved in importation, substantial changes in enforcement and sentencing policies toward those groups could be accomplished without changing the basic posture of American drug policy. Hence, if someone believed that some such change would materially benefit Mexico, it might be possible to make such a change "under the radar," without demanding a major shift in U.S. policy in such a politically charged domain.

ABOUT THE AUTHORS

Sidney Weintraub holds the William E. Simon Chair in Political Economy at CSIS. He is also professor emeritus at the Lyndon B. Johnson School of Public Affairs at the University of Texas at Austin, where he was Dean Rusk Professor from 1976 to 1994, when he then joined CSIS. A member of the U.S. Foreign Service from 1949 to 1975, Weintraub held the post of deputy assistant secretary of state for international finance and development from 1969 to 1974 and served as assistant administrator of the U.S. Agency for International Development in 1975. His many publications include *Energy Cooperation in the Western Hemisphere: Benefits and Impediments* (CSIS, 2007); *NAFTA's Impact on North America: The First Decade* (CSIS, 2004); *Free Trade in the Americas: Economic and Political Issues for Governance and Firms* (Edward Elgar, 2004); and *Financial Decision-Making in Mexico: To Bet a Nation* (Pittsburgh, 2000). Weintraub has also published numerous articles in newspapers and journals. He received a Ph.D. in economics from American University.

Duncan Wood is director of the Program in International Relations and the Canadian Studies Program at the Instituto Tecnológico Autónomo de México (ITAM) in Mexico City. He is also a senior associate at CSIS. Wood is a member of the Mexican National Research System, serves on the editorial board of *Foreign Affairs Latinoamerica*, and has been an editorial adviser to *Reforma*. In 2007, he was a nonresident Fulbright fellow. Between 2007 and 2009, he was technical secretary of the Red Mexicana de Energia, a group of experts in the area of energy policy in Mexico. He studied in the United Kingdom and Canada, receiving a Ph.D. in political studies from Queen's University in Kingston, Ontario.

Contributors

Jonathan P. Caulkins is the H. Guyford Stever Professor of Operations Research at Carnegie Mellon University's Heinz College and Qatar campus. He holds a Ph.D. in operations research from the Massachusetts Institute of Technology.

Nathan Jones is a Ph.D. candidate in political science at the University of California at Irvine.

Eric L. Sevigny is an assistant professor in the Department of Criminology and Criminal Justice at the University of South Carolina. He holds a Ph.D. in public and international affairs from the University of Pittsburgh.

Jonathan Winer is senior vice president in the Washington, D.C., office of APCO Worldwide. Previously, he served as U.S. deputy assistant secretary of state for international law enforcement and as chief counsel and principal legislative assistant to Senator John Kerry. He holds a J.D. from New York University School of Law.